CW00968373

THE SECOND BOOK OF CULLOMPTON

THE SECOND BOOK OF

CULLOMPTON

A Further Celebration of a Devonshire Town

COMPILED BY JUDY MORRIS

HALSGROVE

Title page: *Cullompton Boys' Club Rag Week, c.1964. The Boys' Club was located in Community House, next to the Labour Exchange and under the YMCA. The pram race started at Higher Bullring and the route was along the main street, down Cockpit Hill and back to the Bell for a change over and then finish at Higher Bullring. Winners were Derek Goff and Terry Jones representing Cullompton RFC.* Left to right, back row: *Mike Palmer, Paddy Lane, John Webb, Derek Greedy, Clive Fowler, Roger Veysey, Brian Hales, Derek Goff, ?;* front row: *?, Howard Whitton, Clive Woodland, John Hellier, Terry Jones, ?;* boy at rear: *Russell Dodge.*

British Library Cataloguing-in-Publication Data.
A CIP record for this title is available from the British Library.

ISBN 978 1 84114 625 6

HALSGROVE

Halsgrove House,
Ryelands Industrial Estate,
Bagley Road, Wellington,
Somerset. TA21 9PZ
Tel: 01823 653777
Fax: 01823 216796
email: sales@halsgrove.com
website: www.halsgrove.com

Printed and bound in Great Britain by CPI Antony Rowe Ltd, Chippenham, Wiltshire.

Foreword

I call upon you, my readers, to play your personal part in promoting the well-being of our Parish. Let none say 'I mind my own business, that's enough for me'. That is a sentiment utterly selfish, and wholly unworthy of a Christian or good citizen. The 'common good' should have our constant and warmest concern. He is no true 'Cullomptonian' who does not aim at making Cullompton the best and brightest township in the County of Devon. 'Vivat Cullomptonia.'

Revd G. Forrester: *St Andrews Parochial Magazine*, March 1903

This *Second Book of Cullompton* came about due to the success of the first book. It is very difficult to obtain a copy now and so, rather than just reprint the first book, it was decided to produce a follow-up. A lot of information about Cullompton, its people and its history has, over the years, been published in a variety of forms. My aim was to try to pull it all together in one place; to provide an information source for people researching local history but at the same time provide a book that is interesting to read.

During the Second World War the then vicar of Cullompton, Revd Geoffrey Watkin Grubb, wrote 'A study of English Social History for a thousand years, illustrated from the life of the old market town of Collumpton in Devonshire'. His mentor was Murray T. Foster (1867–1953), a well known local historian. Unfortunately Revd Grubb's work was never published but it is thanks to his research and that of Murray T. Foster and his uncle James Murray Foster that I was able to find out so much about Cullompton.

I would also like to thank another local historian, David Pugsley, who has edited several books providing an insight into Cullompton's past. He very generously gave me his research, which provided me with material for this book.

Many sources of information have been used, including interviews with lots of local people. Some have amazing memories when prompted to remember an event or put names to faces in photographs. The more I found out, the more I wanted to know but, unfortunately, time and words finally ran out. I apologise for anything that has been omitted or may not be as you remember it.

I hope that this book will be as successful as the first and become a source of interest and reference for anyone interested in Cullompton for many generations to come. Thank you to everyone that helped me, I couldn't have written it without your help.

Judy Morris,
Cullompton Town Clerk, 2007

Members of the Fur and Feather Club outside the British Legion, c.1950. Left to right, standing: *?, P. Widgery, ?, W. Denner, ?, ?, W. Yendell, ? , ?, H. Yendell, ?, I. Rutley, ?;* seated: *?, W. Dunn, L. Yendell, ?, ?, ?.*

Left: *St Andrews Primary School production, 1946.* Left to right, back row: *Doreen Rowsell, Brian Chubb, Shirley White, Maureen Wright, Pat Radford, Valerie Aldridge, Brian Gillard, Valerie Broom;* front row: *?, Valerie Biss, Yvonne Isaacs, ?, ?.*

Above: *British Legion Show 1959.* Left to right: *?, ?, ?, ?, Mrs Joan Rutley, Mrs Win Ellis, Mrs Salter, Mrs Luxton.*

Left: *WI, May 1971.* Left to right, back row: *Mrs Kathleen Vicary, Mrs Joan Rutley;* front row: *Mrs Phil Saunders, Mrs Florrie Radford, Mrs Kathleen Lamacroft, Mrs Muriel Coxhead.*

Contents

Foreword		*5*
Acknowledgements		*9*
Introduction		*11*
Chapter One:	How Cullompton Got Its Name	15
Chapter Two:	The Romans to the Normans	19
Chapter Three:	The Plantagenets to the Victorians	25
Chapter Four:	House of Windsor	51
Chapter Five:	Through the Eyes of a Child	69
Chapter Six:	Station Road	85
Chapter Seven:	High Street, Higher Street and Willand Road	99
Chapter Eight:	Fore Street	111
Chapter Nine:	Exeter Hill, Exeter Road and New Street	129
Chapter Ten:	St Andrews Church By Percy Cross	143
Chapter Eleven	The Walronds By Mrs Jane Campbell	147
Chapter Twelve:	In Conclusion	151
Envoi		*154*
Subscribers		*156*
Further Titles		*158*

St Andrews Primary School, 1946: Cannibals and Savages, *a play by ten year olds. The local press reported: 'These ten-year-old children revelled in the individual expression this action demanded. Personal interpretation called for acute analysis and fine personal expression. Solo speaking enhanced group feeling and keen teamwork. Making of dresses and make-up provided most valuable training.'* Left to right: *Bill Bird, Brian Miller, Pat Radford, Brian Gillard, Brian Chubb, Alan Hellier, Jeffrey Heal, Tony Martin, Mavis Wright, Edwin Pratt, John Bradford, Colin Minchinton, Valerie Aldridge, Clarence Bond, Edwin Day and Rodney ?.*

Cullompton Rangers Colts Team, Under 18s, 1956–57. This photograph was taken near Bradfield. Left to right, back row: *Mr Hales, T. Stocker, J. Askew, P. Blackmore, L. Farrant, B. Gunn, L. Denner;* front row: *G. Brown, J. Schimp, G. Cummings, B. Martin, M. Martin, B. Clyst.*

Cullompton Rangers, 1959–60. This photograph was taken in the garden of Dr Shove's surgery in Church Street. Left to right, back row: *H. Barnes, D. Sanders, R. Cherry, P. Blackmore, D. Greening, M. Martin, B. Martin, T. Discombe;* front row: *C. Orton, C. Lane, K. Vinnicombe, M. Ingersent, I. Kernick.*

Left: *Cullompton Rangers 1956/7. The photograph was taken in the garden of Dr Shove's surgery in Church Street.* Left to right, back row: *L. Denner, F. Pratt, K. Vinnicombe, L. Farrant, M. Heale, A. Sanders, G. Veale, Mr Butt, B. Wilson, Mr Buckingham;* middle row: *C. Wellington, P. Edwards, B. Bird, G. Cummings, G. Greening, T. Goff, C. Caines, P. Blackmore;* front row: *M. Lane, M. Martin, B. Martin, T. Stocker.*

Cullompton Rangers winning five cups, 1960. This picture was taken at the Globe Hotel in Fore Street. Left to right, back row: *D. Trevelyan, B. Holsgrove, D. Heale, G. Veale, K. Vinnicombe, R. Cherry, B. Gunn, L. Denner, R. Vicary, B. Richardson, Mr Buckingham;* seated: *D. Whitton, G. Horton, P. Blackmore, B. Martin, M. Ingersent, Mr. Tidborough, C. Lane, I. Kernick.*

Acknowledgements

Mrs Eileen Andrews, Mr and Mrs Patrick Blackmore, Mrs Jean Bradshaw, Mr and Mrs David Broom, Mr Butler, Mrs Jane Campbell, Mrs Joan Castleton, Mr John Chambers, Mr John Chard, Mr Richard Chard, Mrs Muriel Coxhead, Mr Percy Cross, Mrs Marian Dummett, Mr Evans, Mr and Mrs Les Farrant, L. Frayne, Mr Steve Goffey, Mr Tony Goffey, Mrs Janet Hallam, Mrs Shirley Hector, Mrs Audrey Hitchcock, Mr Kellaway, Mrs Marsh, Mr Barrie Marshall, Mrs Pearl Marshall, Mrs Annie Minchin, Alex Morris, Steve Morris, Mr Geoff Munn, Mrs Janet Newton, Mr David Pugsley, Mrs Jenny Rutley, Mrs Caroline Savory, Mrs Thelma Shere, Sharon Snow, Mr Alan Spear, Mr John Spurway, Robert Tinley, Mr Roger Veysey, Nick Walker and Cyril Warren.

Above: *Cullompton Carnival, 1946: 'The Boat Race'.* Seated in boat, left to right: *Geoffrey Osborne, Dick Mitchell, John Spurway, Geoff Spurway, Michael Duggitt, Mike Widgery, Bernard White, John Chilcott, Mike Ingersent;* standing: *?* (man far left), *?* (concealed by oar), *Janet Spurway, Jean Taylor, Percy Widgery, Len Spurway, Mr Phillips.*

Above, inset: *Cullompton Carnival, c.1947.* Left to right: *Perc Widgery, Len Spurway, Michael Widgery, Janet Spurway (Mitchell), John Spurway.*

Right: *Cullompton Carnival, c.1960, Rugby Club float.* Children on the float include: *Tony Lindsell, Malcolm Goff, Janet Goff, Oxlade Brothers, Josephine and Rosemary Rutley, Jane, Judith and Joanna Lambert, Valerie Broom.*

Cullompton Choral Society in the 1960s (the group are standing outside St Andrews Primary School). This picture includes, left to right, back row: *?, Mr Crook, Mr Scott, ?, Mr Ivor Morgan, ?, Ray Cook, K. Law, Reg Ayres, Paul Lambert;* fifth row: *Audrey Warner, Phil Brimmecombe;* fourth row: *Mrs Cadlow, Mrs Joan Rutley, Celia Kerslake, Mrs Cook, Mrs Owen;* third row: *?, Mrs Lamacraft, Joan King, Mrs Benfield;* second row: *Muriel Coxhead, ?, Mrs Butt, Mrs Hutchings;* front row: *Alice Harris, Helen Frost, Sheila Smith, Mrs Salter.*

Introduction

Although Cullompton is Saxon in origin there is evidence that people have been living there at least since Roman times. The settlement has grown up along the banks of the River Culm, Cullompton meaning 'town on the Culm'. Its geology makes it ideal for farming and the quality of its water also makes it a good place for milling. Water power was initially used for grinding corn and processes in textile making but when the cloth industry declined these were converted into paper mills.

Cullompton's location makes it a place that a good many people pass by; indeed, to them it is just a junction on the M5 motorway. It was a staging-post for many years and people would stop-off on their way to Exeter or Plymouth. The town was probably at its most prosperous between the sixteenth and eighteenth centuries when the woollen trade was at its peak and grand buildings such as the Manor House and the Walronds were built and a lot of money was spent on enhancements to St Andrews Church.

In the 1570s the population of England stood at about four million and the population of Cullompton was approximately 5,000, which meant that, at that time, Cullompton was an average-sized country town. Its population declined in the late 1800s as the industrial revolution took hold and the cities in the north of England captured the woollen industry. However, until recent years, Cullompton remained a self-sufficient place, a place where people lived, worked and shopped.

The population of Cullompton is currently approximately 8,600 but it is no longer the self-sufficient country town it once was. Although its population has more than doubled since the 1950s many of the people that live in the town no longer work and shop there. The intention of this book is to show how Cullompton has evolved to become the place it is today, the aim being to ensure that, although the town may be changing, its people will never lose their sense of identity and community.

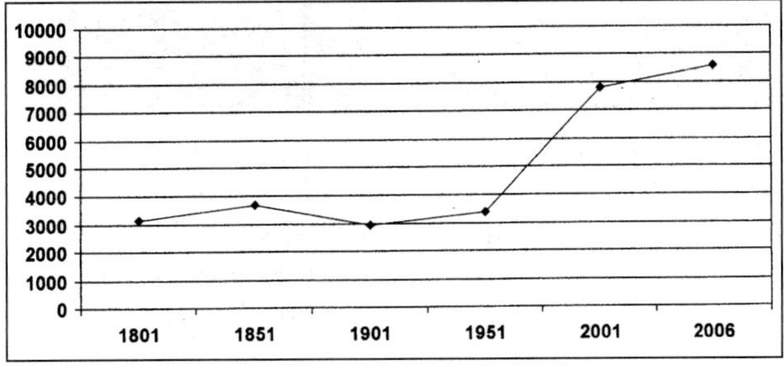

Cullompton population growth, 1801–2006.

Eileen Andrews has lived in Cullompton all her life, she has always worked hard and given a lot of her spare time to ensure that Cullompton's community spirit and sense of identity is sustained. She is Secretary of the Cullompton Community Association and Chairman of the Cullompton Festival Committee and for two years, between 2004 and 2006, she was Town Mayor. These are her memories:

I was born in Cullompton between the First and Second World Wars; among my earliest memories is buying a half-penny worth of sweets that would last me for the whole of a day out. I recall my family going to the Plymouth Navy Day to see my big brother's ship. Mr Burrows drove us down, his car was large enough for us all but it travelled very slowly and the journey took a very long time. I could not travel very well and they had to stop several times to let me out to be ill.

My mother and father would take me on trips to Exmouth on the train during the summer. Mum would make plenty of egg and cucumber sandwiches and we would take a big bottle of lemonade. It was a long walk to the station and the platform would be crowded with daytrippers like ourselves and the sun would be shining bright, although maybe I only recall the sunny days.

The school I first attended was right opposite my home in Victoria Terrace on the site where the Magistrate's Court and Health Centre now stand. When the new Primary School was built I and the other younger ones were transferred there. So we were the first pupils to attend St Andrews Primary School. We were said to be going up Chinatown or to Tokyo, this being the nicknames for the two halves of St Andrews Estate.

I used to love to rollerskate, on the road of course, but sometimes I dared to go onto the pavement but the police would soon spot me and order me back into the road, together with a good telling off.

As a young girl I accompanied my family on the traditional 'Sunday Afternoon Walk', we almost always went a circular route 'up around Knowle and back around Yes'. This was a favourite walk for many Cullompton families. Some would always take the clockwise route, whilst others the anti-clockwise one. There was a small sweetshop about halfway round run by a Miss Martin; my mother would give us a half-penny to get sweets. As we walked along we would overtake or be overtaken by other walkers or we would meet others coming the other way. We used to all greet each other as very well-known friends or at least

Cullompton pantomime, c.1965. Left to right: *Myra Moore, Ann Vile, Margaret Clarke, Eileen Andrews, ?.*

Cullompton Pantomime, c.1966. Left to right: *Ann Vile, Myra Moore, ?, ?, Mary Chubb, Eileen Andrews.*

St Andrews Primary School's production of Robin Hood *(1949–50).* Left to right, back row: *?, ?;* third row: *Raymond Hales, Alan Dummett, Bertha Worly, Linda Nicholas, Geoff Osborn, Michael Hooper, Brenda Wotton, Chris Banfield, Roger Perry, David Chidgey, Graham Radford;* second row: *Mary Chubb, John Tidborough, Ray Stanbury, Janet Pearce, Linda Kerrigan, Brenda Northam, Fred Daniels, Derek Goff, Pam Williams;* front row: *Beryl Saunders, Barbara Fear, Robin Pipe, Dianne Tolhurst, Billy Richardson, Pat Morgan, Carol North, Bill Stocker, Tom Stocker, Tony Heale.*

people one knew well. In those days Cullompton was a small town, everybody knew of each other. Times have changed and I am sorry that walk has changed and that the sweetshop is no more.

Sometimes for a change we would walk up over Old Hill and carry on until we turned back onto the main road to come out at Westcott and thence home.

We had a thriving Cycle Club in the town, which I joined in my late teens. The Club organised many excursions; we rode to places like Sidmouth and Exmouth. Sandy Bay was always a great favourite.

As the years passed my life changed, I married and had five wonderful children. When my eldest was fourteen and my youngest two, I was widowed. Life was far from easy, we were, however, a happy family even with money being so short. I well remember having to make what we called 'special stews' that is to say stews with no meat as I could not always afford it. There were always plenty of good veg and of course dough boys and dough girls – we called some dough girls because they were the better-shaped ones. At Christmas I gave one of the children what we called a big present. The next year it would be one of the other children's turn and so it rotated until everyone had had their big gift.

Cullompton Festival, 1992. Princess Hannah Cockburn and her attendant Laura Ainsworth.

Dancing has always been a great delight for me. I took part in many of the local pantomimes. In fact, I was a chorus girl in the first one. Later I produced several and arranged the dancing in others; we were never posh enough to call me choreographer.

I have always been most interested in my home town and in the early '70s was persuaded to enter local government. As a rookie Councillor sitting on my first few Council meetings I never dreamed that one day I would become Town Mayor. That evening in May 2004, when I returned home after being elected, so many thoughts were coursing through my head that it was impossible to organise them. The next morning I went to the place where I can enjoy my favourite view of Cullompton: the top of Old Hill where the last of the original Scots pines stand. I stood by the gate and looked down over my town. This was a very emotional moment for me, thinking of how proud my dear late husband would have been; also my mum and dad. I wondered what they would have thought, as they passed by that gateway on one of our Sunday walks, if they knew that one day, so many years later, their little girl would look down on the town from there as its newly elected Mayor? I paused for some time. It was then I came down to earth, so very much to do and so little time. I had to get my mind out of the nostalgic past and into the practical present.

The Mayor is of course the Chairman of the Town Council and has overall responsibility for the routine running of the Council. The Chairman of the Council is not a single entity, it is the whole body of the Council and also the Councillors on the various sub-committees that come forward with proposals to be

David Glenn from Cullompton Twinning Association presents Cullompton Town Mayor, Mrs Eileen Andrews, with the gift of a picture from Cullompton's French twin town, Ploudalmezeau in May 2006.

Cullompton Festival: the street market in Higher Bullring, 2003.

debated and voted upon by the full Council. But that did not mean that I did not have a few ideas of my own. I had long thought that Cullompton was not getting a fair crack of the whip from higher authorities, so I fought long and hard for that and with the support of my fellow Councillors, there have been some achievements accomplished. When I left office I felt that there was so much more to do. We have long awaited a swimming-pool and another supermarket.

As Mayor, there were many functions that I was invited to attend to represent my town. At times I wondered how people judged my appearance and the manner in which I conducted myself – for their impression of me would reflect on Cullompton.

To mention just a few such events, I, together with the Deputy Lord Lieutenant of Devon, planted a tree to commemorate the eightieth birthday of Her Majesty the Queen, I gave talks to various local organisations, welcomed the visiting German students at the Community College and attended a social evening with our French friends from our twin town of Ploudalmezeau.

My four girls and my son were so very pleased and proud of me becoming Mayor. They did, however, have one reservation: the fact that they had to make an appointment to ensure that I would be at home when they dropped in, as they often do!

I hit some of the targets that I set myself and feel proud of that. These were, however, not achieved without the wonderful support and constant encouragement I received from my own townsfolk and my fellow Councillors.

I really did my best, good enough or not, so God bless Cullompton and all those who have their homes here in our great town.

Cullompton Town Council, 2005. Left to right, back row: *Cllr Terry Belson, Cllr Ray Weinstein, Town Clerk Judy Morris, Cllr Mike Thompson, Administrative Assistant Janet Hallam, Cllr Brian Mitchell, Cllr Graham Barden;* front row: *Cllr Mrs Pauline Hammett, Cllr Mrs Patricia Cornell, Deputy Town Mayor Cllr Barrie Marshall, Town Mayor Cllr Mrs Eileen Andrews, Cllr Mrs Jane Campbell, Cllr Mrs Muriel Coxhead, Cllr Mrs Vanessa Fyles-Legg.*

Planting a tree to commemorate Her Majesty Queen Elizabeth II's 80th birthday, 20 April 2006. Pictured are: *Town Mayor Eileen Andrews and Deputy Lord Lieutenant of Devon, Air Chief Marshall Sir Michael Stear.*

Chapter One

Cullompton: How the Town Got its Name

It is generally accepted that Cullompton gets its name from the River Culm and means 'the town on the Culm'. The word 'ton' is from Celtic or Guydhelian British, 'tun' or 'tune' being a fortified place, town or village. It is thought that the River Culm is named after St Colomba of Tir-de-Glas who came to the area from Ireland in about 450AD to preach and convert the local people to Christianity. Tradition has it that he set up a preaching station near the river, where two roads intersected. The river became known as 'Colomba's river' which became 'Colme' and then 'Culm'.

The name 'Colomba' means 'a dove' and it was as common in Celtic times as John is today. Among the Celts a 'saint' simply meant a person who had bound himself to Christ's service by vows and not someone whose 'sainthood' needed to be first determined by canonisation from Rome. It was a Celtic custom that wherever a prayer station or 'church' was erected, it should bear the name of its founder.

St Colomba and his companion St Disen established their 'cell' or 'hut' around which a settlement or 'tun' of huts was established. The Celtic name 'Columtune' and later 'Colombton' (i.e. Colomba's tun, or town) was bestowed upon this settlement. Nearby was an ancient holy well, known today as St Georges Well, and it is thought that a chapel was later built there and dedicated to St George, although there is no trace of it today.

A picture of St Colomba used to hang over the high altar of St Andrews Church in the Middle Ages and there was a statue of the saint in the church. It is likely that St Disen preached the gospel in the neighbouring village of Bradninch and founded the first wooden church on the site where St Disen's Church stands today. It is said that both saints later went to Germany. Where St Colomba of Tir-de-Glas died is unknown; there is no record of him being laid to rest in Cullompton.

From about 1677 it was usually either spelt 'Cullompton' or 'Cullumpton' in the parish books. Between 1650 and 1680 tradesmen struck halfpennies and farthings for local use. Six varieties are known for Cullompton, four commenced 'COL' and two 'CUL'. By the mid-nineteenth century there still appeared to be no general agreement on the spelling. The Post Office had it as 'Cullompton'; the railway station sign stated 'Collumpton' and the Ordnance Survey maps showed it as 'Cullumpton'. The Bristol and Exeter Railway timetable had the down train stopping at 'Cullompton' and the up train stopping at 'Collumpton'.

St Georges Well, c.1906 , where St Colomba is thought to have set up his prayer station. Later a church was built on the site and dedicated to St George but only the well still remains today.

COLLUMPTON

TOWN WATER COURSE.

ALL PERSONS

Interested in Maintaining their Right to the

STREAM OF WATER

THAT FLOWS THROUGH THE TOWN,

Are requested to Meet in the PARISH ROOM,

On SATURDAY the 14th of FEBRUARY, 1874,

AT SIX O'CLOCK IN THE EVENING.

February 9th, 1874.

FROST, PRINTER, COLLUMPTON.

PARISH OF COLLUMPTON

Thursday, July 23rd, 1914.

The Ceremony of Receiving and Laying Up the Old Colour of the Highbridge Local Militia (1809—1816) in St. Andrew's Parish Church, and also the Formal Opening of the Upcott Field will take place on the above date.

COLONEL HUGH ACLAND TROYTE

has kindly consented to present the Colour for Laying Up and to Declare the Upcott Field Open.

3.15.—A Procession will be formed in the Higher Bull Ring and proceed to the Church in the following order :—

The Territorials carrying the Colour.
The Reservists.
The Baden Powell Scouts.
The Parish Council.
Members of Friendly Societies.
The General Public.

3.30.—**SERVICE IN THE CHURCH,** and Laying up of the Colour.

4.0.—The Procession will be re-formed and will march to the Upcott Field.

4.30.—**THE FIELD WILL BE DECLARED OPEN,** after which a Free Tea will be provided for all Children attending the Day School.

Tea at 6d. per head for the General Public will be provided. (Tickets may be obtained from Messrs. E. A. Lawrence, Stationer, J. Reynolds, and Mrs. Paul.)

SPORTS for Children will be held in the Evening.

The Band of the G Co. 4th Devons

(by permission of the Officer Commanding) will play until after Tea.

THE TOWN BAND will give Selections during the Evening.

All Inhabitants are requested to decorate their houses for the occasion.

By Order of
THE PARISH COUNCIL.

July 17th, 1914.

Lawrence, Printer, Cullompton.

Above: *'Collumpton': an example of a different spelling, 1874.*

Right: *'Collumpton': an example of a different spelling in 1914.*

During the 1860s and '70s there was a lot of historical research carried out and attention was drawn to the spelling. There was a great deal of correspondence on the subject, published in the *Exeter and Plymouth Gazette* in 1874. This is documented in *The Town on the Culm* edited by David Pugsley and published in 1985 to raise funds for the St Andrews Church Restoration Fund.

It is thought that it was Squire W.C. Grant of Hillersdon who encouraged everyone to fall into line and adopt 'Cullompton' as the correct spelling.

Hillersdon House, home of Squire W.C. Grant who encouraged everyone to fall into line and adopt 'Cullompton' as the correct spelling.

The minutes of the meeting of the Board of Directors of the Bristol and Exeter Railway Company held in Bristol on 23 September 1874 include the following:

> ***648.*** *Cullompton Station. Agreed that in all time tables, tickets, etc. in future the name of the station be spelt Cullompton and that the notice board at the station be altered accordingly.*

The *Tiverton Gazette* on Tuesday 13 October reported that:

> *... the Bristol and Exeter Railway Company, and the Devon and Cornwall Banking Company – the only two important public companies having any connection with the town – have both resolved to adopt the spelling Cullompton for the future.*

The Ordnance Survey, who had used 'Cullumpton' in their first edition in 1809, fell into line with the Post Office, the railway and the bank, etc., by adopting 'Cullompton' when the area was surveyed in 1887 and a revised edition published in 1889.

James Murray Foster was of the opinion that the

correct spelling should have been 'Columpton' and after his death on 2 August 1879 the opposition was led by his eldest brother Lt Col Joseph Foster and his nephew Murray Toogood Foster, but their preferred spelling was 'Collumpton'. Murray T. Foster insisted on using 'Collumpton' for his short history of the town in the *Transactions of the Devonshire Association* in 1910. In 1933 the *Devon & Somerset News* headlined "CULLOMPTON' or 'COLLUMPTON'? That is the question', and devoted three articles by historian F.J. Snell to the subject. Murray T. Foster died in 1953 and when his short history of the town was reprinted in a revised and shortened edition in 1964 all reference to the spelling controversy had disappeared.

Joseph Foster, 1829–1903.

In 1861–62 James Murray Foster spent a lot of time researching the history of Cullompton and he compiled a list of all the different spellings of Cullompton that he came across. There are over 40 different ways in which the name of the parish has been spelt during the 1,000 years since King Alfred the Great in his will (870–875AD) bequeathed the town and lands of 'Columtune' to his younger son Athelward. The confusion between an 'o' and a 'u' in the first syllable has persisted throughout the long history of the parish.

James Murray Foster's List of 40 Ways to Spell Cullompton, published in 1878

1.	*Columtune*	*872*	*King Alfred the Great, Will preserved in Newminster Abbey, Winchester*
2.	*Colitone*	*1080*	*Domesday Book of King William I*
3.	*Colum*	*1080*	*Exon Domesday Book, preserved by Dean and Chapter of Exeter*
4.	*Curemtone*	*1080*	*ditto*
5.	*Columpton*	*1278*	*Gift Deed of Amicia, Countess of Devon, of Columpton Manor, to Buckland*
6.	*Cullington*	*1657*	*Bess's Narrative of the Sufferings of the People called Quakers*
7.	*Colompton*	*1290*	*Letter of Pope Nicholas IV*
8.	*Collumpton*	*1336*	*Deed belonging to St Nicholas' Priory, Exon*
9.	*Cullumpton*	*1630*	*Westcote's History of Devon*
10.	*Collompton*	*1616*	*Tombstone of James Skinner in St Andrews Church*
11.	*Cullinton*	*1068*	*'Carta prima' deed of gift by King William I to Battle Abbey*
12.	*Culuntuna*	*1066*	*No. 3 Deed of gift by King William I to Battle Abbey*
13.	*Coluntuna*	*1067*	*No. 4 Deed of gift by King William I to Battle Abbey*
14.	*Culintuna*	*1068*	*No. 10 Deed of gift by King William I to Battle Abbey*
15.	*Culintona*	*1070*	*Gift deed from Battle Abbey to St Nicholas*
16.	*Colonton*	*17?*	*Grose's Antiq. Of England and Wales*
17.	*Colunp*	*?*	*Quoted in D Lyson's Mag. Brit. as name of Manor, ante King William I*
18.	*Cullum*	*1630*	*Tombstone of Mary Fowler in St Andrews Church*
19.	*Culumpton*	*1406*	*Confirmation Deed of Isabella de Fortibus to Buckland Abbey*
20.	*Cullompton*	*1698*	*Deed of Transfer of land in parish*
21.	*Columton*	*1652*	*Tombstone of Abraham Turner in St Andrews Church*
22.	*Colupton*	*1356*	*Deed of Gift of Town Watercourse by Buckland Abbey*
23.	*Culunton*	*17?*	*Grose's Antiq. Eng and Wales first edition*
24.	*Columbton*	*1586*	*Camden's Britannia, original edition*
25.	*Culmton*	*1538*	*Revd Thomas Moore's History of Devon*
26.	*Colonton*	*1546*	*Chantries Certificate No. XV, made according to Commission*
27.	*Culumbton*	*1586*	*Camden's Britannia. Map in original edition*
28.	*Cullumton*	*1662*	*Tombstone of Mary Day in St Andrews Church*
29.	*Cullumston*	*1666?*	*Local coin, Walter Challis*
30.	*Colomton*	*1651*	*Local coin, Tristram Clarke*
31.	*Cullomton*	*1666*	*Local coin, John Harris*
32.	*Cylmton*	*1797*	*Suggested as proper name by Mr Polewhele*
33.	*Culuntun*	*1100*	*Deed of Gift from Battle Abbey to St Nicholas' Priory*
34.	*Coluntuna*	*1200*	*Deed belonging to St Nicholas' Priory*
35.	*Cullemton*	*1664*	*Local coin, name illegible*
36.	*Colehampton*	*1700*	*Road Book of England and Wales*
37.	*Colump*	*1273*	*Gift Deed of Amicia, Countess of Devon to Buckland Abbey*
38.	*Culumton*	*1400*	*Confirmation Deed of Gift by Amicia, Countess to Buckland Abbey*
39.	*Colampton*	*1788*	*Thesaurus Ecclesiasticus, or Liber Valorum, by John Lloyd*
40.	*Collumston*	*1667*	*Local coin, William Skinner*

Lower Mill with St Andrews Church in the background, c.1925.

Cullompton from Old Hill (the Roman fort was located behind the houses at St Andrews Estate in the background), c.1949.

Chapter Two

The Romans to the Normans

Before the Romans

Before the Romans came to Britain the indigenous Celtic people formed a number of independent nations. The Dumnonii (or Damnonii) occupied Devon, Cornwall and the western parts of Somerset and Dorset. The Dumnonii (their Roman name) were Iron Age Celts, they mined tin and other minerals from Dartmoor, the Tamar Valley and Cornwall and they traded with the Phoenicians and other Mediterranean civilisations long before the Roman invasion.

The Romans

A Roman fort complex was found on St Andrew's Hill by aerial reconnaissance in 1984. A small fort, clearly visible as crop marks on aerial photographs, is thought to have been replaced by a larger fort and that both were built during the first century AD. The whole site is scheduled as an ancient monument.

Trial excavations were undertaken by Exeter Museum Archaeological Field Unit in June 1992. No archaeological features were located in the excavation trenches and the decision was taken to excavate further trenches in the eastern half of the field. These were dug in July 1992 and were subsequently backfilled following the discovery and recording of a large Roman ditch running north–south close to the hedgebank on the eastern side of the field. A total of 22 Roman pot shards were found during the excavations. Small numbers of post-medieval finds and prehistoric flint artefacts were also found, but not in sufficient quantity to indicate exceptional activity in this area.

The Roman army reached Exeter in about 50AD under the command of Vespasian. At Exeter the Romans established a fort to mark the limit of the area of their occupation (on the site where Rougemont Castle later stood). Another fort was constructed at Moridunum, now known as Hembury Fort, near Honiton. Roman roads were built to connect Exeter with Bath and London along the old British tracks.

There are very few remains of Roman settlements in Devon but the fact that some Roman buildings existed points to some sort of truce between the Romans and the Dumnonii. No attempt was made to make slaves of the people and it appears that the Dumnonii were largely left to themselves and probably continued to have a degree of self-government throughout the Roman occupation.

Whilst digging for a sewer in Tiverton Road a considerable amount of sett stones or paving was discovered about 18 inches below the surface, which ran diagonally across the present road. This indicates that there may have been a Roman pathway through the town.

Crossroads, Tiverton Road, c.1910; the remains of a Roman path were found along here.

After the Romans

The Romans withdrew from Britain in about 410 and some 200 years of intense Celtic missionary activity in Dumnonia (the ancient name for Devon) followed. Missionaries from Ireland landed on the coast of Dumnonia and other accessible areas to preach the Gospel of Christ. Among them came St Colomba of Tir-de-Glas and his companion St Disen.

Despite the Roman occupation the people of Dumnonia were mostly pagan. Much of East Devon and Somerset was forest and moorland, such as Exmoor. The only cultivated land was around the small settlements or 'tuns'. The most fertile part of Devon, and therefore the most densely populated, stretched from the River Exe to the present Somerset border and beyond as far as the River Parrett, as much of West Somerset was included in Dumnonia.

It is thought that St Colomba came to the area in about 450AD and set up his preaching station close to the river 'where two roads intersected', possibly somewhere in the St Georges Well area and that it was around this preaching station that the town of Cullompton gradually emerged.

The Anglo-Saxons

The Saxons did not reach Devon until the early years of the seventh century. In 658 they defeated the British at a place called Peonan, which is probably Pinhoe, between Cullompton and Exeter, captured Exeter and occupied the lands of the Exe and Culm valleys. Early in the second half of the seventh century Devon became one of the seven shires of Wessex.

The majority of Devon names are of Saxon origin – particularly those towns, villages and farms ending with '-ton', '-ham', '-ford', '-hayne', '-cot' and '-worthy'. It was common Saxon practice to join '-ton' to the name of a river to describe a settlement on its banks.

Each settlement managed its own affairs and existed mainly in isolation. The laws of King Ina (693) maintained that if a stranger approached a villa or settlement without shouting or sounding his horn then his relatives would have no redress if he was slain as a brigand. A subsequent Saxon law of King Edgar allowed a bell on the neck of his ox or dog to be sufficient warning. Hospitable as they were to strangers, a Saxon stranger had to live ten years or more in the parish before ceasing to be regarded as a 'foreigner'.

For the next 400 years the lands stretching from beyond Taunton through Cullompton down to the shores of Torbay, seem to have passed as a whole into the possession of the Saxon kings. It still belonged to the King at the time of the Norman Conquest and afterwards. The Saxons established a number of large villages in Devon in which settlers lived under royal protection. They gave a tenth of their conquered land for the support of the clergy and of the churches that were built in such villages.

A 'collegiate' church was one around which a number of priests lived and from which they went out to preach and visit the neighbouring farms and settlements. As Cullompton was situated at the main gateway into Devon and already possessed a large Christian community, 'prayer' station and 'holy well', it was an obvious choice for the erection of a 'collegiate' church, of which there were about a dozen in Devon at the time of the Domesday Survey (1086).

The 25th Law or 'Exception' of King Egbert of Wessex (802–809) ordered that one entire hide of land should be given to every collegiate church, service free. Five outlying estates called 'prebends' were given by the Saxons for the support of the priests of Cullompton's collegiate church. A prebend was a landed property, sometimes as large as a manor, set aside and given for the maintenance of a priest. It could be let out and farmed and the rents used to support the priest, or the priest could reside in the prebend. There might be an oratory or chapel-of-ease built on the prebend and sometimes a burying place. The five prebends of Cullompton were:

(i) The Prebend of Uppertone (Upton) at the top of the hill (upper town) on the far side of the River Culm. The connection of Upton with the name of the parish church 'the Rectory of Upton and Cullompton' is found as late as 1610. Until 1680 there was a burial ground there, used by the Quakers, and in 1067 the area of the prebend consisted of 330 acres, including Weaver prebend, and there was a township thereon. There is much to suggest that the original collegiate church stood on the lands of the prebend or manor of Uppertone. Whether it stood where the present church stands or whether it was erected, as so many Saxon churches were, at the top of a hill, to serve as a landmark for the surrounding countryside, is unknown. There is also a quarry at Upton, long-since disused, first worked by the Romans, and from which much of the stone used in the building of St Andrews Church, in the fifteenth century, came.

(ii) The Prebend of Wievre (Weaver) lay on the southern boundary of the parish with Plymtree, adjoining that of Upton. It was later associated with Upton in the rent rolls of St Nicholas Priory.

(iii) The Prebend of Esse (Ash Thomas) lay at the north of the parish, in the present parish of Halberton. There was an ancient chapel and a chapel still exists on the site today.

(iv) The Prebend of Colebroche (Colebrooke) lies near the western boundary of the parish with Bradninch; an ancient chapel existed on this estate at Trinity, probably known as Luttockeswell, now in ruins.

(v) The Prebend of Hineland (Henland) lies in the present parish of Kentisbeare but it was an 'outlier' (outlying estate) of this parish as late as 1876. Outlying land, or islands of land, surrounded by the land belonging to another lord, were common in many Devon parishes from Anglo-Saxon times. Evidence suggests that these prebends provided the sustenance of the priests who served in the adjoining parishes until such time as a parish church was built separate from Cullompton.

The Prebendary of Uppertone was the chief, and probably the best paid, of the five priests attached to the collegiate church. A thirteenth-century record reads 'The Prior of St Nicholas in Exeter holds the church of Columpton, the churchlands of which include Weaver and Ash and Henland and the township of Uppertone'.

The Danes

There is no record of any fighting taking place in the area during the Danish invasions. They conquered Exeter in 876 and overwhelmed Wessex soon after and King Alfred was forced into hiding. Another Danish force crossed from South Wales and landed at Combwich (Cynuit) near Bridgwater in the estuary of the River Parrett in Somerset. This probably represented the first boundary between Devon and Somerset. Alfred emerged from his fortress at Athelney and defeated the Danes at Aethendun (or Edington). Peace was made at the Treaty of Wedmore in 878 and Alfred of Wessex, Lord of the Manor of Cullompton, became the acknowledged King of all England.

During the tenth century the large regions within a shire were subdivided into districts known as Hundreds. The Hundred was originally a unit of taxation, answering for 100 hides to the King's geld (national tax). The Hundred remained an important administrative unit for many hundreds of years. It has been defined as:

> *... a major division of a shire with jurisdiction over a rural area for the preservation of order and the punishment of petty crimes, with the obligation to meet at frequent intervals and the right to hold regular markets. Shires were divided into hundreds and hundreds were sub-divided into units known as tithings or townships.*

Every man, if he claimed to be a 'liege' man (one living under British law), had to be enrolled in a Hundred or be treated as an outlaw. The members of each tithing were to be their own policeman and jury (subject only at a later date to the King's justice of assize). Under this system of mutual liability and suretyship, known as 'frank-pledge', the pivot of Alfred's administration, the people of the parish soon became a peaceable and law-abiding community.

King Alfred died at the age of 54 on 26 October 901 in Winchester. He bequeathed a number of manors in southern England to his younger son Ethelred, including Guildford, Godalming and Cullompton. Further conquests by the Danes in Devon during the tenth century brought the Manor of Cullompton into the hands of the Danish Princess, the Lady Gytha, who married Godwin, Earl of Wessex. She encouraged the building of churches on her vast estates.

Many Danes came to settle in Devon and a considerable Danish settlement grew up on the southwest of this parish running into the adjoining parish of Kentisbeare, where the Danish names Chentesbere, Godric and Alnod are found in the Domesday Survey. It is likely that both Merlesoan and Almer who held the Manors of Aller and Colebrooke in Cullompton were also of Danish extraction. The Danes settled in groups, holding adjoining fields and lands and there is a local tradition that the dwarf-elder, called Dane-wort, usually flourishes at places where the Danes used to live and died. Dane-wort flourishes in many parts of Cullompton parish.

Other Anglo-Saxon manors within the boundaries of the present parish that were created or defined before the Norman Conquest, and perhaps during King Alfred's reign, with their owners and/or occupiers in the time of King Edward the Confessor (1047–65), were as follows.

South of the Parish
The Manor of Langford (Brismer)
The Manor of Colump (Brismer)
The Manor of Chaldon (Semar)
The Manor of Aller (Merlesoan)
The Manor of Upton-Weaver (Torbert)

West and North-west of the Parish
The Manor of Pantesford (i.e. Ponsford) (Sedwin)
The Manor of Hillesdone (Sirewald)
The Manor of Colebrooke (Almer)
The Manor of Bernardesmora, which included Padbrook (Almer)

It was probably during the ownership of Lady Gytha that the land was given to establish the remainder of the five prebends associated with the collegiate church. The prebends of Esse and Hineland lay upon her estate in Cullompton.

Before the Norman Conquest, in the area now comprising Cullompton parish, there were ten separate manors as well as churchlands and prebends. Assessment for land tax and other national taxes were made and collected at the Hundred Court. A roll was kept, called the court roll, which contained a list of the under tenants, villeins or lords of the constituent manors of the Hundred, particulars of their holdings and the date of admission of their successors (who were bound to continue the payment of geld and were supplied with copies of that part of the roll relating to their own holdings).

The Hundred Courts were usually held on an entrenched hill or *kopje*, where the knights of the Hundred had perhaps met for defence against the Danes. King Alfred sought to ensure that such a meeting place should be situated on Crown land, or else he made the meeting place, called the Hundred Manor, into one of his royal manors. The Manor of Cullompton was a royal manor and the Hundred Court met on the hillside, above the farm now known as Whorridge Farm and from which the post-Norman name of the Hundred – Harridge or Hayrigge or Highridge – was taken.

In control of all the Hundreds in the shire was the King's chief officer, called at first the Ealderman (Alderman) and later the Earl of the Shire. Criminal cases continued to be adjudicated at the Hundred Court for some centuries, until the introduction of courts of assize and the appointment of King's Justices. The Hundred system continued for mainly administrative purposes into the nineteenth century; it was the basis of the ecclesiastical sub-divisions of the diocese known as Rural Deaneries and of later local government divisions.

King William the Conqueror and the Normans

King Edward the Confessor (1047–65) nominated his successor as his brother-in-law Harold, son of Lady Gytha and Earl Godwin. The people of the parish rejoiced that the Witan (the precursor of the English Parliament) elected the lord of their manor as King of England in 1065. But the claim to the throne was contested by a foreigner, William Duke of Normandy. During the battle at Senlac, outside Hastings, King Harold was slain and William the Conqueror became the new Lord of the Manor of Cullompton.

Devon remained loyal to the cause of Harold. His mother, Countess Gytha, fled for refuge, first to Exeter and later to Ireland. The following is an extract from the Anglo-Saxon Chronicle:

> *AD 1067 – This year went out Githa, Harold's mother, into Bradan relic (i.e. Flat Holm), and the wives of many good men with her, and there abode sometime, and so departed over the sea to St Omer. This year King William took over Exeter.*

It is possible that women from Cullompton, loyal to Harold, along with their sons and husbands, may well have accompanied Gytha to find refuge in Ireland when William the Conqueror marched this way after capturing Exeter in 1067 and then continued to harry the Normans in Somerset and Devon for some years onwards. There was no outstanding English leader left and within a few years William I had crushed all resistance and divided the country up among his Norman knights as a reward for their services. This was the start of the feudal age. The results of the Norman Conquest on the life of the parish were:

(i) The ancient royal manor of Upton-Weaver was given by the Conqueror to his nephew by marriage, Baldwin, son of Gilbert, Earl of Brionne in Normandy. Baldwin was made Earl of Devon and given as many as 150 manors in different parts of the county to compose his 'barony', this included four other manors in this parish i.e. Langafort (Langford), Pontesfort (Ponsford), Bernardesmore (later Moorhayes) and Columb. He built his castle at Okehampton at which, for the next 200 years, his tenants from the five manors in this parish had to appear in person to pay their taxes. Baldwin never lived here and the Saxons were left on their lands, subject only to the fees they had to pay.

(ii) Local government, on the lines regulated by King Alfred in the Hundred and Manor Courts, was continued but with people now dependent on the Honour of Okehampton. The old Royal Manor of Cullompton was no longer the administrative centre of the hundred, which, for a while, centred around the neighbouring village of Silverton, then known as Sulfertona.

(iii) The Church and the clergy were brought under the control of the Papacy and the compulsory celibacy of all parsons was introduced. It meant that not only parish priests, but almost all professional or educated men could have no legitimate children and no wives to assist in the work of the church. The result was an increase in illegitimacy and bastardy.

(iv) The tenants, and the new lords of the manors are listed in the Domesday Survey. The survey suggests that the population was about 150, excluding women and children, and there were two mills situated on the River Colomb at Langford and Whiteheathfield.

(v) Before the Battle of Hastings had been fought William the Conqueror vowed to build a mighty abbey on the site of the battlefield if God gave him victory. Battle Abbey took many years to build and cost far more than anticipated. To secure the funds for its erection it was necessary to confiscate the endowments of existing churches. The lands belonging to the defeated Harold were a natural target. So it was that the church and churchlands of Cullompton were among the first to be given to the new abbey. The patronage of this benefice and the appointment of its parsons for nearly 500 years was to pass into the hands of monks until the dissolution of the monasteries in 1536–39.

Aerial view of Cullompton, late 1940s.

The monks of St Nicholas in Exeter, by which the name the community of monks from Battle Abbey became known, made drastic changes in the spiritual organisation and ministrations within Cullompton parish for financial reasons. They appropriated the tithes and income of their church here to better maintain their own conventual life in Exeter. The monasteries were free to do as they pleased and the people of the parish had no protector.

The priests were taken away and their stipends appropriated by the monks of St Nicholas and instead of having a parson of their own living amongst them they had to rely on a monk riding or walking over the meadows to give them the sacraments and bury their dead. Every householder was required to make an annual contribution of one halfpenny to meet the huge cost of the new cathedral at Exeter and the church at Cullompton was left to wither and decay. There was no lord of the manor, baron or knight interested to care for the welfare of the people.

When Civil War broke out in England in 1135 Baldwin, Earl of Devon supported the cause of Matilda, daughter of King Henry I. Mercenary soldiers were engaged on both sides by the feudal barons and knights who supported either Matilda or her cousin Stephen, son of Adela, daughter of William I. In Matilda's interest Baldwin garrisoned the Castle of Exeter and it was besieged for three months by soldiers of Stephen, who occupied Baldwin's Manor of Cullompton, and took for themselves such food and support as they could find.

Stephen himself came this way, at the head of 200 knights, to force the surrender of Exeter and the West, but despite the use of battering rams and mines it was only the failure of the water-supply that eventually compelled Baldwin to open the gates.

The manor of Cullompton, with Baldwin's other Devonshire possessions, was confiscated by Stephen and subsequently conferred on the family of Richard de Clifford. In compensation for the damage done to Exeter Cathedral, Stephen assigned to the Dean and Chapter a yearly sum of 150/- to be paid from Baldwin's forfeited manor of Cullompton for 'an everlasting alms for making good the losses which I caused to the same church in a siege'.

How long this 'everlasting alms' was paid is uncertain. On the death of Stephen, Matlida's son ascended to the throne as King Henry II. The scandal of absentee monks reaping financial benefits but ignoring spiritual duties became so great that a decree of the Lateran Council in 1179 required every priory and abbey to appoint a competent priest to take up permanent residence in his parish. The first perpetual vicar of Cullompton was appointed by St Nicholas Priory in 1181.

Chapter Three

The Plantagenets to the Victorians

The Plantagenets, 1154–1399

Henry II: 1154–1189
Richard I: 1189–99
John: 1199–1216
Henry III: 1216–72
Edward I: 1272–1307
Edward II: 1307–27
Edward III: 1327–77
Richard II: 1377–99

Sir William (1181–1231): The first perpetual vicar of Cullompton to be appointed by the prior and monks of St Nicholas Priory in Exeter. He was their librarian or chartulary, in other words the monk in charge of the writing and keeping of the charters, documents, accounts and registers.

Shortly after his appointment the prior and monks of St Nicholas increased their revenue from the parish by securing from Alan de Furnellis (or Furneaux) a grant of the tithes of the mill at Coluptone. The mill was situated on the river Columb close to the boundary of the priory lands of the former prebend of Upton, adjoining Nyewlond (Newlands) and Southwode which belonged to Alan de Furnellis, one of the Justiciars of Henry II. The grant was confirmed in the presence of Bartholomew, Bishop of Exeter (1162–84).

The monks of the priory of Montacute, in Somerset, also owned land in the parish, administered by their small daughter house of Karswille or Carswell, adjoining Coluptone. Since the reign of King Stephen they had possession of Paddockesbroke (Padbrook), La Wetenelonde (Whiteheathfield) and Bernardesmore. Other land in and adjoining this parish was also given to Montacute and/or Karswelle by Hugh Peverell of Sampford Peverell and of Aller manor by William his son and by Roger de Hele, from whose family Hele takes its name.

All that remains of the ancient church is an old Crusader's headstone, or coffin lid, which dates from c.1200. It is preserved against the east inner wall of the south porch. It bears no inscription and this Knight of Cullompton who accompanied King Richard on his Crusade to the Holy Land remains unidentified.

Sir Jocelyne, vicar of the parish until 1265: Changes and consolidation in the ownership of the various lands and manors were frequent at this time. The family of de la Moor were staking their claims on land east of the River Colomb, where later they built Moorhayes. The family of Hilderesdon was in occupation of the manor of the same name. The North Manor of Colomptone, and the largest in the parish belonged to the Earl of Devon. Richard de Langeforde, the grandson of Roger de Langeforde, after whom his manor was named, held Langford, an estate of some 500 acres at the south of the parish. Philip de Furnelis (or Furneaux) held Niewlond (now called Newlands) and Southwood. Henry de Bolley held Upper and Lower Ponsford together with much land in Kentisbeare parish. The Peverell family of Sampford Peverell held Aller Peverell in this parish. Alice de Kideleg, whose family later spelt their name Kilrington and then Killerton bought land at Colebrooke in this parish and in Bradninch.

The grant of a market and fair was a privilege eagerly sought from the Crown by the lord of a substantial manor. The first recorded market and fair held in Cullompton was granted at Westminster on 28 December 1257 by royal charter to Baldwin de Insula (son and heir of Baldwin de Insula, sometime Earl of Devon) and to his heirs. He was granted a weekly market on Thursdays together with an annual fair there on the vigil, feast and morrow of St John the Baptist (24 June). All the fun of the fair was henceforth to be enjoyed by the people of the parish, together with a large influx of visitors and therefore of money. The site of the market and fair lay at first in the churchyard adjacent to St Andrews Church and then just outside it on land stretching down to Cockpit Hill.

Sir Gilbert De Rya (or Rye) 1265–1307: Sir Jocelyn's successor. He was instituted on 26 January 1265, about the same time as the basis of English constitutional government was broadened by the writ of Earl Simon de Montfort in calling two citizens from every borough as well as two knights from every county to sit together in the first English Parliament.

By the end of the thirteenth century the parochial system, with a parson living among the people of the parish was in clear existence. The geographical limits of the manor had become, in general, the geographical limits of the parish and the villa (village or town) superseded the manor as the designation of the area.

The Vicar is assigned in the name of his vicarage all the altar fees, the tithe of hay, and a decent house to the value of half a mark. All the other revenues shall belong to the Prior and Convent of St Nicholas in Exeter.
Taxacio Vicarie Ecclesie Columptone, 1269

This meant that about four-fifths of the income of the vicarage was taken by the monks, and the parson received less than a quarter of the revenue to which he would have been entitled, had the benefice been a rectory. The smaller tithes of wool, milk, butter, cheese, fruit and the young of cattle, generally allotted to the vicar, as well as the greater tithes of all that grows in the open fields, and the rent of churchlands, all went to the Exeter monks. A 'mark' was equivalent to 34 pence, so the value of the vicarage, at half a mark, suggests that he was not overhoused.

The valuable lands belonging to the (north) Manor of Columptone, which for 200 years had belonged to the Earls of Devon, and had been administered on his behalf by a steward or baliff, now followed suit with the adjoining churchlands of Upton-Weaver and passed into monastic hands. In 1278 the widowed and heirless Countess of Devon presented the manor and its lands to the abbot and monks of the new Cistercian Abbey that she had founded in that year on the banks of the River Tavy on her Boclond estate near Tavistock. The Cistercians were to prove excellent landlords for the next 250 years and they did a great deal for the people of Cullompton.

Sir William, Penitentiary (1306/8–1322): In 1316 the Hundred of Harridge, whose boundaries were roughly conterminous with the Rural Deanery of Plymtree, consisted of one borough and five townships or villae, there were:

(i) the Borough of Bradninch and the townships of Plymtrue (Plymtree) with Payhembury and Feniton.
(ii) Childon (Shaldon) with Karswell, Pauntersfoot (Ponsford) and Colmpton (Cullompton).
(iii) Taleton with Bikelegh (Bickleigh), Alre Peverel (in Colmpton) and Wodebyare.
(iv) Thorverton with Cadebyry (Cadbury) and Kentelesbeare (Kentisbeare).
(v) Silferton, with Monk Culm, Upexe and Netherexe.

It is worth noting that the ancient borough of Bradninch was at the height of its prosperity during this period, although it was the small township of Plymtree which gave its name to the Deanery of 15 parishes, in which both the churches of Bradninch and Cullompton were included.

At this time there was no township, as such, of Cullompton and the density of population centred around the north Manor of Cullompton and the Manors of Aller Peverell and Ponsford. However, the Manor of Cullompton must have become one of the largest and most prosperous in the Hundred of Harridge if the figures recorded by Hooker, the sixteenth-century historian and great writer about Exeter, are correct in connection with the payment of 'tenths' and 'fifteenths' in this Hundred:

	Amount Due	**Deductions**	**Amount Payable**
Bradnynche	46s.0d.	nil	46s.0d.
Plymtree	50s.8d.	nil	50s.8d.
Childon (Shyldon)	26s.8d.	nil	26s.8d.
Colomptone	53s.0d.	6s.8d.	46s.4d.
Ponsford	12s.0d.	nil	12s.0d.
Upton-Weaver	6s.8d.	nil	6s.8d.
Taleton	57s.0d.	nil	57s.0d.
Aller Peverell	28s.2d.	nil	28s.2d.
Thorverton	64s.8d.	8s.0d.	56s.8d.
Silferton	42s.8d.	9s.4d.	33s.4d.

On the Festival of St George in 1317 a three-day market and fair was granted by King Edward II to the Abbot of Bocklonde (the successor of the Earl of Devon) as lord of the manor, to be held on his domain. A close connection existed throughout the Middle Ages with this parish (and many others) and St George, the patron saint of England. From an early date a chapel dedicated to St George stood near the ancient Celtic holy well in the area now known as St Georges Well. There was an altar and guild of St George in the parish church, and a figure of the saint was later carved on the exterior of the tower.

In the towns that possessed an abbey or monastic church it is usual to erect a market cross in the centre, or beside, the market ground where the tolls were paid. As Miss Celia Fiennes recorded in her 1695 publication *Through Devon on a Side-saddle,* 'The ancient market cross of this parish, set on stone pillars probably dates from this period'.

Master Henry Steymore, Deacon 1322–33: Within four years of his institution he killed one of his parishioners, named Maurice Potter, who, he alleged, had attacked him with extreme violence one night. His defence was that he had been suddenly assaulted in the dark in his own churchyard by Maurice Potter who had a feud against him and that he had no alternative but to avoid slaughter.

Contrary information was given against him before the Justices of the King and he was convicted and committed to the Sheriff. Steymore fled and, when a new Bishop was appointed to Exeter he appealed to him for justice, asserting that the Archdeacon had exceeded his proper jurisdiction, had denied him the justice that was his due and asked to be reinstated. It would appear that the verdict went in favour of Steymore as he was, indeed, reinstated.

However, the people of the parish then appealed on account of the grievous danger to their souls of having a murderer living amongst them and administering the sacraments. The case went on for seven years and was finally resolved by the passing of a formal sentence of deprivation against Steymore by Bishop Grandisson in a letter to the new Archbishop of Canterbury (Archbishop Stafford 1333–48). Grandisson outlined the case and the protracted investigation of the past seven years and explained that he had been finally forced to deprive Steymore on the grounds that he had failed to appear, or enter a defence regarding the three offences alleged against him, namely:

(i) that he had willfully slain one of his parishioners.
(ii) that he had not continuously resided in, or taken care of his benefice.
(iii) that he had violated the sequestration of the rents and revenues of the benefice and had thus incurred sentence of the major excommunication.

Sir John de Bromleigh, Priest 1334–48: Two weeks after the formal sentence of his predecessor, Sir John de Bromleigh was made vicar, he was probably a relative of Sir Gilbert de Bromleigh, owner of the Tydecombe portion of Tiverton, seven miles away. The times were lawless; bloodshed, murder, rape and cases of homicide were frequent. Local recorded events during Sir John de Bromleigh's time include:

(i) 1334: Langford was granted a charter for a market and three-day fair to be held at the festival of St James. Fifty years later a chapel existed in this parish dedicated to St James and it is thought that this chapel was already in existence at Langford at this date.
(ii) 1336: Sir Oliver de Dinham, who had become lord of the manor of Arle Peverell, was granted licence by the Prior and Convent of St Nicholas, Exeter, to make a watercourse through the lands of his manor from the adjoining monastic lands of Upton-Weaver. In return Sir Oliver agreed to pay the convent one penny for ever at Christmas, to be in sole charge of keeping the watercourse in good repair, and to enjoy but a moiety of fishing.
(iii) 1348: The first recorded Services of National Prayer was held in the parish owing to the onslaught of a terrible plague known as the Black Death. Mortality was very high in Devon between 1348 and 1349. Sir John was one of the victims of the plague together with the incumbents of ten other parishes in the Deanery of Plymtree. The vicars of Bradninch, Burlescome, Halberton, Sampford Peverell and Uplowman were among those infected and killed by the Black Death.

Sir Peter Molyns, Confessor 1349–57: In 1356 the inconvenience, dirt and disease caused by the lack of a proper water-supply, magnified by the incidence and aftermath of the Black Death, led the people to petition the lord of the manor for leave to construct a watercourse of clear wholesome water from the hills on his estate to flow down through the town. From that day the town watercourse has continued to flow through the town. What follows is a translation of the wording of the deed of gift of the Abbot of Bokelond, the lord of the manor, granting and confirming this gift of running water.

Know all men, present and to come, that we Thomas Abbot of Boklonde and of the Convent of the same place, have given, granted, and by this our present writing have confirmed to our whole Homage of Columpton, leave to have a watercourse of clear wholesome water between the ditch of Weremede, the land of my Lord Earl of Devon, and the land of Thomas Vacie unto the High Street of Columpton, over all our domain, and the land of our tenants. In testimony whereof our common seal is hung to these presents. These being witnesses –

Thomas Gambon William Furneaux John Roke
Thomas Facie William Whitemore
Henry Chopyn (and many others)

Given at Bokelonde, the sixth day of May, in the year of the reign of King Edward III, since the Conquest of England the twenty ninth.

The Cistercian monks of Bokelond were famed far and wide for their farming and sheep-rearing efficiency and they did much to improve, till and cultivate their land in Cullompton. The development of the woollen trade which for the next 500 years characterised the town's life and industry can be mainly attributed to them. It was from its flourishing wool trade that England found the means to finance the Hundred Years War with France between 1330 and 1430.

Sir Thomas de Pyltone 1357–61: Excommunicated by the Bishop of Exeter (Bishop Grandisson 1327–69) :

For many offences against God and the Holy Apostolic See... and that the said Thomas is reputed to be a forger and fabricator of letters and seals of the Lord Pope, and in many other ways is guilty in his aforementioned so horrible and detestable excesses to the grave danger of our subject's souls.

Two possible reasons can be gleaned from these words, which caused his excommunication:

(i) that he was a Protestant before the Reformation or
(ii) that his offence was a very common one of issuing 'forged papal indulgences for sins' or fabricated papal letters and seals, authorising their holder to 'hawk' about the country such indulgences or pardons for sin, obtainable merely by paying for them.

Sir Thomas did not submit to what he considered 'episcopal tyranny and injustice' and refused to surrender his freehold or desist from his spiritual duties.

Sir Robert Carpounter 1361: His incumbency lasted two months and it is unclear exactly what happened to him, although the Black Death broke out again in Devon at the end of 1361. It was those in poverty that were hit most severely by the plague, medical attention was non-existent and living conditions were poor. One immediate result was a scarcity of labour and a consequent increase in wages. The corn rotted in the fields, harvests were not gathered, mills could not be worked and much of the countryside went out of cultivation. Land became valueless and people starved.

The rise in wages enabled the labouring classes to free themselves from restrictions and go to work for another master. It is estimated that whereas in 1300 two-thirds of the entire population were serfs, by the time of the Reformation (c.1550) the bulk of the population were free men.

Sir Robert Tholy, Priest 1362–70 and Sir Stephen Hendre, Archpriest 1370–75: During this time the manufacturers of cloth moved from the larger towns to the market and country towns in the west of England, where running water was obtainable to work the fulling mills.

Sir John Burnel, Chaplain and Penitentiary 1375–1411: He remained vicar for 36 years until his death and burial in Cullompton. For three days (September 22–24 1387) the Bishop Brantingham (Bishop of Exeter 1370–1394) stayed with John Burnel at his manse (or vicarage). That he spared the time to visit Cullompton and appears to have been the first Bishop of Exeter to do so, suggests it was to mark a` big and important event. It seems likely that his visit was to dedicate the foundation-stone of a new parish church .

The Houses of Lancaster and York, 1399–1485

House of Lancaster	***House of York***
Henry IV 1399–1413	*Edward IV 1461–83*
Henry V 1413–22	*Edward V 1483*
Henry VI 1422–61	*Richard III 1483–85*

Sir William Sechevyll (Sackville), Chaplain 1411–15 and Sir Edward Fysshacre (or Fyshakre) 1415–33: In 1428 an Inquisition or Official Enquiry was held at Cullompton for the Hundreds of Tiverton, Harygge, Halberton, Uffculme and Hemyock in the presence of Thomas Cheddar and his fellow commissioners appointed by Parliament to collect the subsidy of tunnage and poundage, levied in that year to assist the new King Henry VI. This would suggest that Cullompton was still larger than Tiverton and a more important centre at this period.

Sir Thomas Dalyngtone, Chaplain and Penitentiary 1433–43: In 1436 the dedication of St Andrews Church took place, although this was probably not of its foundation; it is thought that this was the consecration of the church after its rebuilding.

Sir Robert Wylle, Chaplain 1439–61: Fortunes were being made in the West of England during this time through shipping and smuggling as well as the flourishing wool trade and the 'new rich' began to purchase and enlarge their estates.

At this time large bands of unemployed labourers were roaming the country seeking work. These labourers would have been used to build St Andrews Church and when they left Cullompton in search of employment elsewhere, became part of a great mass of vagrant labourers whose grievances and complaints were one of the factors leading up to the outbreak of Civil War in England in 1455, known as the Wars of the Roses.

St Andrews Church was not only built on wool. Rich cargoes, merchandise and wine, illegally smuggled into England on Spanish ships made an indirect contribution. John More of Morehayes was appointed the King's Serjeant-at-Arms in Devon and served on many a commission from 1441 onwards to enquire into whose hands such cargoes had come, and to arrest the felons and confiscate the goods.

In 1460 John More was given a Royal Commission:

> *to make inquisition in the County of Devon touching all insurrections, unlawful gatherings, felonies, murders, rapes of women, extortions, oppressions, treasons and other misdeeds.*

The affluent John More and his wife Elizabeth received a licence on 24 April 1457 to have a chapel in their new house at Morehayes. A few years later he erected a richly carved screen in the new parish church. He was a Justice of the Peace and responsible for 'gaol delivery' at Exeter Prison. He behaved with such uprightness in his various duties during the troubled times of the Wars of the Roses that when the Duke of York succeeded to the throne in 1461 as Edward IV he was given a commission by the new king to urge his loyal subjects in East Devon to 'supply ships well equipped with men, victuals and habitments of war for half a year at their own expense, for defence against the King's enemies'.

The Wars of the Roses, 1455–87

Jealousies between the family of the Earl of Devon, the Courtneys who owned Tiverton Castle and three manors in Cullompton, and Lord William Bonville, Baron of Shute, known to be a supporter of the Duke of York, led to the Courtneys and all their Devon tenants entering the Wars of the Roses on the Lancastrian side.

The Courtney tenants (of the House of Exeter) on the Manors of Langford, Ponsford and Colebrooke and the Beaufort tenants (of the House of Somerset) at Aller Peverell found themselves fighting against their neighbours on the Abbot of Buckland's North Manor at Cullompton and on Sir John Dinham's estate at Whiteheathfield.

The Wars of the Roses represented an intermittent

series of dynastic struggles about who should be king. No fighting appears to have taken place in Cullompton. After a few years of gradually escalating warfare, the throne was taken by the Yorkist line in 1461, the Lancastrians took it back in 1470 and lost it again in 1471.

Sir John Webber, Clerk 1461–80: The King's commission to the Sheriff of Devon and to Sir John Dynham, Knight, Lord of Whiteheathfield, dated 16 March 1470 arrested William Courtney, Knight; High Courtenay, Knight; Peter Courtenay, Clerk (the future Bishop of Exeter); Humphrey Courtenay, Esquire; Phillip Courtenay, Esquire; Walter Courtenay, Esquire; John Secheville, Esquire; Robert Spurway and others. These men were brought before the King in Council and all their castles, lordships, manors, lands and possessions were seized as well as those of George, Duke of Clarence, Richard, Earl of Warwick, John, Robert and Thomas Otter, yeomen and others. This order meant a new owner for the Courtney manors in Cullompton, but the Courtneys were later pardoned and restored to favour.

Sir John Webber added the rood-screen at St Andrews Church which, for those that interpreted his symbolism and colour scheme reveal that, although pardoned he and his people remained, at heart, supporters of the 'red rose' of Lancaster.

The Tudors 1485–1603

Henry VII 1485–1509
Henry VIII 1509–47
Edward VI 1547–53
Jane Grey 1553
Mary I 1553–58
Elizabeth I 1558–1603

Sir John Coryngdon, Canon of Windsor 1480–96: In the attempted rebellions of Lambert Simnel (1487) and of Perkin Warbeck (1497), there is no evidence that Cullompton people played any part although Tiverton was captured by Walbeck's supporters. Finding Exeter was barricaded against them by the local gentry, they marched on Cullompton where they billetted for the night, but these 6,000 men fled as soon as Henry VII with a large army opposed them at Taunton. The King then passed through Cullompton on his way to Exeter to clear up the remains of the West Country rebellion. He remained in Exeter for nearly a month, the first time that a Tudor sovereign came into the far west.

Severe outbreaks of plague in 1485 and again in 1503 raged in this neighbourhood and caused the deaths of large numbers of people.

Despite the wars and intrigues the material prosperity of the people of Cullompton grew. The woollen industry flourished, guilds and fraternities multiplied and families grew rich and affluent, estates were enlarged (Morehayes, Kingsmill and Hillersdon) and upon the proceeds the Church was enriched with new gifts, chantry, chapels, ornamentations and vestments.

Master John Oxenbrigge 1496–1522: The Tudor kings relied on the unpaid services of the local gentry, lawyers and clerics such as More, Kelway, the Cockrams who had recently settled at Hillersdon, and Oxenbridge (spellings vary) for local government. There was no standing army but order was maintained and commercial and religious interests were supported and advanced by Henry VII and Henry VIII. The parish was thriving through commerce and a developing wool trade, begetting large families (John Kelway for example had 14 children, a typical family of the period) who built for themselves larger houses and farms.

St Andrews Church was further enhanced in 1521 with the addition of its famed Chantry Chapel by John Lane, recently settled at Kings Mill, the successor to William Rolt and Bailiff of the town. No records exist to show its cost, the time it took to build or the name of the architect. John Lane and his wife Thomasyn were buried under the original altar of their Chantry.

The Venerable Richard Tollett 1522–28: The five prebends of Cullompton were no more and their stipends were absorbed into the revenues of the Prior and Convent of St Nicholas in Exeter.

Rev John Trotte, MA BD (Fellow of Exeter College), retired to Cullompton from the Principalship of Hart Hall, Oxford (1488–1512). He founded another chantry in St Andrews Church as well as the ancient Almshouse and left sixpence a week in his will for the sustentation of six poor men in the Almshouse. His will, dated 28 January 1522 declared that his executors and overseers should, with the remains of his goods and the debts owing to him:

> *... purchase land as well for the maintenance of a priest for ever to celebrate within the Church of Columpton, as also for the relief of six poor men to have their habitation in an almshouse to be built in that town, and that the same poor men shall have to their sustentation sixpence apiece by the week, to be taken to the revenues for the said lands.*

All chantries and their revenues were confiscated by Henry VIII, and the Royal Commissioners in a certificate dated 15 February 1545, stated:

> *The said Almshouse has been dissolved by the space of one year and a half past by Martin and John Trotte, the sons of the founder, between whom there was a variance for the lands belonging to the said Almshouse, and without the Kings consent.*

At that time there was a marked contrast on leaving St Andrews Church to join the crowds in the market place. The Shambles and Cockpit Hill were dirty and laden with produce and other stalls, as well as tethered animals in the gangway and poultry and ducks running about. Adjoining the Shambles were the 'stocks' for the punishment of delinquents, and the pillory where they might be whipped, while nearby was the 'ducking stool' reserved for the punishment of women of evil repute, and of any accused of being witches. Among the shops hung the sign of the serge-weaver, the serge-dealer, the wool-comber and the chandler. (The chandler was the manufacturer and seller of candles. Up until about 1850 the people of Devon used to light their rooms by rushes, gathered from the swamps, such as those beside the River Culm.) The George Inn was nearby as was the Guild House of the Brethren of St Nicholas. Taverns abounded.

Craft and trade guilds were formed for the protection of their members engaged in such occupations, the development of the skill and the stimulation of commerce. There were also guilds or fraternities connected with the parish church concerned with practical benevolence and charity and collecting contributions from their members. A parish the size of Cullompton would have had about five or six different guilds, each possessing its own property, lands, houses and gardens. Every guild had a religious base and was connected to its own parish church. From as early as the twelfth century the skilled workers of a particular trade in the same town united expressly for the protection of their trade.

The guilds and fraternities in the parish did much to look after the poor and were the forerunners of trade unions. They acted as a friendly society and a religious purpose animated them.

Revd Robert Peryns 1528–49: During his incumbency the papal jurisdiction was overthrown. During the dissolution of the lesser monasteries, ordered by Henry VIII in 1536, the Priory of St Nicholas was removed and its property and lands, including its estate at Upton-Weaver and its tithes and income from Cullompton, passed into the hands of Sir Thomas Denys, the Sheriff and one of the King's Commissioners.

In 1540 King Henry VIII's fifth wife, Katherine Howard, was given the manors of Cullompton, Buckland, Newton St Cires, Plympton, Beer and Yarcombe as part of her marriage dowry. The lands and manors of Cullompton passed from the possession of the Church into the hands of the people who could afford to buy them from the state, and especially the prosperous wool merchants, lawyers and others of the rising 'middle classes'.

The King's Commissioners came from London to Devon and sat for a week or more in Cullompton, armed with royal authority to visit, transfer and abolish all monastic property, settle pensions on ousted monks and make a survey of the present incomes of all benefices requiring every parson to state on oath the amount he derived from his benefice from every source.

The Abbot Toker of Buckland, aware of what was coming, granted free pasture rights and land to many of the people who dwelt upon his manor. The farming tenants were glad to finally own property.

The old manor of Cullompton, given to the second Queen Katherine as part of her marriage dowry, was granted in fee to Sir John Seynt Leger (or St Leger) in 1543. The Upton-Weaver estate, after 500 years in the possession of monks, passed by sale from family to family and much of it into the hands of the Cockram family. The new gentry became Justices of the Peace and in 1546 they secured from the Crown a general pardon for Katherine Freyston, wife of Francis Freyston of Cullompton for having attacked a certain David Blackedon on the highway and stolen his purse, containing thirteen shillings.

The present tower of St Andrews Church was built in 1545. The following local story, quoted in Rev. G.W. Grubb's 'A study of English social history for a thousand years, illustrated from the life of the old market town of Cullompton in Devonshire' (unpublished, c.1940) was passed down from father to son:

The Master Builder set to work to build a tower for the people of Broadclyst between Exeter and Colompton. As he built a quarrel with his foreman became so acute that the latter left him vowing he would build a better tower somewhere else. So Master Foreman was engaged by the People of Colompton to build for them a tower that would excel the other. Riding over to inspect his ex-foreman's work at a later date, the Master Builder from Broadclyst, as the new Tower rising majestic over the River Culme came into his view, at a point on his road near Whorridge Farm, took his life. He was Master no longer.

The tower is 126 feet high and built of rich red local stone. It is said to have been paid for by John and Katherine Manning, new Protestant owners of Upton. Almost certainly a clock was erected on the new tower, the first reference to its repair is found in the churchwarden's accounts for 1616.

In 1547 a licence was granted to John More, gent., and to Elizabeth his wife and to Jane, relict of Henry Botour, to have oratories or chapels within their mansions. The tomb of one John More is still to be seen in the church, while the arms of More impaled with those of Botour occur in the screen in More's aisle in the church.

There was also a public house at Mutterton and frequent entries occur to John Weeks, 'Vitler of Mutterton', whose large family were baptised here.

Bishop William Vivian, Bishop of Hippo 1549–57 and Richard Gammon (or Samson) 1557–59: The latter was the last Catholic vicar of Cullompton. Following the coronation of Queen Elizabeth I the Protestant Prayer Book was restored. Registers of weddings, burials and christenings were henceforth to be kept in St Andrews Church and a new parson was appointed.

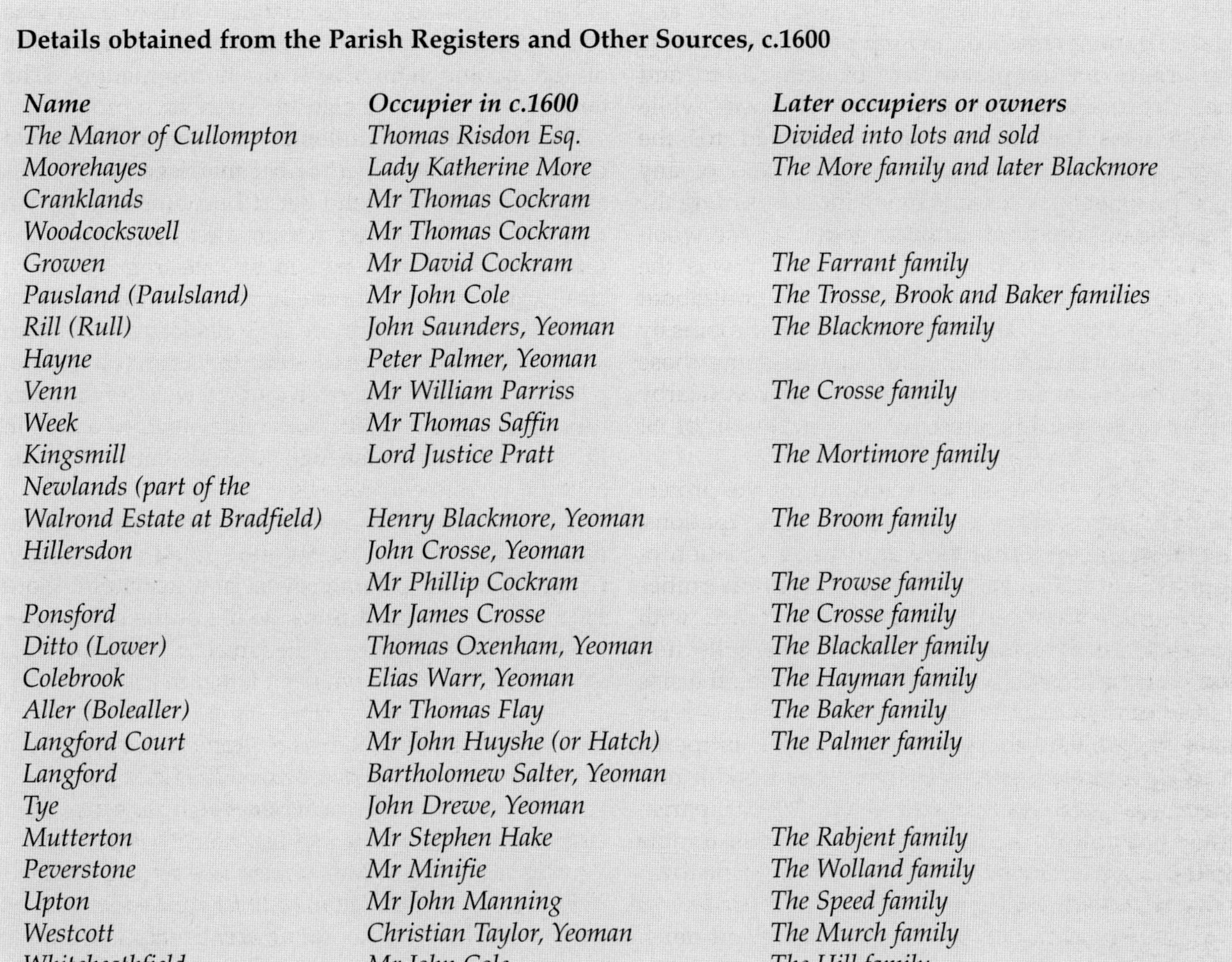

Details obtained from the Parish Registers and Other Sources, c.1600

Name	*Occupier in c.1600*	*Later occupiers or owners*
The Manor of Cullompton	*Thomas Risdon Esq.*	*Divided into lots and sold*
Moorehayes	*Lady Katherine More*	*The More family and later Blackmore*
Cranklands	*Mr Thomas Cockram*	
Woodcockswell	*Mr Thomas Cockram*	
Growen	*Mr David Cockram*	*The Farrant family*
Pausland (Paulsland)	*Mr John Cole*	*The Trosse, Brook and Baker families*
Rill (Rull)	*John Saunders, Yeoman*	*The Blackmore family*
Hayne	*Peter Palmer, Yeoman*	
Venn	*Mr William Parriss*	*The Crosse family*
Week	*Mr Thomas Saffin*	
Kingsmill	*Lord Justice Pratt*	*The Mortimore family*
Newlands (part of the Walrond Estate at Bradfield)	*Henry Blackmore, Yeoman*	*The Broom family*
Hillersdon	*John Crosse, Yeoman*	
	Mr Phillip Cockram	*The Prowse family*
Ponsford	*Mr James Crosse*	*The Crosse family*
Ditto (Lower)	*Thomas Oxenham, Yeoman*	*The Blackaller family*
Colebrook	*Elias Warr, Yeoman*	*The Hayman family*
Aller (Bolealler)	*Mr Thomas Flay*	*The Baker family*
Langford Court	*Mr John Huyshe (or Hatch)*	*The Palmer family*
Langford	*Bartholomew Salter, Yeoman*	
Tye	*John Drewe, Yeoman*	
Mutterton	*Mr Stephen Hake*	*The Rabjent family*
Peverstone	*Mr Minifie*	*The Wolland family*
Upton	*Mr John Manning*	*The Speed family*
Westcott	*Christian Taylor, Yeoman*	*The Murch family*
Whiteheathfield	*Mr John Cole*	*The Hill family*

Revd William Woodroffe (or Woodruff) 1559–73: In 1559 Royal Pardons were issued for 'all the crimes committed by them [listed below], including their reacceptance of the unreformed faith in the five years of Mary's rule, rather than face the stake and a martyr's death'. They were: Sir John More of Morehayes in Colompton, Knight; Simon Keylaye of Colompton, Merchant; George Cockram of Colompton, Merchant; Bennet Collen of Colompton.

Sir John St Leger, the new Lord of the Manor of Cullompton (after the dissolution of Buckland Abbey) was one of the Royal Commissioners who travelled throughout Devon to administer the oath of Supremacy, and to enforce the use of the English Prayer Book in every parish. Cullompton became a favourite centre for the sittings of the Queen's Commissioners during the next ten years. Sir John saw to it that the Queen's injunctions for the removal of the objects of superstitious worship and the use of the English Bible and Prayer Book were quickly obeyed in this parish.

The Queen's Commissioners also held many sittings in Cullompton to settle questions of land tenure and land ownership, as well as to oversee the changes in the ornaments and furnishings of the neighbouring churches, as ordered by the Queen. Manor houses were being built by the new squires and landowners, consequent of the break-up of the monastic estates and churchlands, and there were numerous disputes and questions between squire and farmer that were brought to the Commissioners for settlement.

The trade and taverns of Cullompton benefited from the almost daily visits of churchwardens, suitors and complainants before the Commissioners.

In 1572 Queen Elizabeth I ordered that a muster of soldiers be made in every shire and Cullompton became the centre in this part of Devon. It was expected that they would be trained and the most expert armed at the reasonable charge of the inhabitants of their own parish. Various implements of warfare were supplied by every leading inhabitant of Cullompton according to his means. George Cockram, gent. of Hillersdon, supplied the following weapons: one corselet, two long bows, two sheaves of arrows, one pike, one almen ryvett, plus two steel caps or skulls. His brother, John Cockram, supplied a similar arrangement of arms and these weapons were kept in a large chest in Lane's Aisle in the parish church under the care of the churchwardens. The latter were also given additional responsibilities as a result of the economic changes following the dissolution of the monasteries in 1536–39 and the guilds and fraternities in 1549. These included:

(i) The care of the poor and pauper administration.
(ii) The management of the almshouse and of various charities in land or money left for the poor.
(iii) The relief of passing travellers and of maimed and sick seamen and soldiers and released prisoners.
(iv) The upkeep of roads and bridges.
(v) The care of the parish armour.
(vi) Payment to the constables for the arrest and whipping of rogues and vagabonds, the punishment of immorality, swearing, drunkenness, etc.
(vii) The supervision of the grammar school.
(viii) The destruction of vermin.

The break-up of the monasteries and manors meant that the people of the parish became responsible for every public and charitable duty that others had, until then, done for them. The meeting of the people of the parish to elect churchwardens and other parish officers (such as overseers) became known as the Vestry – so called because it was first held in the vestry of the church. In the Vestry all property owners and householders had an equal vote, and here for the next 350 years they were free to elect their own parish officers with no outside parliamentary dictation, to scrutinise their accounts and to control their activities.

From 1660 to 1685 when an intolerant parliament was largely controlled by the Cavalier favourites of Charles II the greatest interest and care was shown by the people of the parish in the duties of local government and the parish accounts were meticulously kept. When England became strong and prosperous under Queen Elizabeth I and under the large Hanoverian kings, interest in local affairs dwindled and the same parish officers held office year after year.

The Vestry minutes of this parish since 1732 are in existence and contain a mass of interesting information. A tavern in the town was the usual venue for such meetings.

Revd William Jennings 1573–c.85: More than four-fifths of the population of England, by this time numbering some 4 million, lived in the country towns and villages during the Elizabethan era. A country town of an average size contained some 5,000 inhabitants and Cullompton was about this size.

An Elizabethan Act ordered the compulsory wearing of woollen hats or caps on the Lord's Day by every person above the age of seven years. John Drew, the hatter of this town prospered as did the the weavers living in Clampitts and Crow Green. Weavers saw their best days as the local people visited their shops to buy their 'Sunday best'.

The trade of the butchers suffered a set back though as another Elizabethan Act 'forbidding them to kill, dress or permit to be eaten any flesh in Lent or any 'fish day' appointed by law to be observed, or on any Friday'. This act was passed to assist the British fishermen. The Sunday 'joint' became looked forward to but its cooking was not allowed as an excuse for not attending church and further legislation enacted the compulsory nature of Sunday worship.

However, another act allowed exceptions from the observance of fasts and days of abstinence, by obtaining a cheap licence from the curate, so many people took little notice of fast days and days of abstinence. Butchers, for example, obtained licences to kill for the sick and infirm, while the appetites of the soldiers billeted in the town from 1572 onwards more than compensated butchers for closing on 'fish days'.

Money paid for licences was used to assist the poor, according to the statutory proclamations of both Edward VI and Elizabeth I. Trade was flourishing and the people could well afford licence fees. Their interests at that time were eating and drinking and amusements such as cockfighting and bull-baiting. One of Cullompton's streets is now named Cockpit Hill where such cockfights used to take place close to the church and the church-house where the ale was brewed.

The rich merchants, clothiers and weavers were building themselves mansions in the main street, but behind their new houses they constructed cottages – back to back in little courts in which to house their employees. The work took place in the open courtyard or the cottage and workers had to provide their own looms and tools, while the employer provided the materials. Due to the unhealthy and primitive living conditions there were outbreaks of plague in the years 1578, 1579, 1580, 1590 and 1591.

War with Spain led Queen Elizabeth to order a muster of all able-bodied men in 1572 and 1578. Cullompton was the headquarters for the muster of the Hayridge Hundred (or divisions) of Devonshire, where the soldiers of other parishes came to be trained. The threat of the Spanish Armada led to the following local measures of defence in 1586:

(i) The erection of beacons upon the hills surrounding the town, which were watched day and night by 'fit men of good discretion'.
(ii) Standing watches at all bridges and fords in the parish, and on the high roads.
(iii) All trained soldiers and all others 'mustered and charged with armour' were to repair to their parish church (where armour was stored), there to arm themselves and remain, until 'they have direction unto what place they shall repair'.
(iv) Each man thus armed to keep his armour and weapons in good condition, on penalty of a day in the stocks, or a second offence ten days in gaol. He was to be paid at the rate of 8d. a day.

St Andrews Church was chosen as the rendezvous as it was the largest building in the parish, and the churchyard and the market outside also provided a convenient parade ground.

Revd John Milward c.1585–1601: Attributed with the rise of Cullompton Grammar School under the shadow of the Church. However, side by side with a growing interest in education went an extremely low code of morality. Bastardy and vagrancy were common; the number of such papers in the church chest was enormous for a parish the size of Cullompton.

In an effort to deal with begging without a licence the Cullompton constables were responsible for whipping, not only men, but also women and children. The parish possessed its own pillory and whipping-post, its own stocks, which stood in the southwest of the churchyard and its 'cage' or 'lock-up' for the immediate detention of rogues and vagabonds. A hospital or 'House of Correction' for poor people and passers-by who refused to work – the forerunner of the later 'Poor Law' institution – was built in Exeter in 1578. Each parish was rated at one halfpenny per week for the 'relief of the Hospital' as the House of Correction was called, and for the prison called the 'Gaole' which appears to have been part of the same building.

The House of Stuart, The Commonwealth and The Stuarts Restored

James I 1603–25
Charles I 1625–49
Oliver Cromwell 1649–58
Richard Cromwell 1658–59
Charles II 1660–85
James II 1685–88
William III 1689–1702; Mary II 1689–94
Anne 1702–14

Dr Richard Carpenter 1601–26: A disastrous fire within a year of his arrival caused much damage among the old thatched and timbered houses, with the losses adding up to some £8,000. A brief for this amount was issued by King James I for the rebuilding of the houses, and the relief of the homeless. In addition, the Devonshire Justices voted £50 out of the 'Hospital' money, and individually advanced small loans to be repaid at the next sessions.

As a result of the fire two fine Elizabethan-style houses or mansions were erected on the cleared sites in the main street, known as the Walronds and the Manor House (formerly Sellerkes). The former was built by Sir John Peeter or Petre, whose sister Dorothy Petre was married to Nicholas Wadham and was responsible for the building of Wadham College, Oxford.

Whether the fire was due to an accident or some political cause is not known, but in 1605 the failure of the Gunpowder Plot to destroy both the King and the Houses of Parliament gave rise to local rejoicing and demonstrations of loyalty, together with a popular aversion against the Roman Catholic Church, believed to have been responsible for the plot.

As a result of the Gunpowder Plot the laws were tightened against Roman Catholics, who in 1606 were debarred from practicing as barristers or physicians and from acting as guardians or trustees. The parish constables were directed to act as spies on the religious views of all freeholders and to search the houses of any suspected of being Roman Catholic. An entry in the churchwarden's accounts in 1617 reads 'pd for an Excommunication against Mr Sandford', suggesting that this freeholder preferred freedom of conscience to compliance with the orders of King and Parliament.

The times were among the most prosperous thus far experienced by local people. As wealth multiplied in the peaceful days of James I, new and better houses were built and several valuable charities were bequeathed for the poor, or for binding apprentices, while the poor law kept a man from starving. The most valuable charity made to the town was that of George Spicer in 1624, who bequeathed the sum of £300 for the annual binding out of four poor children as apprentices.

Revd Richard Peck 1626–37: Charles I and his Parliament were at loggerheads and people were becoming more and more divided into two parties: the Church (or Anglican) party and the Puritans. The King was a churchman, and the church party became known as the Royal party while the Puritans allied themselves with the cause of Parliament.

The King issued a declaration called the 'Book of Sports' which encouraged and recommended the playing of certain sports and games on Sundays, as this was the only day on which working people could practice regularly. The Puritans considered this to be a direct insult to God.

In 1631 the Justices at the Quarter Sessions at Exeter were 'credibly informed that much disorder and great misdemeanors had been committed in Cullompton by the setting up of the maypole'. It was ordered to be taken down as 'the cause of great outrages, disorderly assemblies and riotous meetings'.

The cutting down of maypoles all over the country, under Puritan influence, caused fierce anger in many places, and the dispute over Sunday observance was one cause of the Civil War. Within ten years the 'Book of Sport' was publicly burned by Act of Parliament (1643) and all persons were forbidden under heavy penalty:

> *... to be present on the Lords Day at any wrestling, shooting, bowling, masques, wakes, church-ale games, dancing, ringing of bells for pleasure or other pastimes and all maypoles to be pulled down.*

Bad harvests and the outbreak of plague, together with the difficulties of transport and a rise in the value of money (through the King's unending attempts to raise funds and taxes) meant that the price of food was soaring.

Maypole dancers in Cullompton, c.1910. Maypole dancing was forbidden on Sundays under the 1643 Act of Parliament.

Farmers gave two valuable charities to the parish: £100 in lands by John Hill in 1631, and Whiteheathfield Farm and other lands by Roger Hill and Anne his wife in 1632.

Frequent mention is made in the churchwarden's accounts from 1600 onwards of the church-house, which was situated in what is now Pye Corner. The church-house would have contained a hall where the ale feasts were held, as well as a kitchen for the baking of cakes and brewing of ale and rooms to store the ale. The churchwarden's accounts for 1610 and the following years record:

In primis received of the pish Money made the last yeare for selling Ale and guiftes £41.13s.

Whereof wee bestowed for things in the Church house the sum of 38s.9d.

The 'things in the Church house' referred to would be the expenses in connection with the brewing of ale and baking of cakes for the succeeding year. The churchwardens were the owners of the church-house and were responsible for its upkeep. Accounts show that the upper part was let out. From 1732 the poor were paid at the church-house and, until the building of the workhouse in 1737 it is likely that it was used for giving a night's lodging to passing poor travellers and strangers. No reference can be found in the Charity Commissioners records, dating from 1818, relating to the church-houses of Devonshire, so it can be assumed that by this time it had passed into other hands.

Civil War

Revd William Skynner 1637–43: Appointed by the Puritan merchant Robert Cockram of Hillersdon. Some 600 parishioners followed his lead in signing the 'Solemn Vow and Protestation' on 22 August 1641, including Mr Cockram himself, Thomas Cockram, George Cockram, George More of Morehayes and Thomas Prowse the Elder who was a close friend of Mr John Pym MP who was responsible for its wording (parish registers of Cullompton 1641). In the preface to his will dated 13 February 1642 Thomas Prowse wrote:

Being now resolved to use my best endeavours to exterminate those locusts and caterpillars who have now invaded this Countie of Devon, and doe endeavour as much as in them lye to alter the fundamental lawes of this Kingdom of England, and that which is most dear to a Christian, the Protestant Religion now established within the said Kingdom, in which Religion I am now resolved to live and die...

It would appear that the local people truly believed the Parliamentary cause was the side of justice and religion and that those that fought for the King were the enemies of God. In general, London and most of the towns with commercially minded Puritan middle-classes, as well as the seaports and the east and south of England supported Parliament. Behind the King were the old-fashioned country squires, churchmen and Roman Catholics. Exeter, Plymouth and for the most part Devon with its ports and Puritan spirit were 'Roundhead', while the Cornishmen were strongly 'Cavalier'.

In the course of the Civil War two men of Cullompton were hung and quartered by the highway by the Cavaliers, and were later buried in the churchyard. The registers contain these significant entries:

21 Sept 1643	*John Fry was buryed, being hanged by the King's Army*
4 April 1644	*Moses Pudgley was buryed, being hanged by ye King's Party.*

In the neighbourhood were three strongly Royalist houses, that of John Ackland at Columb-John, Peter Sainthill at Bradninch and John Were at Silverton. These became strongholds of the Cavaliers. Frequent sorties were made by Sir John Ackland from Columb-John and his troop though Cullompton. To keep their support in Cornwall it became essential for the Royalists to capture Exeter and the surrounding district. A strong force was sent under Prince Maurice, nephew of Charles, in 1643. They marched through Cullompton and took possession of all the roads round Exeter, while the Cornish Cavaliers defeated the Parliamentarians at Torrington and marched on Exeter from the west.

Throughout the course of the Civil War, the parish had troops stationed among them, on one side or the other. Royalist troops, for example, were stationed in Cullompton between 1643 and 1645 in order to protect their stronghold at Exeter and prevent the town from becoming a base for an attacking army.

Dr William Schlater 1644–54: On 20 September 1644 prior to an attack on Exeter, Charles I captured Cullompton from the Roundheads and passed the night at the Cavalier stronghold of Peter Sainthill at Bradninch. A year later, following the greatest battle of the Civil War at Naseby (14 June 1645), the Earl of Fairfax was sent into the West Country to regain Parliamentary control. On 15 October 1645 Fairfax marched against Cullompton. The defending Royalist soldiers were under the command of Lord Millar who was hated by the Puritans of Devon. The people of Cullompton rose in the rear of the Cavaliers, holding their town in support of the oncoming Parliamentary forces of Lord Fairfax. Lord Millar and his dragoons were put to flight and ended up in Tiverton.

The church bells of Cullompton rang out a welcome to Lord Fairfax, 'Black Tom' as he was known to his soldiers, and a Council of War was held in Cullompton. The captured Cavaliers were confined within the church. Lord Fairfax sent Major-General Massey with his horse from Cullompton and Colonel Weaver with a brigade on foot, to march over the hills to capture Tiverton, while he and some 7,000 men pressed on after the retreating Cavaliers towards Silverton and Exeter. Oliver Cromwell also joined the fray and with his 'Ironsides' marched through Cullompton to join Fairfax.

The winter was one of the hardest known in Devon, the lanes were blocked with snow and mud which hindered proceedings. Garrisons were left at Cullompton, Bradninch, Tiverton and Silverton and Fairfax made his headquarters at Ottery St Mary until the weather improved and he was able to continue. Exeter surrendered to Fairfax in April 1646.

Revd William Crompton 1654–62: In 1657 Peter Atkins of Padcott and Cranford left an endowment on these lands whereby for perpetuity eight of the most 'deserving, godly, religious and earnest of the poor of the Parish were to receive ten shillings apiece annually for their better-relief.' The charity has since been merged with Cullompton United Charities.

The Society of Friends (Quakers) was established in 1658 – their original meeting house was at the top of New Street to which they attached a 'yard' or burial-ground, which is sometimes referred to in the church registers. It became so full that in 1681 a further Quaker 'burying place' was in use on Knol Hill. On the accession of Charles II some 15 persons were taken from the Quakers' meeting place in Cullompton to gaol for breaches of the restrictions placed upon Nonconformists:

> *... the Constables of Cullompton with one Captain Prowse and a rude rabble attending them, came to the Meeting there, pulled the Friends from their seats, threw them on the ground, and dragged them along the streets, kept some at the Inn with a Guard of Soldiers all night, and would not let them have lodgings for their money. Next day they carried them before some Justices, who, for refusing to swear, sent fifteen of them to prison, namely; Humphry Sprague, Thomas Dyer, Richard Jacob, Roger Brown, Samual Deeke, John Brice, George Parnel, Thomas Carter, Thomas Burgoign, Ric Linington, John Hutchins, Bartholomew Weeks, Christopher Richards, Christopher Osmund and Alexander Richards, at whose house they were met: and at the same time the Justices issued a Warrant to distrain their Goods for the Charges of conveying them to Gaol.*

William Crompton was ejected from the vicarage, together with his wife and three children because he had not been episcopally ordained. He was driven from the parish at the orders of the King under the 'Act of Uniformity' which demanded unfeigned assent to the newly revived and restored Book of Common Prayer, its exclusive use in every parish church and episcopal ordination for every holder of a benefice.

The Act of Indulgence in 1672 allowed Nonconformist clergy and their congregation to worship freely as long as their meeting places were duly registered and licensed. Imprisoned clergy, dissenters and Quakers were freed from prison. Mr Crompton returned to minister in the private houses of those that preferred his ministry to that of his successor at St Andrews Church. He obtained a certificate in 1695 at the Exeter Quarter Sessions where he was registered as a 'Dissenting minister in holy orders' and continued in Cullompton for more than 25 years, becoming the first Dissenting Pastor of Cullompton. His growing Nonconformist congregation built a meeting house for him in 1695 at the bottom of Cockpit Hill. The chapel remained until 1814, when it was taken down and its successor was erected on the same spot.

Until the time of Charles I the mode of travelling for all was on horseback or in a farm wagon. During the time when the Puritans ruled England some public coaches started running from London to other towns. The stage-coach system was introduced in 1658. In four days a traveller could reach London at a fare of 40s. for the 200 or so miles. Each principal stopping place was called a stage and here at the inn the horses were changed, and new passengers taken up while others alighted.

As many as 32 coaches a day passed through Cullompton and their principal stopping places were: the White Hart Inn and the Half Moon Inn for the coaches and The Red Lion for the stage-wagons.

Prebendary John Gilbert 1662–81: In 1679 there were 91 burials in Cullompton. In the following year there was a tremendous fire and the number of burials rose to 132. The fire in 1680 burnt many of the thatched and easily combustible houses of the town. There was no fire-engine and people had only buckets in which to convey water.

Revd Samuel Dicks (or Dyke) 1681–1719: Ogilby's map of the Bristol to Exeter road of 1698 shows only one route from Exeter to Cullompton. It began at St Marys Chapel in Exeter, near to what is now Sidwell Street roundabout, and proceeded via Tiverton Road and Stoke Hill into a place called Stoke Post where the route dropped to Stoke Canon and then towards Killerton. The route crossed the Ellerhayes Bridge to cross the River Culm, where it turned towards Bradninch. The route dropped into Bradninch and then descended to Padbrook Bridge and crossed a culvert at the entrance to Cullompton.

A West Country rebellion broke out almost immediately after the death of Charles II. His brother, James II, suspected of being a Roman Catholic, at heart, came to the throne. The bastard son of the late King, the Duke of Monmouth, laid claim to the throne and issued a call for all Protestants to rise in his favour. The strong Protestant and Nonconformist spirit of the West Country merchants was soon aroused and they flocked to join his standard. The Lord Lieutenant of Devon was Duke of Albermarle, who with the troops he could raise, retreated to Exeter. The Duke of Monmouth, instead of pursuing him marched to Taunton.

The Duke of Albermarle advanced to Cullompton and set up his headquarters against Monmouth's forces. As the Lord Lieutenant of Devon was in the town with his forces and trade was good the people of Cullompton supported James II. Monmouth was defeated at the Battle of Sedgemore on 6 July and, when it was learnt that the Duke had been captured and beheaded for high treason in London on 15 July a thanksgiving service was held in St Andrews Church.

Monmouth's followers, taken prisoner after the Battle of Sedgmoor, were brought to Cullompton and confined within St Andrews Church. Some 80 of these prisoners were executed at Exeter by the orders of Judge Jeffries, Chief Justice of England. His severe measures of repression throughout Somerset, Dorset and East Devon began to alienate support for James II. The people of Cullompton were aghast at the whippings and imprisonment of many of their neighbours as well as the sight of heads and quartered trunks set up by the wayside and in town.

In 1688 King James II ordered the removal from his office of George Saffin, of Paulsland, as an Alderman of Exeter in pursuit of his policy of replacing Protestants with Roman Catholics. Local indignation was high as Saffin was respected. The birth of a son to James II, which it was felt might threaten the advent of a Roman Catholic dynasty, strained the loyalty of England. This time, when the King's son-in-law William, Prince of Orange and Duke Nassau, landed at Torbay with a great fleet, there were few that did not support this fourth West Country rising against the Crown.

The Revolution of 1688/9 was bloodless. Part of the army of William of Orange was stationed in Cullompton for some weeks and William of Orange passed through Cullompton en route for London. Parliament declared William and his wife Mary (daughter of James II) as King and Queen and there was rejoicing in the town. The churchwarden's accounts show the following:

Itm. *Pd ye ringers when the King was proclaymed £1.7s.0d.*

Itm. *Pd Humphry Ffinimore and others for gathering wood for bonfire when the present King was proclaymed 1s.6d.*

Itm. *Pd John Pratt for a hogshead of sider 15s.0d.*

Itm. *Pd John Hill for a hogshead of sider 19s.0d.*

Itm. *Payd. For six pounds of powder, spent ye Crownacon day 7s.0d.*

Itm. *Payd ye Ringers the Rejoicing Day, ordered by the Convention 15s.0d.*

Explorer and author Ellis Veryard bought a house in Cullompton. The house in the main street where he lived from 1704–14 has ever since been known as Veryards and his second son, John Veryard became a doctor in the town.

The House of Hanover

George I 1714–27
George II 1727–60
George III 1760–1820
George IV 1820–30
William IV 1830–37
Victoria 1837–1901

George Derby 1719–33: The vicar was a very wealthy man in his local community and his income was secure for life. The duties were very flexible. The patronage – i.e. the right to present the new vicar whenever there was a vacancy – was an asset of considerable financial value. That value could not be realised directly by presenting the new man in exchange for payment or other *quid pro quo*. That was simony, and in that case the presentation was void and the right of presentation passed to the Crown.

It would have been a disaster for the patron if the Crown presented a young clergyman who might remain vicar for many years. But the patronage could be used to advantage to present a relative or friend to the living, and the patronage itself could be bought and sold.

Prior to 1839 the vicar's income was derived from tithes in kind. During the eighteenth century the patrons showed very little interest. They were the Sellick family who lived at, what is now, the Manor House Hotel. After the incumbency of Vicar Derby they failed to make any presentation within the statutory six months, so the right of presentation lapsed, first to the bishop and then to the King.

Revd John Wilcocks 1733–56: John Wilcocks was presented to the parish by George II, which represented only the second time in the parish's history that a vicar was exercised by the Sovereign. He was a clergyman's son, born in Mid-Devon and was exceptional as he lived in the town and held no other living. He initiated several material improvements:

(i) The churchwarden's accounts show a great increase in amounts spent upon sacrament bread and wine. In 1737 cushions were ordered by Vestry to be made for the communion rails, in order that the communicants might more reverently kneel for administration of the sacrament.

(ii) The establishment of a Singing Gallery, and the development of music and orchestras of St Andrews Church. In 1747 the Vestry agreed to pay a certain Nicholas Welshman £36 'to erect a loft in the middle aisle for the singers to sit in'.

(iii) The establishment of a bell foundry in the old Almshouse, from which in the course of the next 50 years over 400 bells were cast for churches in Devon and other parts of England. The inconvenience and expense of using someone from out of the parish to repair and recast the church bells led to the passing of the following resolution:

Ordered that the bells of the Parish be cast in some part of the Almhouse, and that the Parishioners of the same find a Bellfounder to carry on his work, proper ffowell (fuel) to run his mettle, to dry his moulds, and sufficient brick to build an oven to compleat it in lieu of the expense of carrying bells to Taunton.

In response to this invitation of the Vestry, Thomas Bilbie, a Freeman of Bristol who possessed a bell foundry in Chewstock (Chew Stoke near Bristol), came to Cullompton and set up in the Almshouse the West of England Church Bell Foundry, paying an annual rent of £1.13s.4d. to the overseers for the premises. Here, for nearly a century, the bells of St Andrews Church were attended to at considerably more reasonable cost than before.

(iv) The recasting and rehanging of the Peal of Eight Bells, which were probably erected originally when the tower was completed in 1549.

(v) The development of Baptists and Methodists in the parish. John Wesley preached in the parish on many occasions, though never in St Andrews Church. He was a frequent attendant at services. In his journal in 1755 he records that he 'heard the minister there preach an excellent practical sermon, and he always made it his practice to attend the morning service therein.'

A Wesleyan Society was formed in Cullompton soon after John Wesley's first visit to Cullompton in 1746. A Wesleyan chapel was built in 1764 and a schoolroom in 1765, on a site behind one of the taverns of the town, named the Half Moon Inn (now Tavy Textiles). The chapel was rebuilt in 1806.

A Baptist chapel was erected in 1743 and was served by ministers from Prestcott in Culmstock parish until 1751, when its first resident pastor, the Revd Nicholas Gillard was appointed. He was to remain here 50 years. A larger Baptist chapel was built on the same site in the next century.

The Sellick family failed to make any presentation within the statutory six months and so **Revd Thomas Manning 1756–77** was appointed by the bishop.

The Vestry minutes of this time show that a lot of time was taken up with such matters as law suits, quarrels among weavers, defaulters among the overseers, and the misuse of charity money and outdoor relief by the poor who spent their pay at the 'hucksters-shops'.

It was insisted that every poor person in receipt of parish relief must wear a 'badge' to distinguish him from a normal citizen and various attempts were made to prevent the entry of 'badge wearers' in the 20 or more taverns of the town. Bull-baiting and cockfighting were other diversions and the cause of several riots. But the imposition of a tax upon Devonshire cider from 1763 to 1766 brought matters to a climax! Feelings throughout Cullompton and the neighbouring villages ran very high.

Scarcity of corn and bread in 1766 provoked further riots. On 31 July a mob of Cullompton and Bradninch people destroyed the mills of Mr Sainthill on the River Culm, who was accused of overcharging.

The coronation of King George III in 1761 was marked at Cullompton by the expenditure of ten guineas by the overseers of the poor from parish money:

paid to the several societies of Combers, Weavers and Husbandmen, and other inhabitants of the town in such a way as should be thought most proper for celebrating the day.

Richard Crosse, a deaf and dumb miniaturist painter was living at Knowle House at this period and his brother Henry occupied Bolealler. The invention of Hargreaves's 'Spinning Jenny' in 1767 began the process of removing the spinning wool from the country cottages to the town factories, and with it the beginning of the decline in the size of Cullompton's population.

Revd John Veryard Brutton 1777–1814: John Brutton was presented to Cullompton by Alice Sellick, daughter of William Sellick, who lived next door to Veryards and had known him since a boy. His elder brother, Henry Brutton, was one of the most prosperous landowners in the area, and served as a churchwarden in 1777 and 1781. He later gave £200 towards the erection of a church school.

On 1 October 1792 a meeting was held at the Half Moon to consider the construction of a navigable canal from Taunton to Topsham. Francis Colman (of Hillersdon) accepted the chair and Henry Brutton, attorney at Cullompton, was appointed secretary and solicitor. John Rennie surveyed the route from Topsham to Taunton and included branches to Tiverton and Cullompton.; only the Tiverton branch was built.

In 1795, riots took place in Cullompton as a consequence of the scarcity of wheat. The following are extracts from Vestry minutes of the period (it is also worth noting that in 1801 Cullompton was the ninth largest town in Devon with a population of over 3,000):

1788: The Sunday School children may be encouraged to attend and enjoy the Sunday services. Ordered that the rood-loft be put in order for their use, and neat wainscoting of a proper height erected to make it safe.

1801: It being represented to the Vestry that there is a quantity of pilchards at Plymouth to be disposed of, Ordered that the Overseers immediately purchase four hogsheads for the purpose of applying them to the use of the poor, in order to lessen the consumption of bread corn, agreeable to the directions of a late Act of Parliament.

But many of the poor died through under-nourishment in the great potato famine of this year, which spread from Ireland to Devon and caused a tremendous increase in the price of bread.

Owing to the great scarcity of Corn, Potatoes and other Necessaries of Life... immediate application to be made to the Farmers of the Parish and Neighbourhood, representing the urgency of the case, and earnestly recommending them to send a proper supply of Corn and Potatoes at a fair reduc'd price, which the Parish will undertake to guarantee the payment of...

Provisions were sold at the church at reduced prices and one of the farmers responded so handsomely to this 'earnest parochial recommendation' that in 1801 the Vestry passed the following minute:

This meeting being held for the purpose of making some compensation to Mr Joseph Bussell for his extraordinary care and trouble in supplying the Poor with Bread and Corn during the late scarcity and dearth, and he, having declin'd to take any pecuniary compensation for the same. IT IS ORDERED by this Vestry that the sum of Ten Guineas be taken out of the Poor Rates, and applied for the purchase of a Piece of Plate, and that the same be presented to him with the following inscription –

'Presented by the Parish of Cullompton to Mr Joseph Bussell for his gratuitous and benevolent exertions in providing a constant supply of Bread and Corn for the Poor during the late Scarcity. 5 Sept 1801'.

The practice of cockfighting and other public diversions, were considered to have a direct tendency to promote and encourage vice and immorality. It was felt that such behaviour was too much practiced in the parish, and so were ordered to be suppressed in 1805 with the full vigour of the law. There was a public outcry in the town. This law had little effect , so that cockfighting and bull-baiting were finally abolished in 1835 by Act of Parliament.

The last 20 years of Mr Brutton's vicariate were marked by the Napoleonic Wars, in which many of the sons of Cullompton lost their lives, including the three sons of the Squire of Hillersdon. The Cullompton Volunteer Company was formed in 1794 under the command of Captain Jarman, an old Marine Officer.

James Dean, surveyor, listed the following improvements to be made to the turnpike from White Ball to Exeter:

From the White Ball Inn, through Cullompton to Exeter... at Five Bridges take down a barn and linhay on the left and widen the road to 20 feet. At the entrance of Cullompton town, in Willand, take down a cottage to the left adjoining to the churchyard and throw the scite into the road; reduce Stoneshall Hill by digging the summit five feet down; at Five Bridges take down a Barn and linhay on the left and widen the road to 20 feet. At the entrance of Cullompton by the toll-gate cover the drain on both sides of the road, and reduce the footpath by the turning on the right: here ends the jurisdiction of the Tiverton Trust.

On the Exeter road the following improvements should be made: take down the shambles in Cullompton and throw the scite into the road, follow the present road to the foot of Cullompton Hill, then enter the inclosures on the left, and skirt the high grounds beyond Bradninch Town, then follow the present road by Killerton to Stoke Hill, reducing the intermediate hills by digging down their summits and lengthening the slopes on their sides.

(*Sherborne Mercury*, 26 February 1810, p.2)

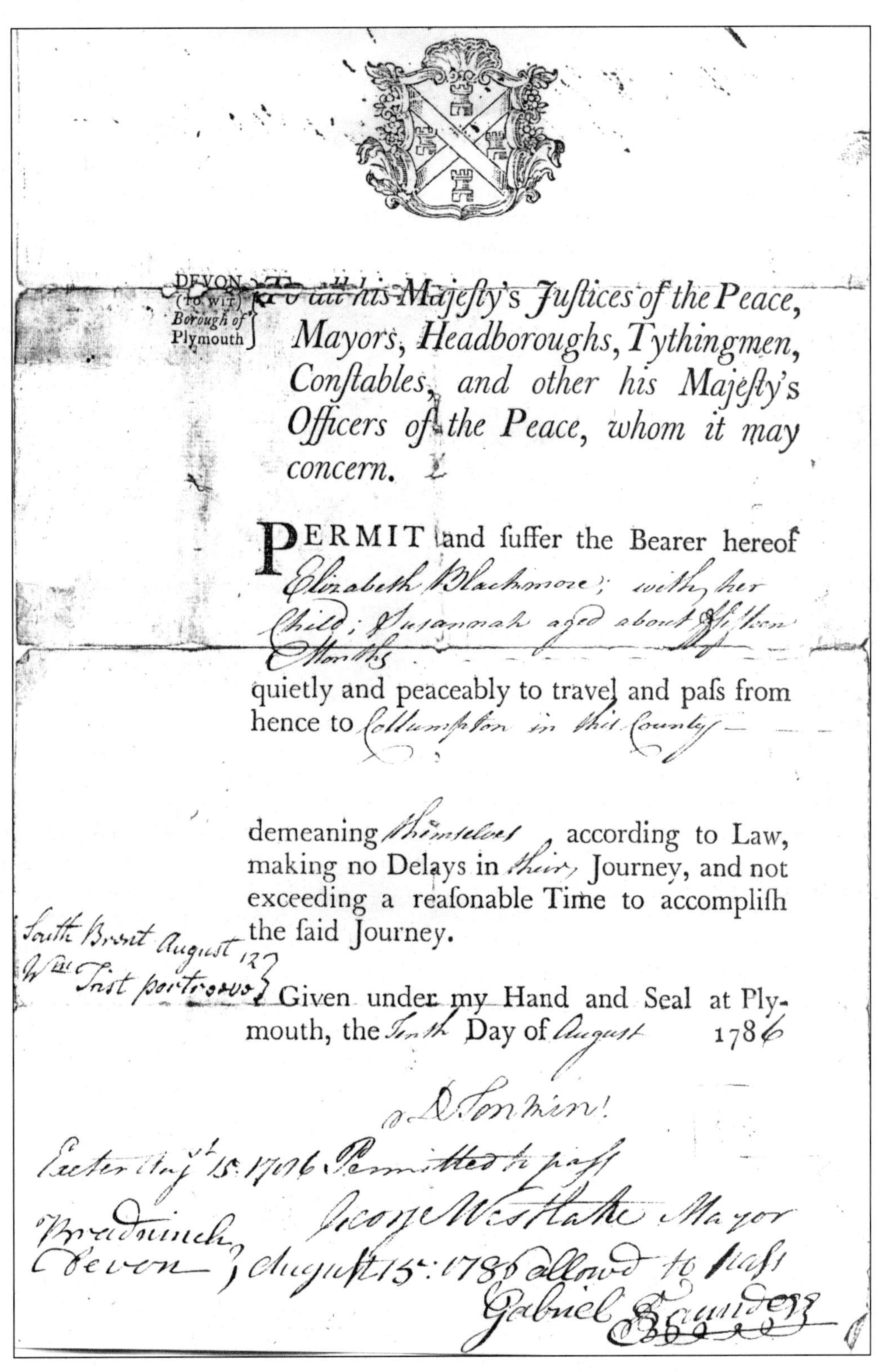

DEVON (TO WIT) Borough of Plymouth } To all his Majeſty's Juſtices of the Peace, Mayors, Headboroughs, Tythingmen, Conſtables, and other his Majeſty's Officers of the Peace, whom it may concern.

PERMIT and ſuffer the Bearer hereof Elizabeth Blackmore; with her Child; Susannah aged about fifteen Months

quietly and peaceably to travel and paſs from hence to Cullumpton in this County

demeaning themselves according to Law, making no Delays in their Journey, and not exceeding a reaſonable Time to accompliſh the ſaid Journey.

South Brent August 12
Wm Trist portreeve

Given under my Hand and Seal at Plymouth, the Tenth Day of August 1786

Tonkin

Exeter Aug 15. 1786 Permitted to pass
George Westlake Mayor

Bradninch Devon } August 15: 1786 allowed to pass
Gabriel Saunders

Permission to pass through Cullompton for Elizabeth Blackmore and child; 10 August 1786.

2404 A/PS 99

Globe Tavern, Exeter, 4th March, **1817.**

Exeter Turnpike Roads.

AT the *General Monthly Meeting* held this day, the Report of the last *General Road Committee,* having been read, and their Resolution to recommend to this Meeting----

" That Fifty per Cent. be allowed the several Parishes within this Trust, " calculated upon the amount of their last year's Compositions, for the cur- " rent year ending Michaelmas 1817, and that the same be notified to them " by the Clerk, with directions that they do forthwith pay the amount of such " abated Composition to the respective Surveyors within whose District any " such Parish may be situate; and that such Surveyors be authorised to " demand the payment thereof, and in case of refusal that the performance of " the Statute Duty be immediately enforced *to its full extent*"----

Resolved, That the Report of the General Road Committee be *confirmed,* and the measures recommended therein be immediately adopted.

Entered, *H. M. ELLICOMBE, Clerk.*

Gentlemen,

I have the pleasure of stating, that your Parochial Composition in lieu of Statute Work, for the year commencing Michaelmas last and ending Michaelmas next, is, in pursuance of the above Resolution, reduced to the sum of £ 3 —— *, which sum you are requested to pay forthwith to Mr.* Newbery *the Turnpike Surveyor of your District, it being understood that such immediate payment is the only condition on which such abated Composition will be admitted.*

I am, your obedient servant,

Exeter, 5th March, 1817. H. M. Ellicombe

P. S. Your Arrears *of Composition may be paid at my Office, any Tuesday or Friday, between the hours of ten and one o'clock; which amount, by Mr. White's statement, to £* 5 . 14 . —

FLINDELL, PRINTER, EXETER.

Contribution to road maintenance costs, March 1917.

DEVON, to wit. } *To the Keeper of the House of Correction for the said County, and also to all Constables and other Officers of the Peace whom it may concern, to receive and convey; and to the Church-Wardens or Overseers of the Poor of* Cullompton *in the County of* Devon *to receive and obey.*

WHEREAS Mary Chapple on the 5th Day of Jan Inst was apprehended in the Parish of St Mary the Apostle wandering and begging And whereas the said Mary hath been by me one of his Majesty's Justices of the Peace in and for the said County examined, adjudged, and convicted to be a Rogue and Vagabond; and hath, in Consequence of such Conviction, been committed to and confined in the House of Correction, in and for the said County, ~~for the Space of seven days~~ pursuant to the Statute in that Case lately made. And whereas upon Examination of the said Mary taken before me upon Oath, (which Examination is hereunto annexed) it doth appear that the last legal Settlement of the said Mary is in the Parish of Cullompton These are therefore to require you, the said Constable, to convey the said Mary to the Parish of Cullompton in the County of Devon ~~that being the first Parish in the next Precinct through which ought to pass in the direct Way to the said Parish of to which to be sent, and to deliver to the said Constable or other Officer of such Parish in the next Precinct,~~ together with this Pass, and the Duplicate of this Examination of the said Mary taking his Receipt for the same. And the said Mary is ~~to be thence conveyed on in like Manner to the said Parish of~~ there to be delivered to some Church-Warden, Chapel-Warden, or Overseer of the Poor, to be there provided for according to Law. And you, the said Church-Wardens, Chapel-Wardens, and Overseers of the Poor, are hereby required to receive the said Person and provide for her as aforesaid.

Given under my Hand and Seal, this 6th Day of Jan in the Year of our Lord 1814

Wm Ellicombe

Vagrancy Bond, possibly for a Mary Chapple, 1814. At that time people found to be unable to support themselves were returned to their parish of birth to be cared for.

DEVON, to wit. } ***To the Overseers of the Poor of the Parish of*** Cullompton ***in the said County.***

THESE are to authorise and require you within Six Days after Demand thereof, to pay to John Davey Constable **the Sum of** Ten **Shillings being the Reward appointed by Act of Parliament, for apprehending** two **Vagabonds named** Elizabeth Parker & Abraham Parker **within the said Parish, and bringing him before me, one of his Majesty's Justices of the Peace for the said County, to be dealt with according to Law, upon the said** John Davey **producing and delivering to you this Order and giving you his Receipt for the same.**

Given under my Hand and Seal, the Twentieth **Day of** January **in the Year of our Lord, One Thousand Eight Hundred and** Twenty Four

W Barker

Received the above Sum,

Vagrancy Bond for Elizabeth Parker and Abraham Parker: January 1824.

Roads in Britain until 1870 were either 'Turnpike' or 'Parish'. Parish roads were inferior to the turnpikes and served local needs within the parish boundary. Four waywardens were elected annually at the Easter Vestry, to superintend the maintenance and upkeep of the 38 miles of parish roads. They were unpaid. Under the Highways Act of 1835, the Poor Law authorities were empowered to raise the Highway Rate; 3d. in the pound was annually levied for this purpose. About £160 per annum was raised and one man was employed regularly upon the roads in the parish. Whenever required assistance was provided for him, generally at the expense of the farmer or landowner whose land abutted onto the road being trimmed or repaired.

The nineteenth century patrons paid much more attention to the business side of patronage. Vicar Brutton, who had acquired the patronage, sold it to Alderman Daniel of Bristol for £16,000 but refunded £2,000 when the tithe income was found to be lower than anticipated. Daniel presented **Revd Walker Gray 1814–19**, who had married Daniel's daughter, Emily in June 1813. The patronage was an investment to provide an income for a daughter and son-in-law. In addition he also gave them the patronage.

In 1814 the apprenticeship system in the parish was changed. Compulsory binding of all poor children as apprentices ceased and every man was now at liberty to follow the occupation to which he felt most suited. Apprenticeship became voluntary.

Although Waterloo was yet to come, the peace following the Peninsula War was celebrated in Cullompton by a public dinner on 23 June 1814 in Fore Street, 50 to a table. Each table had a nominated president and all attending were to line-up four-deep, per table, in the Linhay Field. Beef and cider were served. Mr Upcott had a table for 100 persons. Other presidents included Messrs Brown and Davy, Robert Baker, Samual Upcott and Mr Sellwood. The Drum and Fife Band beat 'The Roast Beef of Old England'. (This information was taken from a handbill found in a chest and recorded by J.M. Foster, 1868.)

In 1816 Walker Gray gave sufficient land, which he owned at the top of Exeter Hill for the erection of a Church Day School. Two schoolrooms, one for poor boys and the other for poor girls, were built and opened for instruction in 'reading, writing and arithmetic' and (for girls) in needlework. The cost of this Church Day School was met by two gifts of £200 each by Henry Brutton and by the Trustees of the late Miss E. Pryor who had left money for benevolent purposes in the town. A grant of £100 by the National

COLLUMPTON, DEVON.

To be Let

BY AUCTION,

At the VESTRY ROOM,

IN COLLUMPTON,

On SATURDAY the 20th Day of SEPTEMBER, inst.

AT THE HOUR OF 4 IN THE AFTERNOON,

For a TERM of 7 YEARS,

To commence at Lady-Day next,

THE FOLLOWING

PREMISES.

All that WELL-ACCUSTOMED

CALLED THE

Three Mariners,

Situate in the Fore-Street of the TOWN of COLLUMPTON, and now in the possession of Mrs. ELIZABETH SEARLE.

ALSO, ALL THAT ACCUSTOMED

SHOP & DWELLING HOUSE,

With Outhouses adjoining, situate in the said Street, & now in the possession of Mr. Wm. TAYLER.

The Tenants will be required to pay all Rates and Taxes chargeable on the PREMISES, and to keep the same in Repair.

N. B. There is an OVEN on the last mentioned PREMISES, which might be converted into a Bakehouse.

☞ *Particulars may be had by applying to*

Mr. HILL, *Assistant Overseer, Collumpton.*

Dated 8th September 1834.

ROWE, GENERAL PRINTING-OFFICE, COLLUMPTON.

The Three Mariners (now Tavy Textiles), available for let in 1834 (note the spelling of Cullompton).

Society completed the required total of £500.

A Select Vestry was appointed for the first time in 1818 'with the like powers and duties as are prescribed in a Bill lately introduced into the House of Commons, and now in progress.' It was ordered that twelve gentlemen should henceforth compose this 'Select Vestry' and from this date it gradually dealt with all the work formerly undertaken by the Vestry meeting of all interested parishioners. The last step in the gradual evolution of local government from the Hundred and Manor Courts of Saxon times to the Parish Council had been taken.

Walker Gray appointed **Revd John Templer (1819–30)** as curate and later sold him the patronage. The prosperity of the parish reached its peak at the end of the eighteenth and the first half of the nineteenth centuries. The average rental of land stood at 30s. an acre and at a Ministry of Health enquiry in 1854 it was stated that 'in a parish containing 7,370 acres only 100 acres were common or waste land, 3,900 were found to be arable and 3,000 meadow and pasture land'.

The wool trade was still flourishing and the number of looms employed was nearly 500. There were also 40 'manufacturers, small capitalists, chiefly in the serge flannel trade'. With the expiration of the Charter of the East India Company in 1858, who used to purchase the Cullompton serges for their trade with China, a death-knell had been struck and before long the Midlands and the new industrial cities in the north of England captured the English woollen industry and the population, which in 1841 was 3,900, steadily dropped as trade languished. By 1941 it was just 2,900.

The local press during these difficult economic times provide an insight into the everyday struggles of Cullompton people. The following advert appeared in the *Exeter Flying Post* on 28 June 1821:

... to be sold by auction at the Golden Lion Inn in Cullompton... Two dwelling houses, Courtlages, Orchard, Garden and Premises with a small factory attached, which has been some time passed used as a Hosiery Manufactory... and in the occupation of George Fowler... Also all that Meadow near, in the occupation of Mr W. Melhuish, miller containing about 3 acres.

The same year, 1821, the following was recorded in a local newspaper:

A man named Mortimer died last week at Collumpton of voluntary starvation. He had a small property by which he had been supported for some years but finding he was likely to outlive it, as it was reduced to about 150/- and feeling the apprehension of want more than the natural love of life, he came to the resolution of ending his days by starvation. To effect this dreadful purpose he took nothing but water for a month before he died...

Similarly, Padbrook Farm was also put up for sale, as revealed in the *Exeter Flying Post* on 6 September 1827:

To be sold by Private Contract, for the remainder of a term of 99 years determinable on the decease of the survivor of three healthy lives, aged 36, 32 and 23, all that very desirable Farm called Padbrook, situated adjoining the town of Cullompton, comprising a very complete Farm-house, and all necessary appendages... excellent enclosed farm yard, and about 88 acres (more or less) of very superior pasture land, orchard, tillage ground and irrigated meadows, now in the possession of Mrs Hewitt as tenant until Christmas 1829, at the clear yearly rent of £162.

John Templer died on 14 December 1829 aged 46 leaving a wife, Sarah, and five children. The only way Sarah could raise money was to sell the patronage but this was not straightforward. To preserve the patron's right she appointed a 'stop-gap' vicar. As **Revd John Hodge (1830–34)** was 78 when he was appointed it was unlikely that he would hold the living for long. In fact, there is no evidence that Hodge ever came to Cullompton; he appears to have been a 'caretaker' vicar.

William Sykes took over as curate and resident minister on 29 August 1830. At this time the town had 695 houses and a population of 3,410. He moved into the vicarage and ran the parish. He was vicar in all but name. In 1831 Sarah Templer sold the patronage to Sykes's 'uncle by marriage', Richard Benyon de Beauvoir. After Hodge's death, Richard Benyon de Beauvoir presented the living to William Sykes on 20 December 1834 to give him the official title as well.

Revd William Sykes 1834–57: William Sykes's early years were far from happy as people grumbled about paying their tithes. The new vicar seemed a rich man and many refused to pay. Some farmers went as far as leaving some of their fields unsown and their crops unharvested to avoid paying tithes in kind. In 1836 the Tithe Commutation Act was passed by Parliament, and all tithes in kind were commuted to a fixed rent charge.

The vicar of Cullompton's income was fixed at £400 per annum at the tithe commutations of 1839 and 1841 as the equivalent of what he would previously have received by way of tithes. By way of comparison the weavers went on strike against their employer, William Upcott, in 1842 as they were earning no more than six shillings a week. A typical household weekly budget at that time was as follows:

House rent	1s.5½d.
Shoes and clothing	1s.0d.
Soap and candles	0s.6½d.
Coal	1s.0d.
Food for five persons	2s.0d.
TOTAL	5s.0d.

Mr Sykes opened a small school for gentlemen's sons at the vicarage.

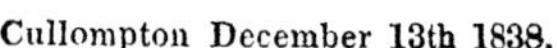

Cullompton December 13th 1838.

Sir,

CULLOMPTON TITHE COMMUTATION,

EXCLUSIVE OF UPTON WEAVER.

The Committee this day appointed at a Meeting of Land and Tithe Owners, beg to press upon your attention the necessity of your immediately electing either to merge the Great Tithes of your own Lands in Cullompton, exclusive of Upton Weaver, in the Freehold and Inheritance thereof, or to set a value upon them for a Rent-charge in lieu thereof, in order that at the next Meeting of the Tithe Commissioners, to be held here on the 28th instant, the Return required by them may be made.

The Committee will deliver, on a personal application to them, or the Vestry Clerk, the Form of Merger approved by the Tithe Commissioners.

The Committee also request you to meet them, or to direct your Tenants to meet them, at the Payhouse, in Cullompton, on one of the Days mentioned below, at 10 o'Clock in the forenoon, with a Statement of the separate quantities belonging to you of

Arable,

Meadow,

Pasture,

Orchard,

Woodland, &

Common Lands.

If the Great Tithes of your Lands do not belong to you, the Committee call your attention to the necessity of your being prepared by agreement with the Tithe Owner, to state the sum at which the Great Tithes may be commuted, or to be prepared to submit your case to the Award of the Commissioners thereon.

I am, Sir,

Your obedient servant,

ELIAS BAKER,

Chairman of the Committee.

The Town Quarter	.	19th	December.
Eastculm do.	.	20th	
Ponsford and Knowle do.		22nd	
Southculm do.	.	24th	

ROWE, GENERAL PRINTING-OFFICE, COLLUMPTON.

Tithe notice, 1838.

Victorian Cullompton

On 28 June 1838 Queen Victoria was crowned and there were celebrations in nearly all parishes, including Cullompton:

Here the national Anthem was sung about the streets at an early hour in the morning, and the town was a scene of general rejoicing, the houses being all gaily decorated. A grand procession was formed, which perambulated the town, after which there was Divine Service in the Church, where the Rev. W. Sykes, the Vicar preached a very excellent and appropriate sermon. The poor to the number of 1700 were bountifully fed. The gentlemen and tradesmen dined at Hodge's Half Moon Inn, J. Leigh Esq. most ably presiding.

In the afternoon, the Ladies of the town provided a gratuitous tea for the Sunday school children of all denominations; and there were rural diversions, which were kept up on Friday with great spirit, and the whole of pleasantly.

Exeter and Plymouth Gazette, 1838

In 1839 a disastrous fire almost completely devastated the lower half of the town and destroyed all the old houses in Crow Green and the site of the present New Street. It is thought that 145 dwellings were burnt to the ground plus over 170 farm buildings. One young man was killed.

DREADFUL FIRE AT CULLOMPTON

The *Western Luminary and Family Newspaper for Devon, Cornwall and Dorset*, 8 July 1839

Yesterday between 12 and 1 o'clock, just before the congregation were about to leave church, an alarm of fire was raised in Cullompton and flames were seen issuing from a chimney in a small street, near New street. The fire when first discovered was slight and had timely aid been afforded there is little doubt it would have been extinguished without much further mischief but before any measures could be taken the sparks from the burning chimney had communicated themselves to the roof which was of thatch, and in an instant was in full blaze. The fire rapidly then extended itself to New street and from thence ran, with fearful violence to the houses and cottages continuous.

Measures were taken to check it, and the local engines were soon on the spot, but the wind blowing briskly from the NW carried the sparks to a great distance by which the flames broke out simultaneously in various quarters of the town, to the consternation of the inhabitants, and those engaged in extinguishing them.

An express was immediately sent to Exeter for assistance and the fire engine of the West of England fire brigade, under the superintendence of Mr G.W. Cummings, was the first to arrive at Cullompton, followed very shortly afterwards by the West Middlesex and Sun engines. At the moment of their arrival the scene that presented itself was truly awful. From New street the flames had communicated on both sides of the road until they reached the Town Green, from whence they had extended more or less all over the town. Houses in the neighbourhood of the White Hart were observed on fire at a distance of a full quarter of a mile from the spot where the flames first broke out. In this neighbourhood between the above Inn and the Red Lion the property is very valuable and the exertions of the West Middlesex engines were directed in its preservation. The West of England tried to cut off the communications between New street and the Green, which was done effectually though with the greatest labour, the men having to work in narrow streets with the fire blazing on both sides of them, by which the heat was intense. The Sun was also occupied in the very centre of the flames. By the joint exertions of these and the local engines, a good supply of water having been obtained, by degrees the fire was got under, but not before no less than 130 houses were burnt to the ground and property to a great extent damaged and destroyed. It was not until a late hour last night that the fire was extinguished, and the engines played upon the smoking ruins all night, until 5 o'clock this morning.

As many would suppose the town of Cullompton presents a most melancholy appearance after this truly awful fire. Hundreds of poor families have we fear lost their all. Whole streets have been burnt down: in fact, nearly two thirds of the town may be said to be destroyed. Near the White Hart the destruction of ruinable property is very great. A great number of houses continuous to the bank are total wrecks, but that building is, we believe, uninjured. It is some consolation however to be able to close this sad narrative without recording the loss of any life. One poor fellow, a sweep, was seriously injured by the fall of a partition on his back, but he is not dead and hopes are entertained of his recovery. We have heard of no other casualties.

Nothwithstanding that the West Middlesex people forcibly took possession of a pair of post horses ordered expressly by the West of England, the latter engine passed its competitor on the road 5 miles this side of Cullompton, and in doing so the men gave three hearty cheers. It is to be regretted that the West of England was thereby prevented from being sooner at the fire; and it is probable that some property which has been destroyed might have been spared. The West Middlesex broke down on the road.

LATEST PARTICULARS – Since the above was written we understand it has been ascertained that 145 dwelling houses are burnt to the ground, and in addition to that number, including out-houses, barns etc. upwards of 170 buildings have been totally destroyed. It is impossible to calculate the amount of the loss when it is considered that not only the buildings but also a great deal of furniture and stock-in-trade in them must have been burnt scarcely £100 for each building will cover it, and that will make a total loss of somewhere about £15,000. We fear however it will be found to be much greater. We are informed that the respectable inhabitants in the town, vied with each other in their exertions to save the furniture of the poor from the burning cottages, many of whom were in a state of most deplorable distress and anguish. It is truly fortunate that this awful calamity did not occur by night, or the loss of life might have been great. The hopes expressed above for the recovery of the sweep who was injured by a fall of partition have, we regret to say, not been realised. The poor fellow expired this morning. Business is quite at a stand still in the town and the scene of desolution is truly distressing, no objects presenting itself to the eye in every direction but blackened rafters and dismantled buildings.

Calamitous Fire at Cullompton

(Reprinted repeatedly in all Exeter newspapers, July 1839)

On Sunday the 7th instant, a fire broke out at Cullompton, in this County, which raged with great violence for several hours, and consumed upwards of 100 houses, and reduced to the utmost distress the inmates of nearly the whole of those houses.

Perhaps the Public have seldom been appealed to in a case in which distress was more extensively felt by a similar visitation; not only were many hundred persons deprived of houses, furniture and clothes, but the greater number of them lost even the very means of exercising their calling, the following morning finding them without looms or tools to recommence their labours.

The inhabitants of Cullompton have assembled and formed Committees for various purposes, but as the cases of distress are numerous and the amount of suffering afflicting to an extent almost beyond description, the Public are invited, nay, urgently implored to contribute by subscription to the alleviations of such a mass of human misfortune and suffering.

Steps are also being taken to communicate with Bankers in London, and important bodies, to co-operate in extending information of the calamity, and receiving the Contributions of the Benevolent and Charitable.

Signed by the request of the Inhabitants of Cullompton,
at a Public Meeting held on the 9th day of July 1839
Wm Sykes, Chairman

Subscriptions will be received by Tristam Walrond Whitter, Esq.
Treasurer at the Bank at Cullompton, and all the Banks at Exeter

Fire at Cullompton

(Published in all Exeter newspapers August/September 1839)

The Committee deem it their duty gratefully to acknowledge that the Appeal to the Public on behalf of the Sufferers by the late Fire has been answered to an extent far surpassing their utmost expectations.

They have satisfaction of adding that they have been enabled by the large funds thus placed at their disposal to assist many, and to more fully relieve others, who had not the means wherewith to make good any part even of their loss.

The Committee believe that they have funds sufficient to give aid in such further cases as can reasonably be presented to them.

It affords the Committee the greatest pleasure to be able to express their approbation of the good conduct of the general body of applicants, who shewed an honest desire to keep their claims within, rather than to exceed, the actual amount of their losses, and to add that the sums hitherto distributed have been received with thankfulness.

There are still claims collectively to a large amount under consideration, the allowances of which, wholly or in part, demands the strict attention of the Committee. The Committee will not fail to publish their account of the application of the funds as soon as that account can be made up.

Signed by the request of the Committee
Wm Sykes, Chairman, 24 August 1839

On 8 November 1839 there was a fire opposite the White Hart and six houses were burnt down.

These were the 'good old coaching days' and as many as 32 coaches a day would pass through the town, some without stopping to change horses. They carried both passengers and mail to Exeter, Plymouth and Cornwall from Bristol, Bath and London. The Royal Mail from London arrived every morning at 8 o'clock after a 20-hour run from London and the return mail coach from Exeter passed through the town at 6 o'clock in the morning. Several coaches came through from Exeter every afternoon on their way to Taunton, and a midnight coach often woke the dwellers of the High Street as it rumbled through the town. At 7 o'clock in the morning the stagecoach for Bath and Bristol delayed for half an hour at the Half Moon Inn in the main street while its passengers partook of breakfast in the coffee room. Post wagons came in from Tiverton and Honiton and stage wagons set out regularly for Exeter, Bath and Bristol.

The churchwarden's accounts show that the cost of sending a letter to London in 1689 was 2s.6d. In 1739 the short distance 'post' to Exeter was charged at 6d. In 1805 the cost of postage to London was raised to 9d. The uniform rate of the penny post was introduced by Rowland Hill in 1840. The building of the Bristol–Exeter Railway in 1842 (when the population stood at just over 3,900) saw an end to the mail coaches and the town became the new centre of a postal district east of Exeter as far as the Somerset border.

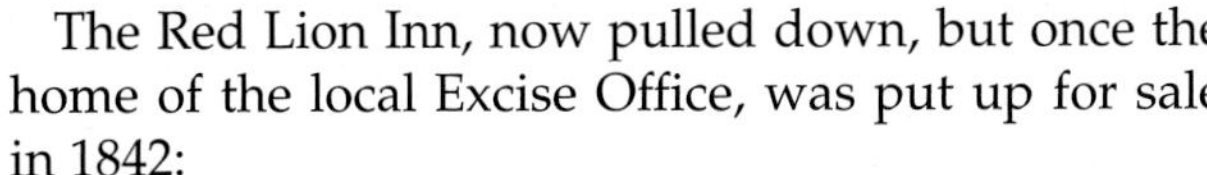

The Red Lion Inn, now pulled down, but once the home of the local Excise Office, was put up for sale in 1842:

> *Inn, malthouse and brewery situate in the most open and public part of the High Street, late in the occupation of Mr John Frost, jnr deceased... The excise yard has been kept at the inn for many years... stabling for 40 horses in a Spacious Yard, behind the inn.*
> (*Exeter Flying Post*, 15 September 1842)

The following year the Red Lion Inn was destroyed:

> *On Monday morning last a fire broke out at the Red Lion, Cullompton, which burned with great fury for some time, consuming the premises and those adjoining. There are eleven dwelling-houses and cottages destroyed; the whole property is insured in the Yorkshire and Farmers offices. Owing to the great exertions of the West of England Company's brigade of firemen the Half Moon Inn was preserved.*
> (*Woolmer's Gazette* 11 March 1843)

In 1849 the chancel of St Andrews Church was pulled down and rebuilt and in 1850 the Cullompton Benevolent Society was formed.

In 1854 a survey looking at the sewerage, drainage and supply of water and the sanitary condition of the inhabitants was carried out. The table below is a return of the births and deaths in the parish between 1847 and 1853.

Year	**Births** Total Births	**Deaths** Under 5 years	Above 5 years & under 10 years	Above 10 years & under 20 years	Above 20 years	Total deaths	Deaths from epidemics, endemic & contagious disease
1847	*138*	*29*	*4*	*6*	*69*	*108*	*8*
1848	*121*	*25*	*1*	*3*	*65*	*94*	*12*
1849	*133*	*37*	*5*	*8*	*63*	*113*	*19*
1850	*121*	*33*	*5*	*8*	*64*	*110*	*32*
1851	*110*	*35*	*10*	*8*	*58*	*111*	*37*
1852	*101*	*18*	*5*	*4*	*49*	*76*	*20*
1853	*120*	*22*	*5*	*8*	*65*	*100*	*35*
TOTAL	**840**	**199**	**35**	**45**	**433**	**712**	**163**

The Report states that:

> *... assuming the average population of the parish, during the period to have been 3,600, the above return shows a mortality rate of 28.3 in the thousand. The deaths from epidemic, endemic and contagious disease appear to have been nearly 23 per cent of the whole number of deaths, and to have carried off 1 in every 156 of the population annually.*

The Report also states that:

(i) The town is without lighting of any description with the exception of two lamps in front of the Sessions House.

(ii) The total number of vagrants that applied for lodgings between February 1850 and February 1854 was 2,349, of whom 1,324 were relieved. There are three common lodging-houses in the town of the lowest and dirtiest description; they are subject to no control as the Lodging-houses Act has not been put into operation here. The justices have now been ordered to enforce the Act.

(iii) There is no public drainage in the town and a great deficiency of privy accommodation; particularly amongst the poorer classes.

(iv) The town is partly supplied with water from the Town Lakes, which is managed by a company called The Cullompton Watercourse Club and partly by wells. But the watercourses through the streets are much polluted by refuse matter.

(v) That typhus and other epidemic diseases are generally very prevalent here; more so than in any other parish in the Union.

(vi) That the parish churchyard is a very old ground and is full to repletion; and that further burial accommodation is much required.

In 1854 St Andrews churchyard was closed for further burials and a new public cemetery was procured on the hillside above Tiverton Road in 1855 at a cost of £350. In 1857 the Vestry empowered the newly constituted burial board to borrow £1,000 on the poor rates for the purpose of erecting two identical cemetery chapels, one for the burial of members of the Church of England and the other for Nonconformists.

Revd Robert Pinkney 1857–61: In January 1860 he initiated proceedings against the Revd Reginald Shute, vicar of St Mary Steps, Exeter, for marrying two Cullompton couples knowing that they were not resident in Exeter. In May 1859 Shute married George Luxton, cabinet maker, and Lydia Burrows;

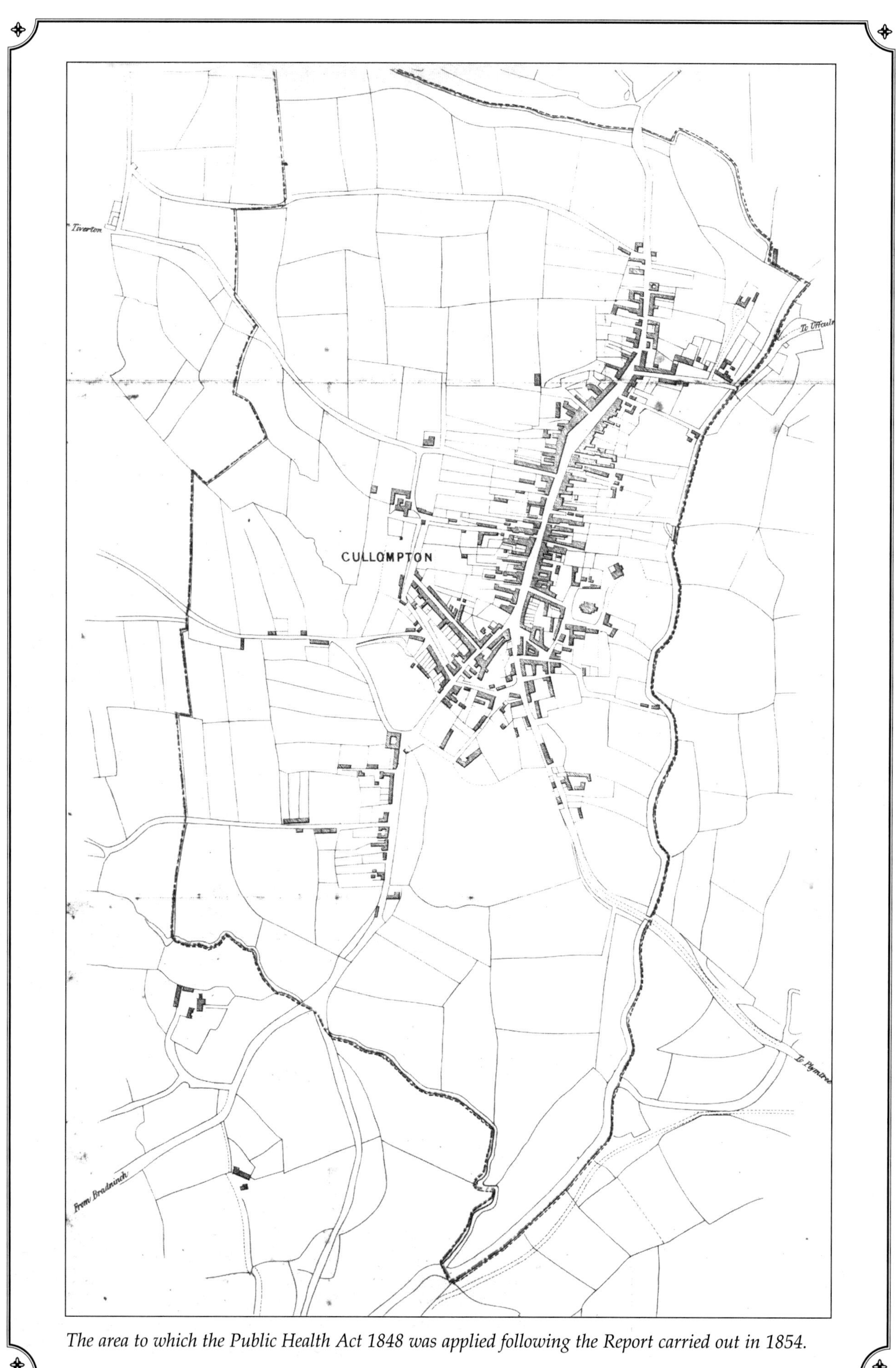

The area to which the Public Health Act 1848 was applied following the Report carried out in 1854.

and in October 1859 he married George Hornsey, butcher, and Ann White, a domestic servant, in the employment of Mrs Prudence Upcott. The reason Hornsey gave for not getting married in Cullompton was that he believed no-one in the parish liked Mr Pinkney. It is worth noting therefore that if you are studying your family history and looking for a marriage in Cullompton before 1860 you may have to look somewhere else instead!

In 1859 Charles Biddlecombe Ewens bought a site next to the vicarage and built a fellmonger's yard. The smells from the yard were highly offensive and Pinckney successfully sued Ewens for nuisance. On 29 July 1861 he was awarded 40s. damages. As a result Ewens closed the yard and moved to new premises at Court, at the far end of the town. Less than two weeks later Pinkney moved out as Sykes had sold the patronage to Mrs Chave who presented the living to her husband **(Dr Edward William Tanner Chave 1861–64)** and then transferred the patronage to him as well.

In 1862 the Volunteer Fire Brigade was established and vied with the Upper Culm Vale Rifle Corps (established in 1860) for popularity among the men of the parish. Under the captaincy of Mr John Walrond, the rifle corps established its firing range at the top of Colebrooke Lane, while its armoury occupied the site of the present Town Hall. The corps changed its name several times and was successively known as: 5th Administrative Battalion of the Devonshire Regiment, 3rd Volunteer Battalion Devonshire Regiment, 5th Devon Rifles Volunteers, 'A' Company 3rd Volunteer Battalion Devonshire Regiment and 'G' Company, 4th Devonshire Territorials.

In 1863 an open-air dinner for 1,300 people was held to celebrate the marriage of the Prince of Wales to Princess Alexandra of Denmark. There were well-laden tables on either side of the main street.

Revd Francis Bazett Grant 1864–72: In 1870 the 'Forster' Education Act marked a turning point in education. New local schools were built at a total cost of £2,318. Some £1,408 was raised by voluntary subscriptions, the sale of the old schools realised £75 and grants from the National Society, the Educational Department and the Diocesan Board of Education amounted to about £800. The schools were placed under the control of the vicar (who was to superintend the religious and moral instruction of the scholars) and nine other persons, contributors to the funds and members of the Church of England.

Between 1870 and 1890 the average school attendance doubled and redoubled as did the money spent on the education of each child.

In 1870 turnpikes were abolished. There were ten miles of turnpike road running through the parish, administered by four different turnpike trusts. These were:

(i) The Exeter Turnpike, which ran from the top of Exeter Hill from the Exeter direction.

(ii) The Tiverton Turnpike, which ran to the entry of the Tiverton Road into the main street and also, by another branch, to the 'College' Turnpike Gate, in what is now Higher Street.

(iii) The Honiton Turnpike, which ran as far as the entry of Lower Street (now called Station Road) into the main street.

(iv) The Cullompton Turnpike, including the remainder of the main road through the town in the Willand direction.

Letter sent from Cullompton Post Office, 25 December 1872.

Revd Lewis Francis Potter 1872–87: The decision was taken in 1872 to light St Andrews Church by gas instead of the candles that had been used until then. This also helped to warm the church.

Improvements were made to the Lower Bullring in 1878, including the erection of a lamp for the safe guidance of the bewildered traveller at that intricate part of the town. The lamp was later taken down to make way for the 'ever increasing traffic' and the plinth now stands in the CCA Fields and bears a plaque commemorating the town's twinning links. Further progress was made in 1882:

> *For once in the history of its existence the quiet little town of Cullompton was all astir on the occasion of the inauguration of the new Assembly Rooms, situated in Tiverton Road. The event seemed to draw forth all the energy and enthusiasm of the inhabitants, who assembled in large numbers to celebrate the opening of the building, the want of which has long been felt in Cullompton. Hitherto there has been no large hall or meeting-place in the town and this led to the acquisition by five enterprising tradesmen of the structure formerly known as the Independent Chapel.*
> (*Exeter Flying Post*, 12 March 1882)

The general decay in agriculture from 1875 onwards led to the beginning of a continued migration of farm labourers to seek work elsewhere. The decay in the woollen industry and its general removal to the north of England accelerated this migration and the population fell considerably. Farm cottages began to fall into a state of dilapidation. The development of easy methods of transport and the motor car led to the gradual introduction of a new way of life. **Prebendary John Gerrard Davis 1887–93** was in post to witness these changes.

Above: *Cullompton Fire Brigade, c.1900.*

Right: *Cullompton Fire Brigade attend a chimney fire at Lower Knowle Cottages, c.1958. Norman Gooding and Clifford Hodge are on the ladder.*

Chapter Four

The House of Windsor

House of Saxe-Coburg-Gotha

Edward VII 1901–10

House of Windsor

George V 1910-36
Edward VIII 1936
George VI 1936-52
Elizabeth II 1952–

Cullompton Parish Council held its first meeting on 31 December 1894 when it took over from the Parochial Committee. Councillors attending the first meeting were: Messrs Chas B. Ewens, John Rew, Edwin Lawrence, J.P. Grant, Fred A. Manfield, James P. Baker, Murray T. Foster, Robert Farrant, Thomas Mitchell, Charles J. Upcott, Charles Grainger, Frank Sellwood, John James, Frank Leach and William Poole. The first Clerk was John Reynolds.

Chairmen

1894–1904	Mr Chas B. Ewens
1904–17	Mr Frank Sellwood
1917–19	Mr Thos Mitchell
1919–37	Mr Tom Grant
1937–44	Mr C. Taylor
1944–45	Dr E.S. Cardell
1945–46	Mr W.E. Woolcott
1946–66	Mr S. Hill
1967–70	Dr B.E. Hammond
1970 - 1971	Mr Neville Jones
1971–81	Mr D.J. Whitton
1981–89	Mr Les Rowe
1989–95	Mrs Marian Dummett

In 1994, to celebrate the Town Council's centenary, it was decided that Cullompton should have a Town Mayor to perform civic duties and represent the town at civic functions, etc. The title of Chairman was changed to Town Mayor, although the powers and responsibilities that go with the title remain the same.

Town Mayors

1995–96	Mrs Marian Dummett
1996–98	Mrs Jane Campbell
1998–2000	Mrs Muriel Coxhead
2000–02	Mrs Linda Holloway
2002–04	Mr Graham Barden
2004–06	Mrs Eileen Andrews
2006–present	Mr Barrie Marshall

The events in this chapter are taken, in the main, from the Council minute books, and provide an insight into life in Cullompton during the twentieth century. The information is presented in chronological order, as a series of short entries to reflect the town's changes, developments and progress through the century.

Vicars

Revd George Forrester 1893–1904
Revd Charles Harris 1904–13
Revd Robert Noble Phillips 1913–21
Revd Cecil William Jameson 1921–29
Revd Henry Southcombe Bunny 1929–37
Revd Geoffrey Watkins Grubb 1937–46
Revd John Gwynn Downward 1946–51
Revd Edward Guy Hammond 1951–60
Revd Bertram W.M. Berdoe 1960–66
Revd John Hedley Mardon 1966–77
Revd John Victor Matson 1977–90
Revd David Anthony Saunders 1990–98
Revd Philip Sourbutt 1998–present

April 1895: Decision to establish Fire Brigade.

May 1895: Fire Brigade to consist ten members: Captain Frank Sweet, Sub-Captains C. Taylor and W. Galpin, W. Hawkins, Chas Brooks, J. Brooks, A. Chick, J. Broom, W. Pearcey and W. Stone.

June 1895: Meeting called to discuss complaints from parishioners regarding new bridge in Station Road (Palmers Bridge), which had been left in a dangerous condition. There was a complaint that there had been no consultation with parishioners and it was agreed to write to the County Council.

October 1895: The Property Committee was instructed to investigate the possibility of purchasing some property to the rear of Parish Rooms with the aim of providing a large public room.

March 1896: The Council took possession of a seat in Willand Road presented to the public by the Mercantile Association.

January 1897: The County Council proposed taking the main roads out of the hands of the District Council. The Parish Council agreed to write to the County Council requesting that they allow this Council to undertake the maintenance of the roads in the parish by contract or otherwise.

March 1897: The chimney of the Parish Rooms fell and caused considerable damage to the roof.

June 1897: A letter dated 4 June was sent from Mr Burrow offering to present the Assembly Rooms (later renamed the Victoria Hall) to the parish on the Queen's diamond jubilee for the use and benefit of the parishioners according to a scheme to be arranged between himself and the Parish Council. The gift was accepted by the Council on 17 June 1897, presented to the Council on 22 June 1897. The deed of conveyance was issued in January 1898.

January 1898: Use of the hall was granted to the Boys School during alterations to the classroom at the school.

April 1898: It was resolved that the Council instruct the Clerk of the Burial Board to write to Mr Chudleigh making him an offer of £200 for an acre of land to be taken from a line from the present division of consecrated and unconsecrated portions and to include the hedge on the east side of the land. Mr Chudleigh offered to accept £250 in May 1898, but in July 1898 he accepted the lower offer of £200.

1898: New offices were built for the Devon Constabulary, now the offices of Thorne & Carter in the High Street.

February 1899: Mr Baker enquired if any information could be given regarding the purchase of the Parish Room property with the proceeds of the sale of the Town Hall (the site to be used for the new police station) and whether any balance remained from the said transaction or what was done with such balance.

26 July 1899: A letter was received from Mrs Upcott of Manor House calling attention to the flooding of their premises in cases of storms. She was sent a courteous letter of reply pointing out that the Sanitary Committee had endeavoured for some years past to relieve the sewers of all the water it could, and had endeavoured to obtain Mr Upcott's permission to take the stream of water running through their back premises from the sewer into another channel but had failed to obtain the necessary consent, which if done would, to a certain extent, relieve the outfall.

October 1900: A letter was read from Lord Clinton regarding a testimonial to General Buller and the Devonshire soldiers. It was resolved that a committee be appointed to receive subscriptions towards same.

January 1901: The Parish Council of Cullompton expressed its sincere sorrow at the death of its honoured and beloved Sovereign Lady Queen Victoria.

September 1901: Plans of Parish Rooms – Mr Warren asked to modify the plans by doing away with the WC at the end of the entrance leaving the passage straight through to the yard and providing a WC in the yard further back near the wash house and another on the first floor.

5 February 1902: The revised plans were presented to

General Buller entering Cullompton, August 1906.

the Council and were approved subject to provision being made for an exit from the large room through the engine room and also at the back of the said room. It was agreed that the Council should advertise for tenders.

26 February 1902: The tender of £775 from Labdon & Son was accepted for carrying out the above work.

3 April 1902: A public meeting was held to decide how to celebrate the coronation day.

September 1902: A loan of £850 was granted from the Local Government Board for the purpose of providing Council Offices.

October 1902: A notice was issued to terminate the tenancy of the Fire Brigade Station. Mr Labdon was to look after the fireproof safe and the furniture was to be removed to the Victoria Hall during rebuilding.

1902: Discussion took place regarding plans for the fire station and 'it was considered that the engine station will be sufficiently large to accommodate both Fire Engines.'

February 1903: Discussion took place regarding the question of fixing the tablet removed from the late Parish Rooms. It was resolved that the said tablet be fixed in the Committee Room of the new Council Office together with another one showing the circumstances under which it was so fixed. These are still on display on the wall in the Council Office.

It is worth mentioning that the original Town Hall was on the site of the building now occupied by Thorne & Carter but this was sold to the police for the building of the police station with cells at the rear and court room above. The Parish Hall was then purchased and rebuilt to include provision for the fire-engines at the front.

31 May 1905: The subject of bathing on Sundays was brought up and it was resolved that a committee be asked to consider the matter and report back at the next meeting.

28 June 1905: It was resolved that two notice boards forbidding bathing on Sunday after 1 o'clock be fixed, one at each end of the footpath leading through Highbanks.

4 February 1907: It was reported that some unpleasantries occurred between the firemen at a fire at Ashill. It resulted in one resignation being sent in and, after some discussion, it was resolved that the Captain be asked to attend the next Council meeting with a report on the incident and that the Property Committee investigate the matter and bring up a report.

Fire Brigade Revels: Plenty of Drink at Nine Pence an Hour

Extract from the *Daily Mail*, 1 March 1907

The Captain and every member of the Cullompton (Devon) Fire Brigade have been called upon to resign by the Parish Council. This drastic step is the result of an alleged orgy to have been held by firemen at a fire at Ashill recently. A new brigade is to be appointed on Saturday. In the meantime, the town and an extensive agricultural district are without the services of a brigade, the members having stated that they will not act if a fire breaks out.

The allegations brought against the firemen were that, on being summoned to a fire at Ashill, they reached there at ten at night, and finding the fire practically out proceeded to enjoy a festive evening. When the Captain gave the men the orders to go home, one of them said 'What can you have better than this? There's plenty to eat, plenty to drink, and ninepence an hour.'

After this the Captain it is asserted went to sleep and two of the firemen began fighting. On the return journey in the morning the men stopped for two hours at a public house, where in the words of Mr Force, a member of the Parish Council, they finished themselves off. All the firemen were summoned to appear at last night's Council meeting.

The Chairman, Mr F. Sellwood, read a letter from the brigade captain, Mr Sweet, in which regret was expressed that there had been a 'row among the firemen'. 'But', added the Captain, 'it was a bitter cold night and they drank rather freely to keep out the cold.' The cider was strong, as he himself found out, but whether it was that or the smoke he did not know. This sentence caused a roar of laughter.

The Captain went on to state that after seeing about the fire he went into the farmhouse about the insurance. While there he was informed that two of the firemen were fighting. Eventually he gave orders for the things to be packed up, and they started off home. On the way they stopped at a public house 'to have their horses roughed' (laughter). During the halt the men started quarrelling again. The letter concluded 'please overlook it this time, and all are very sorry'.

Mr Gibbings, one of the members of the Parish Council, who went to Ashill Farm to investigate the complaints, said the information obtained went to show that only two firemen were sober. Mrs Chilcott, the farmer's wife, in mentioning the conduct of one of the firemen, said 'if I had been a man I should have given him a good hiding'. It was further stated that when the firemen found themselves in trouble they tried to implicate a constable named Babb, suggesting that he also had too much to drink. Mr Gibbings said there was no foundation whatever for this suggestion.

November 1907: A resolution was made to purchase a hand bier for the cemetery, at a cost of £14.15.0.

25 March 1908: The Committee recommend that a spot near Highbanks appears to be most suitable if the consent of the owner and tenant can be obtained. A shed might be erected at a cost of about £25 and with the co-operation of owners and occupiers of other places, at which bathing also now takes place, might be made the one bathing place for the town. Season tickets at a nominal charge are being issued to induce the public to co-operate.

27 May 1908: Communication from Mr Horne, agent to Mr Wyndham, consenting to the erection of a bathing shed near Highbanks.

8 July 1908: Shed erected at a cost of £13.14.8. A charge was levied at 1s. per annum for adults and 3d. for all children under school age. Ladies had their own bathing session on Tuesdays and no bathing was permitted on Sundays after 10a.m. Posters were procured and circulated warning all persons attempting to bathe elsewhere that they would be trespassing and liable to prosecution.

30 September 1908: An application was received for 26 allotment plots in the higher part of town. It was resolved that it would be referred to the Properties Committee to investigate.

21 March 1909: Loudwills Carriage Works in High Street (now Clark's Court), and storage sheds in Station Road went up in flames on the same night. Both properties belonged to the West of England Trading Company whose managing director was Charles Reynolds of Lavington House, Fore Street.

The fire near the station was discovered at 2a.m. by postman Sidney Denning, who raised the alarm. Captain George Brooks was soon on the scene with one of Cullompton's fire-engines. He was amazed to notice that there were five different fires in various parts of the building. In view of the seriousness he sent for the second fire-engine. On the premises he found a number of petrol and oil cans, some empty, some part-full, and a board saturated with petrol which looked as if it had held a candle.

The second fire-engine had just arrived when the news came through that the carriage works was also on fire. That was also a serious fire and the Tiverton fire-engine was called for. At the back of Loudwill's premises George Brooks found a petrol can and a quantity of shavings which were saturated with petroleum.

A year later a serious fire was discovered at the Round Tree Mills in Frog Street, Exeter, this also belonged to Mr Reynolds. It was clear that no-one had broken in and on the premises the police found a bag of shavings, half a hundredweight of cotton waste and seven-gallon oil cans.

This time Mr Reynolds was arrested and charged with arson, with intent to defraud the North British and Mercantile Insurance Company. By the time this last fire happened, it appeared Mr Reynolds had been very unfortunate with fires:

23 October 1896: Station Mills at Cullompton burnt down and he received £2,236.

2 July 1897: The same mills were burnt again, with an estimated damage of £1,500.

25 January 1909: Cricklepit Mills in Exeter burnt down, £2,841 received.

21 March 1909: two fires at Cullompton; Reynolds received £2,704 for the station fire and £377 for the one in High Street.

At the first trial at Exeter June Assizes the jury could not agree. At the retrial Mr Reynolds was found guilty and sentenced to five years in proson. His appeal to the Court of the Criminal Appeal failed and he died in prison.

28 May 1913: Resolved that the Clerk write to the Manager of the Great Western Railway urging the need for a better train service.

25 June 1913: In a letter from Sir Fredrick Upcott it was stated that it was the desire of himself and the family to make over the Chapel Field at the rear of Victoria Hall to the inhabitants of Cullompton as a recreation-ground, in the hope that it may be acceptable and of lasting benefit to the inhabitants in memory of their dear father and mother who lived for so many years in Cullompton.

The Chairman also informed the meeting that Miss Upcott had given a Bath Chair formerly used by her late father for the use of anyone needing such in the parish.

29 October 1913: Mr Plumpton reported that he had received instructions from Sir Frederick Upcott to sink a well and fix a pump in the recreation-ground. The Property Committee met there and recommended that it be placed near the entrance gate about 12 feet from present railings and from the thorn hedge at rear of Victoria Hall.

28 January 1914: The deed of gift of the Upcott Field was presented and read by the Chairman.

April 1914: Plans for public conveniences in Upcott Field were accepted and submitted to the District Council. The plans had to be approved by the Sanitary Inspector before tenders could be invited for carrying out the work.

11 May 1914: The question of organising the proposed collection for the steam fire-engine was discussed and it was resolved that the town members of the Council undertake the collecting of the town,

Plaque on the wall behind steps leading to the Upcott Field which was gifted to the town by the Upcott family in 1913.

while the farmers were responsible for the country district of the parish. The Clerk sent out notices soliciting subscriptions from the interested public who may have been outside the parish and those owning property within the parish.

27 May 1914: A complaint was received respecting the noise caused by pig killing at Higher Street. It was resolved that Mr Burnard be asked to try another method of killing to prevent the annoyance.

26 August 1914: It was resolved that there should be an alteration of the figures in the agreement to purchase the steam fire-engine from £100 to £102.10.0 to include horses.

May 1915: The Cullompton estate was for sale and included ten farms in Cullompton and Halberton totalling 1,400 acres and generating an income of £2,330 per annum. One of the farms was Padbrook. It was let to Thomas Mitchell at £220 p.a. and enclosed 143 acres. It included a 'stone and slated barn with water wheel outside for driving machinery'.

1916: The first meeting of the Cullompton WI took place in a house in New Street. The founder was Mrs Gidley, wife of the local doctor. At first they knitted socks for the troops and made flannel shirts for the hospitals. At one meeting there was a talk on pigs by a local farmer. As meat was rationed during the First World War the ladies decided that those who could would take a pig and fatten it in their back gardens.

August 1917: Houses in the parish:

Under £8 rateable value	419
Between £8 and £16	168

No vacant houses were suitable for working classes at this time. The number of new houses for working class people that were considered necessary was about 20. It was considered probable that suitable sites could be acquired by agreement. It was not expected that private enterprise could be expected to provide the necessary houses required at the close of the war.

14 February 1918: In response to an advertisement for land for use as allotments, the only offer received was from Mr E. Lawrence of land adjoining the cemetery and Upcott Field – this being offered at £5 per acre.

27 November 1918: A letter from the District Council regarding a housing scheme was considered, sites suggested included Higher Street, near the station, Dray Field in Exeter Road, Colebrooke Lane, Tiverton Lane (Shortlands Orchard or the next field) and Mr Bowerman's orchard in Higher Street. The Clerk wrote to owners enquiring if they would be willing to sell an acre or less and on what terms.

It was also resolved that the Council call a public meeting to discuss the question of a War Memorial to the town's fallen heroes.

30 December 1918: The report to the District Council regarding housing recommended that Mr Sellwood's offer should be accepted and Mr Darts considered, it being thought desirable that 24 cottages instead of 20 should be provided.

3 July 1919: At the Parish Meeting the Committee appointed for the purpose laid the suggested plans for the War Memorial in the church and in the Higher Bullring before the meeting and explained some of the details. The estimated cost stood at under £600, with subscriptions being £581.

September 1919: It was resolved that 34 cottages be recommended to be built near the Exeter Road for the Poundapitt District.

October 1919: A letter giving the dimensions of the proposed houses was considered. The Council was not satisfied that these plans were suitable for this district and asked the architect to submit other plans.

31 March 1920: It was resolved that a meeting of parishioners be called to consider the question of electric lighting for the parish.

16 April 1920: The architect attended and produced plans for the housing schemes and explained the layout and details of suggested houses in Exeter Road and Tiverton Road. Questions and criticism were invited and reasons given for various details. It was resolved that a portion of the Exeter Road houses should be with parlour and those on the Tiverton Road site should all be with parlour.

Summer 1920: Various events took place to celebrate the end of the First World War, as outlined below.

1921: Cullompton welcomed a royal vistor to the town in May.

Report of the Peace Celebration Committee to the Council

21 June 1920

The Committee appointed by the public meeting on 3 July 1919 to carry out the various celebrations in connection with the Peace beg to report that they have completed their duties which may be as follows:

1. *A collection was made throughout the Parish, £106.4.8 was received.*
2. *On Peace Day 19 July (which was very wet) a service was held in the church at 3p.m. Tea for the children and old people (pensioners) in the various halls and schoolrooms. The sports had to be postponed. Bonfire and fireworks at Opelands at 11pm.*
3. *On 24 July the sports were held in a field at Georges Well.*
4. *On 25 July a smoking concert with refreshments was held in the Victoria Hall for returned soldiers and sailors, about 200 being present.*
5. *On 16 March 1920 the second entertainment was given for the remaining returned soldier and sailors in the Parish Room and about 100 sat down.*
6. *It was decided not to give medals to the children as the funds did not amount to nearly as much as was anticipated.*

The Committee met on nine different occasions

Crowds flocked to see the Prince of Wales.

A Royal Visitor

From the *Tiverton Gazette*, May 1921

It was not known until the previous Saturday that the Prince of Wales would be passing through Cullompton. A large crowd gathered near the War Memorial in the Higher Bullring. About 50 ex-servicemen paraded under Lieuts. C. Stone and F.J. Embery, together with Boy Scouts, under Sergt. Marlow, Girl Guides and Brownies under Mrs Alleyne, Mrs Pyne and Mrs Webb. The town was gaily bedecked with flags and bunting. Several arches were erected, one by Major Sellwood's employees near the Tannery with the inscription 'God Bless the Prince of Wales' and another at the entrance to the Bull Ring with the words 'Welcome to our Prince'. Major Sellwood and Capt. Croft arrived a few minutes before the Prince to tell of His Royal Highness's approach.

The Prince was welcomed by the Chairman of the Parish Council, Mr Tom Grant and shook hands with each ex-Serviceman. The Vicar, Dr Alleyne, Dr Gidley and members of the Parish Council were then presented. Mr G. Ingersent was wheeled before His Royal Highness, as one of the town's oldest inhabitants. Mr W. Denner, smith, approached the Prince and asked for his acceptance of a gilded horseshoe as a token of good luck. The offer was accepted with thanks. The Prince then got into his car and drove slowly through the town amidst much enthusiasm. The Town Band under Bandsmaster S. Nex played selections. Mrs Gidley's efforts were mainly responsible for the success of the proceedings.

1922: It was announced that electric light cables were to be installed.

February 1924: The status of the Post Office was changed to that of sub-Post Office.

27 August 1924: Parish Meeting held to discuss the purchase of a new fire-engine to replace the old steam fire-engine. On a show of hands (25 for and eight against) it was agreed to purchase a Dennis Motor Trailer Pump; a loan of £450 was obtained for the purchase.

1925: An application was made to the District Council for 24 houses to be built at Stoneyford. Mr Grant offered the land at cost price.

June 1925: Mr Burrows and family stated they were willing to give the parish the first allotment field in Tiverton Road provided the parish will purchase the upper field. At the public meeting held on 10 July it was agreed to purchase the upper field for £350 and a loan was obtained for the purchase.

August 1925: Mr A.R. Hammett appointed the Clerk to the Council at an inclusive salary of £67 p.a., Mr Reynolds having resigned after over 40 years due to ill health.

1925: W.H. Grant Esq. of Croydon presented two almshouses to the parish and A. Burrow gifted the allotment field adjoining the cemetery to be known as Burrow Field. The deeds were placed in Lloyds Bank.

September 1926: The captain of the fire brigade brought the Council's attention to the unsatisfactory method of calling the brigade together i.e. using a steam siren at Messrs Sellwood's property. It was agreed that the fire brigade revert back to the use of maroons to call the men together.

The WI were granted permission to use the small Committee Room at the Parish Rooms for a lending library one evening per week.

October 1926: A discussion took place regarding the delay in the fire brigade attending a fire at Weaver due to the usual lorry being unavailable resulted in the captain of the brigade being instructed to take the first available lorry, and arrange with other lorry owners to assist in cases of emergency.

The captain of the fire brigade was also empowered, in the case of country fires, to despatch two firemen using motor cycles to the scene of a fire in advance of the fire-engine. Sixpence a mile to be allowed for the use of their motor cycles.

February 1927: The Council met to consider plans for houses at Stoneyford. It was agreed that 12 parlour type and four non-parlour type should be erected.

September 1927: Signs were erected in Higher Bullring stating 'motors park here' provided free by the Automobile Association.

Devon County Council granted permission to use the Parish Rooms as a 'Child Welfare Centre' once a fortnight.

November 1927: Mr Pearcey of Growen offered to put sheep in the Upcott Field to 'eat down the grass'.

November 1927: The small Committee Room in the Parish Rooms was put to use as County Library once a week.

April 1928: The library had developed more than was anticipated and a request for the use of a large room was granted.

January 1929: The Council agreed to sell 2.5 acres of land above the Upcott Field to Tiverton Rural District Council for housing at a price in the region £100 per acre.

March 1930: Mrs Clitsome drew attention to the insanitary method of the collection of household refuse in open carts and it was resolved that the Council consider provision of a covered cart for this purpose.

January 1931: Formal notice was received for the transfer of the Cullompton Elementary Schools to Devon County Council.

July 1931: Streets were officially named and each house given a number: Duck Street was renamed Duke Street (no reason given), Church Lane became Church Street, Tiverton Lane became Tiverton Road, Higher Bullring was renamed High Street, Lower Street was changed to Station Road.

8 March 1932: Mr G. Brooks resigned as Captain of the Fire Brigade after 25 years of service. He attended his last fire at Mr Veysey's butcher shop.

September 1932: The GPO agreed to install a telephone kiosk on paving outside the police station (now Thorne & Carter Estate Agents).

June 1933: A drowning occurred at Palmers Bridge.

August 1936: A meeting was held to discuss the disposal of the Victoria Hall. An approach was made by the County Education Department regarding its use for school purposes. The reserve price was fixed at £200 and the sale, which eventually took place on 13 April 1938, saw the property go to Miss L. Hill.

June 1937: Estimates were obtained to provide

Above: *Parading to St Andrews Church to celebrate George V's silver jubilee, 6 May 1935.*

Left: *Cartoons of Cullompton personalities published in the* Western Morning News, *July 1938.*

Cullompton Volunteers, 1939. The photograph was taken outside the British Legion on a Sunday morning just before Church Parade. Later that day whilst sitting through the service in St Andrews Church the vicar left the pulpit and came back to announce to the congregation that war had been declared. Left to right, back row: *? Price, Alec Mortimore, Cliff Denner, Bert Bradford, ?, George Rugg, ? Montiffe, Peter Patterson, Bob Chidgey, Dick Milton, Jack Dyer, Bill Hill;* third row: *Dick Miller, Bert Dommett, Jack Clist, Cyril Warren, Jack Parsons, Maurice Ellicott, Dennis Heale, George Jolliffe, Alf Perry, Bill Purslow, Gerald Murray, Vic Tidborough, Fred Whitton, Monty Payne, Albert Mitchell, Fred Osman;* second row: *? Gill, Bert Jefferies, Rolf Mitchell, Reg Hales, Cecil Shopland, George Young, Jack Hake, Jumbo Lyons, Bill Wood, Kenneth Sanders, John Little, Frances Heale, ?, Tom Batting, Ken Saunders, Arthur Wright, Jo Chidgey, Ron Holmes;* front row: *Ted Sampson, Spencer Shopland, ?, Archie Ellicott, Bob Crispin, Eric Batten, RSM Morrison, Captain Batten, RSM Ingersent, Percy Palfrey, Stan (Toot) Butt, Tom Jolliffe, Roy Biss, ? Palfrey.*

electric lighting to the Parish Rooms. The work was completed in August 1937.

1938: As remembered by Mrs Doreen Phillput (née Knowle):

> *The proceeds of the annual carnival was allotted to the St John Ambulance Brigade to help provide an ambulance for the town which was badly needed. Doreen Knowles raised the most money from various collections and was declared Carnival Queen for that year, being crowned in the Parish Hall together with her page boy and four attendants.*
>
> *The carnival parade started in Station Road and after the judging of the floats and other entries proceeded via High Street, Fore Street and Exeter Hill to the Cullompton Hotel where the Carnival Queen presented the awards to all the prizewinners. The day ended with a dance at the Assembly Rooms with music from the Freddie Burrows Dance Band. Photographs of all the events were taken by Mr Cross who had his shop in Fore Street.*
>
> *The following year Cullompton got its first ambulance which was garaged behind the doctors' surgery opposite the police station (now Thorne & Carter).*

1939: The Parish Rooms were commandeered for ARP purposes.

June 1940: A letter was received from a London school thanking the townspeople for the cordial welcome they had given to the children evacuated from the capital.

September 1940: Permission was granted for the removal of a tree outside the Baptist Church in Higher Bullring to allow room for the erection of an air-raid shelter.

October 1942: The Council's attention was drawn to the practice of sending children from the junior school to take cover in the trenches during air-raid alerts. This was considered dangerous and the County Education Committee was asked to provide surface shelters or some other more suitable protection for the children during air raids.

March 1944: A meeting was held to consider a suggestion that the Cullompton Hotel, being up for sale, might be acquired as a cottage hospital.

August 1944: A meeting was called to consider a request from the RDC for an estimate of the number of houses required in the parish in connection with the postwar housing schemes. It was tentatively estimated that 100 houses would be required.

August 1945: A special meeting was called to consider celebrations following announcement of cessation of the war against Japan. It was unanimously agreed that the public be asked to display flags and bunting. It was also resolved that Messrs Jefferies or Mitchell be asked to cater for a tea for the children on VJ+2 Day. It was also resolved that the Chairman and Clerk arrange for sports and a bonfire and to obtain permission for a house-to-house collection to meet expenses.

May 1947: A letter was received from the Fellowship of St Andrews Church asking the Council to explore the lack of adequate facilities for young people, particularly in respect of tennis-courts. It asked the Parish Council to obtain some site for conversion into one or more public tennis-courts and further, wanted to know if any steps were being taken with regard to the provision of a public swimming-pool. It was

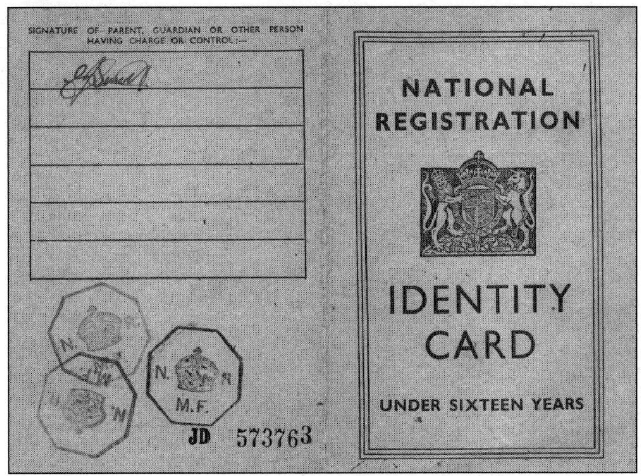

SIGNATURE OF PARENT, GUARDIAN OR OTHER PERSON HAVING CHARGE OR CONTROL:—

NATIONAL REGISTRATION

IDENTITY CARD

UNDER SIXTEEN YEARS

M.F.

JD 573763

A National Registration Identity Card. Such documents were issued during and following the Second World War.

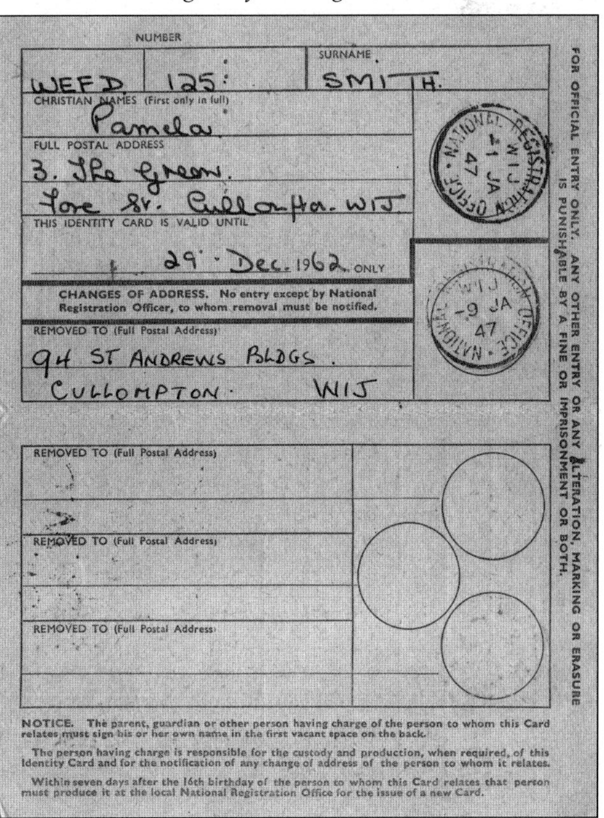

NUMBER: WEFD 125

SURNAME: SMITH.

CHRISTIAN NAMES (First only in full): Pamela

FULL POSTAL ADDRESS: 3. The Green. Fore St. Cullompton. WIJ

THIS IDENTITY CARD IS VALID UNTIL 29 · Dec. 1962 ONLY

CHANGES OF ADDRESS. No entry except by National Registration Officer, to whom removal must be notified.

REMOVED TO (Full Postal Address): 94 ST ANDREWS BLDGS. CULLOMPTON · WIJ

REMOVED TO (Full Postal Address)

REMOVED TO (Full Postal Address)

REMOVED TO (Full Postal Address)

FOR OFFICIAL ENTRY ONLY. ANY OTHER ENTRY OR ANY ALTERATION, MARKING OR ERASURE IS PUNISHABLE BY A FINE OR IMPRISONMENT OR BOTH.

NOTICE. The parent, guardian or other person having charge of the person to whom this Card relates must sign his or her own name in the first vacant space on the back.

The person having charge is responsible for the custody and production, when required, of this Identity Card and for the notification of any change of address of the person to whom it relates.

Within seven days after the 16th birthday of the person to whom this Card relates that person must produce it at the local National Registration Office for the issue of a new Card.

St Andrews Primary School Christmas play, 1946.

resolved that the Clerk contact the Secretary of the Parish Councils Association to ascertain the possibility of resuscitating the pre-war scheme for a swimming-pool.

July 1950: It was agreed that one of the two cemetery chapels should be used as a mortuary as it was little used.

August 1950: A letter was received objecting to a mobile fish and chip stall in High Street on certain evenings. The Clerk reported that the matter was being investigated by the Local Food Office.

March 1951: The Council recorded a strong protest against the rapidly increasing County rate and urged that every economy should be made to prevent further increases.

May 1951: A letter was received from the Secondary Modern School asking if the swimming-pool planned some years ago would materialise as the Education Authority was anxious that the children should be taught swimming. After discussion it was resolved that the Clerk reply that it was unlikely and the Council was not in favour of increased expenditure on the present education rate.

Head Weir, where local people used to go to swim and after which Head Weir Road is named.

June 1951: Mr Whitton referred to the fact that the police station was unmanned at night and at certain times during the day. In view of the heavy traffic and the urgent need for quick contact with the police, it was resolved that the matter be referred to the Chief Constable of Devon.

September 1951: An invitation was received from the Scouts for the attendance of the Chairman at the official opening of their new headquarters in New Street.

May 1952: Considerable discussion arose over the proposal of the County Fire Service to build a new station at Shortlands at a cost of £7,000 but it was pointed out that this was outside the jurisdiction of the Council.

August 1952: A meeting was held to consider steps to be taken in response to an appeal for funds for relief following the disastrous floods in Lynton and Lynmouth and North Devon. It was unanimously agreed that a house-to-house collection be made. The total collected was £378.6s.4d.

June 1953: Reference was made to the County Development Plan which provided for a bypass to the town but after a good deal of discussion it was agreed that the Council take no action.

September 1953: It was resolved that a public meeting should be held to allocate surplus coronation funds and to endeavour to ascertain if various funds such as those remaining from the jubilee, swimming-pool and public hall could be merged for some other purpose for the good of the town.

At a public meeting on 2 November 1953 a committee was appointed to investigate the possibility of a public hall, swimming-pool, playing-fields, tennis-courts or any other project for the good of the town to which funds that were already extant could be allocated.

Above: *'Best in Show' plus other prizes – Ivor and Reg Rutley at the 1953 Flower and Vegetable Show.*
Below: *Cullompton Carnival float, c.1970.* Left to right, back row: *Angela Metcalfe, Katrina Thompson, ?, Suzzane Pulce, Sharon Metcalfe, Lorraine Metcalfe;* front row: *Stephen Long, Richard Lane, Louisa Lane, Gareth Squance, Michelle Smith, ?.*

October 1954: A letter was received from the County Council drawing attention to non-compliance of certain traders with the regulations as to shop closing hours and the limitation of commodities for sale on Sundays. It was resolved that the press be asked to stress the matter and that the Chamber of Commerce be asked to co-operate.

November 1954: Invitation received to the official opening of the new fire station.

November 1954: In view of the continuance of excessive noise from car and motor cycles in the Higher Bullring after cinema shows it was resolved that the management be asked to draw to the attention of patrons these complaints and to ask the police for their co-operation.

July 1955: It was agreed a typewriter should be purchase for the Clerk at a cost of £33.10s.0d.

December 1956: The Gas Works in Station Road was closed.

April 1957: A letter was received from the Chamber of Commerce expressing concern about the decline in the market and the subsequent effect on trade.

August 1957: Due to lack of support it was decided to withdraw the Market's Livestock Certificate.

January 1958: It was proposed by the Head Postmaster in Exeter that Post Office counters be closed at 6p.m. However, it was resolved that the Council could not support the proposal on the grounds of public demand.

October 1958: Another fire took place in the town:

£250,000 Tannery fire puts 100 men out of work

Blazing like a mighty torch, with white flame spouting from every window opening and leaping 100 feet upward through the fallen roof to play upon the rolling clouds of smoke, the tannery of Messrs Sellwood Bros. was on Friday evening a glowing spectacle which cast in contrast the shadow of unemployment into over 100 Cullompton homes.

(*Devon and Somerset News*, Wednesday 22 October 1958)

May 1960: A party of 26 children, with their leaders Miss Caslake and Mr Wheeler, set off on the first ever continental tour organised by Cullompton Secondary Modern. The children caught the 7.45a.m. train from Cullompton Station to catch the boat train from Victoria Station in London to Dover. From Dover they caught the cross-Channel steamer *Roi Leopold III* and arrived at Ostend at 8.55p.m. From there the party continued to Bruges and went on various trips to France, Holland and Belguim.

November 1963: Mr Mingo raised the question of why the Rural District Council had given licence for the cinema to open on Sundays. The Clerk was instructed to write to the RDC pointing out that the Council hoped that the Sunday Cinema Act would be used to have some control over the type of film shown.

20 May 1964: Mr Cole raised the question of smoking at meetings. It was decided that there should be no smoking until 8.30p.m

1964: The railway station at Cullompton closed due to the decision to make cuts on the nationalised railway.

12 May 1965: The Clerk read a letter from Brig. Appleton which set out what was proposed at the old school. The existing building would be demolished and a scheme prepared to include both a health centre and a Magistrates' Court. Although a new branch library was required, the site was considered too small for such a purpose.

12 March 1969: A letter was read from the headmaster of the primary school requesting that the recreation-ground be fenced. After discussion it was resolved to place boulders to mark the boundary.

October 1969: The bypass was completed.

April 1971: A letter was received from the Community Association asking the Council what financial help it could offer towards the provision of a sports and recreation centre for the town. Mr Saunders, Chairman of the Association presented to the Council the proposals to provide these facilities at Lower Mill. This site was the only one where planning approval had been given by the County Council Planning Committee and the idea was to provide football and rugby pitches as well as tennis-courts and ground would also be available for a swimming-pool. Unfortunately the owner of the land would not sell piecemeal and therefore the total 30 acres (or thereabouts) would have to be purchased at the total cost of about £12,000. Discussion followed and the following resolution was passed:

For the purpose of providing recreational and sports facilities at Lower Mill this Council contribute £1,000 per year for a period of ten years commencing financial year 1971/2 to the Cullompton Community Association subject to consultation with the Treasurer of the Tiverton Rural District Council and that this Council be represented on the Governing Body.

1 April 1974: Under the Local Government Act 1972 Cullompton Parish Council became Cullompton Town Council. The titles of Chairman and Vice-Chairman were retained (rather than employing the titles of Mayor and Deputy Mayor).

14 May 1975: The sale of the old police station was announced when a letter from the Devon and Cornwall Police Authority was read to the Council. Mr Lawrence said it would be a pity if the clock on the front of the building was taken down and should be left there as there was no other clock for public use in the town.

Mr Hill asked when the law would be put in force regarding double yellow lines. The Chairman said the order had been approved in the *Tiverton Gazette* during this week. Mr Hill said the town would be choked to death with yellow lines and no-one would be able to stop in the town, which would lead to the demise of the town. Mr Venner said he had to wait 10 minutes in a bus to pass Labdon's yard, while Mr Vicary said it took 40 minutes to go from his shop at the bottom of town to the one at the top. Mr Labdon said it was due to selfish parking by motorists. The Chairman said a car park was in view but it could not be made public at this time. It was resolved to wait at least another month.

Mrs Martinscroft reported that St Andrews School was in a crucial state. The school was built in 1937 for 200 pupils but by this 1975 it had 461 pupils using 13 classrooms and one hall. The canteen, built to feed 100, was catering for 350. The toilet facilities had not been increased since the school was built and were most unhygienic. School managers were repeatedly told a new school would be built, but had seen no developments on this. The headmaster requested another classroom and had applied repeatedly for another mobile classroom but had not seen any progress.

April 1976: The Commercial Inn was renamed the Pony & Trap.

1977: The M5 was opened from Bristol to Exeter.

9 November 1977: Dr Hammond asked what would happen to Queensway (situated on the site of the current Somerfield supermarket) when it closed down. The Chairman said he hoped another industry would take it over and give employment, although it was an ideal site for a car park and he believed that the local authority might purchase it.

14 February 1979: Mr Allen reported that the sub-committee had visited Colyton and Axminster to have a look at their sports halls and had come to a decision that a sports hall was necessary in Cullompton. However, at this stage it was unclear as to how big the hall should be or where it should be located. Mr Foster felt it should not be positioned on educational land, and that it must have the full support of all the people of Cullompton. Mr Allen thought the Culm Valley was deserving of a sports hall and he did not see why the townfolk should have to use the facilities of neighbouring communities.

14 May 1980: A rambling discussion discussion took place regarding the lack of progress in the provision of a sports hall and where it should be sited. It was agreed to invite the District Planning Officer to meet the Council and discuss possible sites.

14 May 1980: Mr Goffey invited members of the Council to join the march to Tiverton Town Hall to demand the District Council improve industrial and recreational facilities for Cullompton.

17 September 1980: Mr Rowe explained that it had been made quite clear to him that if Cullompton pressed for a complete amenities complex it could be between 10 and 20 years before anything would be done. If the Council opted for the sports hall work would hopefully be started in early 1983. It was therefore proposed by Mr Rowe, and seconded by Mr Doyle, that a sports hall be built on Mid-Devon District Council land at Exeter Road with sufficient land remaining to expand the amenities in the future.

8 October 1980: A letter was received from Bradninch Town Council requesting the Council's support concerning the withdrawal of the crossing patrol at Cullompton Comprehensive School. It was agreed to give full support to Bradninch Town Council. It was also agreed that there was a real need for a crossing patrol in Exeter Road. It was felt that Devon County Council should be responsible for this instead of passing it over to local charities. A pelican crossing for the site was also suggested. It was agreed to write to Devon County Council and the Road Safety Committee for their support on this matter.

8 October 1980: It was stated that the traffic congestion outside Willowbank School was a serious hazard. The situation had become extremely dangerous. It was agreed to write to the County Council again stating that the Council were not happy with the situation and that something should be done immediately. A one-way system was suggested.

8 July 1981: Mr Dunning stated he was pleased with how the toilets had been built in Station Road, and that their appearance was a credit to Cullompton. He suggested that the Rotary Club go ahead with the landscaping around the toilets now that the builders had finished.

10 February 1982: A letter was received from the headmaster of St Andrews School requesting that Upcott Town Pump be removed from the Upcott field as it was causing inconvenience. It was agreed to ask the Rotary Club to remove the pump.

10 February 1982: A letter was read from Mrs Duffin, supervisor at Cullompton Playgroup. Mr Doyle proposed that the playgroup be allowed to use the Parish Rooms at a rent of 50p per session, and the playgroup be responsible for their own cleaning, on a weekly basis subject to existing bookings. The charge was amended by Mr Whitton to £1 per session.

14 July 1982: Mrs Dunning proposed, seconded by Mr Simmons, that there be no smoking during Council meetings. This was agreed by the Council.

8 December 1982: Mr Hake reported that an agreement had been signed enabling the youth club to use the day centre (Community House).

15 April 1983: Mrs Dunning proposed, seconded by Mr Doyle and agreed by the Council, that the name of the new sports facility should be Culm Valley Sports Hall.

The building of the Culm Valley Sports Centre, c.1982.

BUCKINGHAM PALACE

From: The Lady-in-Waiting to H.R.H. The Princess of Wales

27th September 1990

Dear Mrs. Dummett,

The Princess of Wales has asked me to write to thank you very much for the splendid bouquet of flowers that was so kindly presented to her yesterday on behalf of Cullompton Town Council.

Her Royal Highness was delighted she was able to visit Cullompton and was extremely touched by the warmth of her reception. It was a most successful and interesting visit and one which The Princess particularly enjoyed.

Her Royal Highness would be grateful if you could pass on her best wishes to Andrew Bowers for a very enjoyable and successful visit to Seoul in 1991.

Yours sincerely,

Sarah Campden.

Viscountess Campden

Mrs M. Dummett

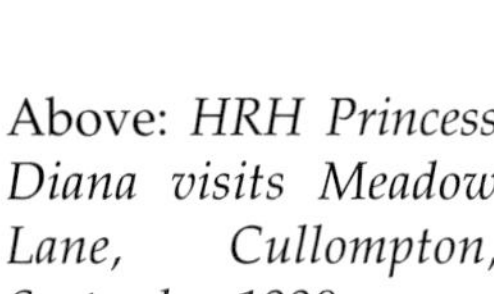

Above: *HRH Princess Diana visits Meadow Lane, Cullompton, September 1990.*

Above, right: *HRH Princess Diana is presented to the Chairman of the Town Council, Cllr Mrs Marian Dummett, during her visit to Cullompton on 26 September 1990.*

Right: *Thank you letter from HRH Princess of Wales following her visit to Cullompton in 1990.*

15 April 1983: Mr Dunning explained that the property in Middle Mill Lane would need skilled services to convert it to a youth club and these were not available under the Manpower Services. Mr Dunning proposed, seconded by Mr Doyle, that the Council write to Devon County Council asking for support for a youth club to be built in the grounds of Cullompton Comprehensive School.

8 June 1983: Mr Wilkinson said that this was a growing town with a larger population than Pinhoe, whose railway station had just been reopened. He proposed that the Council write to the Western Region of British Rail stating that it was hoped discussions would recommence regarding the future of the station.

8 June 1983: The Council agreed to underwrite any losses incurred when the outdoor swimming-pool at Cullompton Comprehensive School was opened to the public during school holidays.

12 September 1984: The Council announced that planning permission was being sought for a youth club to be built behind the sports hall in Meadow Lane.

11 February 1987: A letter was sent to the Police Authority requesting additional traffic warden cover.

13 July 1988: A letter was sent to the Police Authority requesting increased foot patrols following an article in the *Express & Echo* entitled 'Terror Town'.

13 July 1989: Dr Rhys-Davies and Dr Martin addressed Councillors regarding their proposals to build a hospital in Cullompton.

October 1989: An ambulance station was opened in Station Road.

26 September 1990: HRH The Princess of Wales visited Cullompton to inspect the Red Cross personnel and watch displays and demonstrations of their skills in the Culm Valley Sports Centre. She then visited the John Tallack Centre and Mrs Hannah Curtis, youth club leader and Mrs Kay Gordon, tutor to the local course for the training of pre-school playgroup leaders, were presented to her. The Princess was then escorted to watch a practical session for playgroup leaders attended by a group of young mothers. At the end of the visit the Princess was presented with a bouquet, on behalf of Cullompton Town Council by Andrew Bowers (aged 13) a member of Cullompton Scout Troop who had been selected to attend the World Scout Jamboree in Seoul (South Korea) in 1991.

23 April 1991: It was reported that can and glass banks were now in position and in use at Station Road car park.

Cullompton Fun Run which started at Cullompton Football Club, 1992.

25 July 1991: A meeting was held to discuss the enhancement scheme for Higher Bullring.

1 April 1992: A public meeting was held to discuss complaints about rowdiness from young people gathering outside the Magistrates' Court. Youngsters felt that the claims were exaggerated, and an investigation took place to assess the provision of meeting places for young people in the town centre.

27 April 1992: A meeting was held between representatives of Devon County Council and Mid-Devon District Council to discuss the future economy of Cullompton. It was agreed that the major stumbling block to improving the economic viability of the town was traffic and parking.

June 1992: Exeter Museum undertook archaeological excavations in the field belonging to the Town Council above the cemetery in Tiverton Road.

13 January 1993: Councillors were invited for a guided tour of the new Woodmill Hospital. It was closed and in receivership in October 1993 and despite a lobby for it to become become a community hospital it was sold privately in November 1993.

7 July 1994: It was agreed that the Magistrates' Court car park should be rented on Saturdays for an annual rental of £150 to provide short-stay shoppers with parking.

1 September 1994: It was resolved that, with effect from 1 January 1995, the Chairman of the Council assume the title Town Mayor and the Parish Rooms be renamed the Town Hall.

6 July 1995: It was resolved that an additional Council meeting is held each month to discuss current planning issues and applications.

30 May 1996: Discussion took place regarding the possible redevelopment of the site of Clark's Motors for a supermarket.

7 November 1996: The decision was taken to purchase a bus shelter for Higher Bullring, with a total cost of approximately £3,000.

5 June 1997: It was resolved that the Council pay the cost of providing five dog bins at an estimated cost of £250 each in anticipation that MDDC will fund an equal number. It was also requested that the local community be made aware that they are expected to clean up after their dogs.

4 September 1997: It was resolved to recommend the refusal of the planning application for a motorway services area at Station Yard.

2 October 1997: It was reported that an in-line skating facility had been constructed in Meadow Lane and was proving very popular with young people.

16 October 1997: Discussion took place with Mid-Devon District Council's Development Control Manager with regard to the proposal to construct a food retail outlet on land adjacent to Forge Way (including Station Road car park).

20 November 1997: Discussion took place regarding the planning application from Barratt Bristol Ltd for residential development and Phase I of Northern Distributor Road at Court Farm.

19 March 1998: No objections were raised to the planning application from Westcountry Housing Association for the demolition of 56 dwellings and erection of 54 dwelling units with associated curtilage parking, highway improvements and play/open space provision at Haymans Close/Orchard Way.

2 July 1998: It was resolved to hold a public meeting to understand the views of the local community with regard to a planning proposal to erect a food store, diner and petrol station on land off Station Road (between the petrol station and the Weary Traveller).

4 November 1999: A report stated that the developer has decided not to proceed with proposals to construct a supermarket on land adjacent to Forge Way.

2 November 2000: It was resolved not to continue leasing St Andrews car park to Mid-Devon District Council when the lease expired on 31 March 2001. It was resolved to accept an offer from Cullompton traders to pay the annual rent of £1,100 to enable St Andrews car park to become a free, limited-stay shoppers' car park

18 January 2001: It was suggested that the Council set aside money to carry out general maintenance work around the town, including such things as gutter and path weeding, keeping public rights of way in good order, etc. It was resolved to investigate a partnership with Devon County Council and Mid-Devon District Council, in an attempt to ensure there is no overlapping of work, that it is carried out to their standards and, where applicable, they make a contribution towards the cost of providing the service.

15 February 2001: It was reported that a CCTV system would be installed in High Street/Fore Street during the first week of March.

1 March 2001: The Farmers' Market was cancelled this month due to the Foot and Mouth outbreak.

3 May 2001: It was resolved to write to the Highways Agency asking when Cullompton had its name changed to McDonalds! It requested an explanation as to why the name of a commercial venture was detailed on a distance sign alongside the names of other towns but not the name of the town in which the said fast-food outlet was located.

8 December 2001: The launch of *The Book of Cullompton* took place at the Town Hall. It was compiled by the Town Clerk and Town Councillors with many contributions from members of the public.

Cullompton St John Ambulance Officers at the Town Picnic in 2002 (they had their faces painted with Union Jacks to celebrate the Queen's golden jubliee). Left to right, standing: *Debbie Vinnicombe, Ray Newland, Margaret Billingham;* crouching: *Leanne Chandler.*

3 June 2002: The Town Council organised the first Cullompton Town Picnic at the CCA Fields to celebrate the Queen's golden jubilee.

6 March 2003: It was resolved to buy a new coat for the Town Crier at a cost of £595.

20 March 2003: Concern was expressed by local businesses about a new traffic management scheme in Fore Street which meant that private cars were unable to use the loading/unloading bays. A meeting was arranged with a traffic warden.

17 April 2003: It was resolved to write to Devon County Council Highways requesting that the Traffic Order is amended to permit private cars to park whilst loading/unloading in bays in Fore Street.

3 July 2003: The Council agreed to accept the principle of taking responsibility for the vacuum sweeping of Cullompton's pavements.

21 August 2003: It was resolved to write to the Police Authority requesting an increase in foot patrols due to complaints about anti-social behaviour in the town centre, particularly during the evenings.

September 2003: Cullompton Town Council was granted 'Quality' status. It was one the first three Town/Parish Councils in England to be given this award.

4 December 2003: A planning application was discussed for the erection of a Tesco supermarket on Western Way industrial estate. Council requested a meeting with the Planning Officer and developer to discuss highway issues.

The planning application for a park at Court Farm was also discussed. Refusal of plans was recommended as the soil height needed to be reduced as there was potential to create drainage problems.

8 January 2004: The planning application was discussed for the erection of a shop unit with flat above and erection of 33 sheltered apartments at the former Clark's Garage site, High Street. Clark's Court was completed in July 2006.

Above: *Cullompton Police Sergeant Jackie Chinn and Binka at Cullompton's 'Celebration of Christmas Lights', November 2003.*

Below: *Cullompton Ace Majorettes parading at Cullompton's 'Celebration of Christmas Lights', November 2003.*

5 February 2004: Councillors were advised that the planning application has been submitted for the redevelopment of the Toad Hall site. Planning was approved and Toad Hall was demolished to make way for Heyridge Court, which was completed in 2006.

September 2006: A planning application was received for the completion of Northern Distributor Road and the erection of Phase II housing at Court Farm.

Left: *Footpath Walk organised by Cullompton Town Council to survey the parish footpaths, May 2004.* Left to right: *Terry Belson, Shaun Holvey, Eileen Andrews, ?, Sue Newall, ?, Judy Morris, Brian Mitchell, Barrie Marshall, Graham Barden*.

Cullompton Town Picnic 2006

Binka trying to decide the winner of the fancy-dress competition.

Cullompton Army Cadets erecting the tents.

Cullompton Youth Café Project.

Cullompton Town Crier, Gordon Pring, attends all the local community events and is a great ambassador for the town.

Chapter Five

Through the Eyes of a Child

This section comprises a series of interviews with seven people who grew up in Cullompton in the seven decades between 1920 and 1990 to provide an insight into how childhood and Cullompton has gradually changed. Marian Dummett wrote down her own memories while the other contributors were interviewed.

Children of the Twenties

Pearl Marshall (née Mitchell) and Joan Castleton (née Mitchell)

Pearl Mitchell was born in 1921 and her sister Mavis Joan (usually known as Joan) was born in 1924. They lived with their parents, younger sister Pamela and brother Eddie at 46 Exeter Road. Their father Gilbert Mitchell was a builder, as was his father and many of his cousins and uncles. He built the first three bungalows and some houses in Brooke Road (as you enter Brooke Road from Exeter Road).

Pearl and Joan went to school on Exeter Hill where the Magistrates' Court is now located. They started school when they were about four years old and left when they were 14. Joan remembers that her first teacher was Miss Labdon and the headmistress was Miss Wise. They liked Miss Wise as she would let the children stand around the heater in the winter to warm themselves. Other teachers they remember are Mr Baker the PE teacher, Miss Parker, Miss Button, Mr Newman and Trevor Jones the music teacher.

At break time Eddie Nicholas would bring a tray of freshly cooked buns from the Co-op (which was situated where the library is now located) and sell them to the children through the school railings for a halfpenny each. They can still remember the taste and smell of those buns!

Cullompton School, the school that Joan and Pearl attended from age four to fourteen, it was situated on Exeter Hill where the Magistrates' Court is now.

Their house in Exeter Road had two bedrooms and the three sisters shared a double bed in one bedroom. It had no inside toilet and no electricity. Bath night was once a week in a tin bath in front of the fire. There was no heating in the bedrooms but they sometimes warmed their bed with a hot brick. They had a chamber-pot under the bed in case they got caught short in the night and the only light they had in the bedroom was provided by a candle.

Hot water was boiled in a 'copper' and their mother took in washing to earn money. Before she married, their mother Lily, was a cook at Padbrook Farm and she was also in the Royal Air Corp during the First World War. She married their father in 1921.

As children they played games such as hopscotch and paper chase in the street; Exeter Road was fairly quiet then. There were two ladies called Jeffreys who lived in Colebrooke Lane and would come into town a couple of times a week to do their shopping in a pony and trap. They also remember Obi Luxton and his horse and cart. He would collect parcels to take to Exeter and bring back anything people wanted. He lived in Exeter Hill and kept his horse and cart at the back of the Pony & Trap, which is how it got its name, as it was formerly the Commercial Inn.

At Christmas they would usually be given a doll and a book each and sometimes a game. They also received nuts and an orange and a penny in the bottom of their pillowcase. Children were expected to go to Sunday school and chapel. They went to the Methodist Church and can remember a Sunday school outing to Exmouth on the train. For pocket money they picked wild primroses and violets and sold them to Joe Dyer for 1d. a bunch. The flowers were sent by train to London where they were sold on the markets.

They could catch the train to Exeter for 9d. return but they would walk to Bradninch or Tiverton to watch the carnivals and, if they went to Tiverton, they would take a few pennies with them to spend in Woolworths. They also liked to go into Tiny Hellier's shop in Fore Street. They felt like 'Alice in Wonderland' as the shop was full of small toys and all sorts of fascinating things.

When Pearl was about 12 or 13 their father bought a motorbike and sidecar and he would sometimes take his family on outings, usually to Exmouth.

Pearl and Joan remember the 'lamp lighter' who lived at 11 Crowbridge Cottages. He would come along every evening at about 5p.m. to light the street lights. He rode a bicycle but had a 'gammy' leg so

Above: *Lily Gillett (mother of Pearl and Joan Mitchell). She married Gilbert Mitchell in 1921. During the First World War she served in the Royal Flying Corp. and was stationed in France.*

Above: *Ways Lane, Pearl lived in Ways Lane from 1942-46.*

Exeter Road in the 1930s where Pearl and Joan were born and spent their childhood.

would only pedal with one foot.

The Police Sergeant at that time was Sgt Kellaway, who lived at the police station (now Thorne & Carter). Joan once accidently threw a stone at a car and broke its window. The police came to see her parents and she was 'frightened to death'.

When Pearl first left school she worked at Cullompton Weavers in High Street. It was a small shop, just one room really. She wasn't too keen on using the knitting machine and so she left and went to work in Frisby's shoe shop. Frisby's opened every morning at 8.30a.m. and closed at 6p.m. on Monday, Tuesday and Wednesday. Thursday was half-day closing in Cullompton so she got to go home early but Friday the shop stayed open to 7p.m. and on Saturday it didn't close until 8p.m.

Barrie and Joan Marshall. Barrie is the current Cullompton Town Mayor and son of Pearl Marshall (née Mitchell).

Joan left school and went to Fox's factory in Higher Street where she learnt to invisibly mend the fabric as it came off the loom. Later she went to work at the jam factory which was situated where Ploudal Road is now located. The factory made jam according to the fruit in season and they also pickled onions, etc. Joan made the jam, poured it into the jars and labelled it. She also washed jars and peeled onions. Before it was a jam factory it was a sweet factory. Manuel Copp was foreman when Joan worked there and his family were also connected with the Regal Cinema in High Street.

At that time it was quite easy to find work locally as long as you were prepared to work hard. It cost 6d. to go to the cinema and the Young Farmers' dinner dance at the Cullompton Hotel was 2s.6d. They had to give their mother most of their earnings; Pearl earned 7s.6d. a week at Frisby's and gave all but a shilling to her mother.

The girls were never allowed to go into the many pubs in the town but they did go to dances at the Assembly Rooms (now the Masonic Hall) where they waltzed and quickstepped to dance bands. The Assembly Rooms, at that time, was owned by the Half Moon Inn (now Tavy Textiles) but no alcohol was available in the Assembly Rooms. They can also remember going to picture shows at the Victoria Hall, when entry was 2d.

They can remember the water running in the gutters in the main street and in Ways Lane, swimming at Highbanks and Head Weir and fishing in the stream in Exeter Road. They remember nuns living at the Walronds. Their favourite sweetshop was Easterbrooks and Phil Osmond used to cut their hair.

In 1939, when she was 17, Pearl went to live in Hayes, Middlesex with an aunt and it was here that she met her future husband. She moved back to Cullompton in 1940 and married in 1941 at Tiverton Registry Office. Her husband was in the Navy during the war and she stayed in Cullompton. At first she lived with her parents at 8 Exeter Road and then moved into a house in Ways Lane. The rent was 10s. a week. There was no electricity, the toilet was at the bottom of the garden and water was collected from a pump at the end of the lane. In 1946 Pearl and her husband Cyril and two children, Barrie and Susan, moved back to Hayes.

When Joan was 14 she met her future husband Bill. He was working at the Cullompton Hotel as a bell boy and went on to help the chef in the kitchen. He later worked at the tan yard but then came the war and he was called up. They were married at St Andrews Church in 1942, when Joan was 18. Neither Pearl or Joan had a formal wedding dress as both money and material were in short supply. Pearl wore a blue and grey dress for her wedding, the reception was held in her parents' house and her Aunt Rose made the wedding cake. Joan had a blue dress and a burgundy fur fabric coat. Later, when she washed the dress, it shrank. When Joan's husband was demobbed he worked for her uncle as a builder but work dried up and in 1947 they moved to Hayes to be near Pearl as her husband was able to find Bill a job there.

Both Pearl and Joan have very fond memories of Cullompton and come back at least once a year to stay with Pearl's son Barrie, who is the present Mayor of Cullompton. He and his wife, also called Joan, now live in Crow Green not far from the house where Joan and Pearl grew up.

Child of the Thirties

Mrs Marian Dummett (néeMilford)

I was born at the end of October 1929 so one could say that I am well and truly a 'Child of the Thirties'. The cottage at Growen where I was born had two rooms downstairs and two bedrooms, one of which was more like a landing.

At the time I was born my mother was 42 years old and I have heard it said that one of my older sisters was so disgusted at Mother having me at that age; she wouldn't look at me for couple of months. Ironically this sister had her youngest son at the age of 42.

I had four sisters. They were aged 20, 18, 17 and nine when I put in an appearance so one might say that I was an 'afterthought' and like an only child. I slept in one room with Mother and Father and my sisters, all four of them, in the other room. We slept in iron and brass bedsteads – they would be worth a fortune now – on a feather mattress. This had to be shaken and turned every day. Around the bed was a valance – not as they are today but made from white cotton with embroidery around the edge. The quilt was also of a white thick embossed material. Imagine having to wash these items when all the water had to be pumped or drawn from the well, heated in a copper burning sticks and logs. Then ironed with a flat iron heated in the range, which by the time one had walked from the fire to the table on which the ironing was being done, was half cold.

When I was five years old my sister Doris got married and left home. Young people now must have their own space. I am now 75 and I have never had a bed of my own – a room would have been something else.

We had no water indoors – the pump being on the wall at the back of the house. When each winter it became frozen, all the water had to be dipped from the well in the field next to the house. I remember the most important thing, instilled into me as a child – was don't go near the well. There was no electricity; our light came from a candle in a candlestick upstairs and an oil-lamp downstairs. I remember one of Mother's first jobs in the morning was to trim the lamp and refill it with paraffin for the evening. I can still remember how creepy it was in bed with just one candle, shadows everywhere.

One must realise that we had no television or wireless as we know it and that all our knowledge of the outside world would come from stories told in books. At this time I had read a book about wolves and I could see wolves everywhere in those shadows. Looking back, why a wolf would want to come to our house I have no idea – such are the fears and imaginations of the young.

All the cooking and heating of water was done on a black leaded range, burning logs and coal. This had to be lit before anyone could have a cup of tea or breakfast. One of my first memories is of the cold. In winter we were always cold. It was quite usual to have chilblains and chaps on your feet, legs and hands.

Our toilet was a bucket with a piece of wood on the top with two holes. When this bucket became full the contents were buried in the garden – Father grew the best cabbages around. The actual lavatory building

Growen, where Marian spent her childhood. 1930s.

Marian Dummett (née Milford) and sisters, c.1935. Left to right: *Florence, Betty, Marian, Doris and Lucy.*

was a lean-to on the back of the house – no door, no light. This was alright in the summer but when the evenings were dark it was a nightmare. If one wanted 'to go' one had to ask 'who will come with me'. This caused quite an upset, as no-one else would want to go out into the dark and cold. There was one good thing: there was always a chamber-pot under the bed.

Living in the country we only went into 'town' (Cullompton) on Wednesday and Saturday. Mother would dress me in my best clothes. She always made our clothes – in fact I must have been working before I bought my first off-the-peg dress.

On Wednesday she bought odds and ends and on Saturday she paid the bills. As a child I remember the highlight of our day was either the visit of the baker, Mr Vigar, the butcher, Mr Veysey, or Mr Kemp from the International Stores. He would come on a Tuesday by bicycle to take the order that would be delivered (also by bicycle) on Wednesday. The baker and butcher would deliver twice a week and the children would fetch the milk from the farm in a tin can each morning. I can still remember the smell in some of the shops. Rawlings was of coffee being ground; Reynolds was wonderful, paraffin, string and all sorts of smells mixed together. The best shop was the International Stores. They had tins of biscuits all along the counter. We used to buy broken biscuits, which would be put in a brown paper bag.

Arthur and Vera Packer lived next door to us and as children we would play around the fields and the house. We would go into the hayfields and cornfields and generally mooch about, we had very few toys. Vera had a dolls' pram which I always envied. Eventually I was given a secondhand pram which my granny 'did up' for me but it was never like the one Vera had.

I was not allowed to join the Guides or anything like that as we had no transport (only the very rich had cars) and would have had to walk to town in the dark.

As my sisters were older than I was they worked at Fox Brothers and one Christmas I was lucky and had a white baby doll, to be followed the next year by a black doll.

My father was a thatcher; he died when I was 15. As a child many times I wouldn't see him for days as he would be gone to work when I awoke in the morning and when he got home in the evening I would be in bed. His only means of getting to work was by bicycle and he would ride to Butterleigh, Bickleigh, Tiverton, Linley and once, Stoke Canon. As I remember he was a little man who always wore a cap. He had one suit of clothes, which he wore for weddings and funerals and apart from special occasions when he wore shoes, he always wore hob-nailed boots. He must have had to work hard to keep us. He also grew all our potatoes and greens in our very large garden. His main hobby was keeping pigeons. At the beginning of the war all pigeons had to be handed to the government for war work. Father said he could not allow his pigeons to go through this so he killed them. He also liked cider. Each weekend we would go to the farm with 'a jar' to fetch father's cider for the week.

In those days mothers did not go to work, they had enough to do at home. Mother did, however, go up to the farm scrubbing for Mrs Pearsey. She must have had a very hard time managing. Father worked solely for farmers, thatching ricks and cottages. Farmers were not always very prompt payers. In fact one man used to pay father in apples or a duck and one offered a dahlia root.

As a young child I can remember feeling safe but we had very few displays of affection. In fact I can never remember seeing my father and mother kiss or hold hands, although they must have – they had five daughters!

I don't honestly know how my mother managed with six adults and one child living in that very small house. Although the furniture was basic, everything was polished and starched. We had lino on the floor of the living room with coconut matting but Mother's pride and joy was her dresser full of china. The kitchen was very small and just a scrubbed table, a stool for the water buckets and a meat safe on the wall and cobbles on the floor. We did however have good food which Mother cooked herself. She was in service at Knightshayes before her marriage so she was able to cook really fancy stuff sometimes. She did have a very strict code of behaviour. We were not allowed to talk at the dinner table and always had to start tea with a piece of bread and butter, no margarine, that was for cooking. I cannot remember ever having tinned food. Mother bottled all the fruit from the garden in Kilner jars to keep for puddings after dinner: junket, blancmange, stewed fruit and always suet pudding on Sunday. The first time I encountered tinned peas was when I was 'taken home' to my future husband Eric's house for Sunday tea. I must have been about 16 then.

Although we all lived at home at one time, my sisters were so much older than me that we were never playmates. They were out to work from 6.30a.m. to 6.00p.m. each day. Even though I was the youngest, when I became able, I too had my little jobs to do. Tear up paper into squares for the loo, collect eggs, break up sticks to light the fire and of course, always, fetch the milk from the farm.

Cullompton Carnival, 1933 – one of the many carnivals Marian would have watched. On the side of the lorry is written 'C.L. Barons, 7 Duke Street'.

At all times we had a cat, a dog, usually a couple of rabbits, chickens and sometimes ducks. The chickens and ducks were for eggs and meat and when the hens were laying well Mother would put some in a jar covered with water glass to keep for when they became scarce.

We also hatched our own chickens. Children growing up with no knowledge of things like this certainly lose out. I can remember quietly peeping under the broody hens to see the eggs hatching into tiny chicks. We fed the chickens on potato peelings, which had to be boiled on the range, and mixed with barley meal – it smelt awful.

Our lives revolved around the seasons. In the spring we picked primroses and daffodils, in the summer we played in the fields and hoped to get a rabbit to take home from the cornfields. In the autumn it was apple picking. These were stored under the bed to keep for Christmas. We picked hazelnuts and chestnuts and of course blackberries which were made into jam. As well as this gathering there were plums and blackcurrants to be picked from the garden trees and bushes. Father used to cover the gooseberries with flour and say it was poison so that we would not eat them. The blackcurrants were made into jam and into a drink for when we had coughs; I always seemed to have one. They always said I had a weak chest. In fact each summer on our only trip to the seaside Mother used to tie a handkerchief on my front and over my back to stop the water getting to me.

In the winter our main occupation was keeping warm. At Christmas, however, we would pick holly to take indoors and always gathered a tree from the woods. One did not buy Christmas trees in those days. I can remember having a stocking with just a few little things in it, nothing like today. We always had one of our chickens for dinner and Mother would cook an ox tongue. In those days nothing was wasted. When Mr Pearsey cut off the lamb's tails and castrated the little rams we would go up to the farm with a bowl and bring home the tails and testicles which Mother would cook. I thought they were lovely then but I could not eat them now.

When I became old enough for school, I had to walk about 1½ miles into school each day. I stayed to dinner, firstly taking a packed lunch and later having a cooked dinner. We used to have free milk and 1d for dinner. When the weather was bad country children were sent home early. I was never very fond of school and loved the holidays.

After my sister Doris was married she went to live in Silverton. That was like going to another country. I could then go to Silverton for part of my summer holiday. Mother used to put me on the train at Cullompton Station in the care of the guard and my sister would meet me at Silverton. I loved those times. My brother-in-law made a little wooden seat for his bicycle (on the crossbar) for me and they would take me for picnics to somewhere called Chain Bridge. There was a bridge made of chain over the River Exe, which jumped up and down when you walked over it. Then there was the Methodist Sunday school treat. Everyone walked from Silverton to the top of Christcross. There a wonderful tea was laid out and afterwards we ran races, sang songs and said bits of poetry. We thought it was really magic.

Remembering this has brought me to Sundays at home. Lots of things were out of bounds to me like the shed or the top of the rec. and Joe Dyers. All we did there was drink lemonade, so I could never make out why this was so. But anything to do with Church was okay. Of course when going to church down our lane we would get our shoes muddy so we carried clean shoes in a bag to change before we got into town.

From a very early age Sunday was spent walking to and from church. We had morning Sunday school, afternoon Sunday school and in the evenings church with Mother. Father would never go. He said Christians stayed home and I used to worry that Mother and I would go to heaven and Father would go to hell. Such was the teaching at that time. We had to learn a text each week and then a passage from the Bible. At Christmas we were given a tea party with jellies and cakes and a prize of a book if you had attended regularly.

As children we would pick primroses at Easter to trim the church and on Easter Sunday take eggs to the service to be given to the hospital. In the summer we were taken on 'the outing'. This was the only time most of us went to the sea. Usually it was Teignmouth and we would go by train. The excitement of going through the tunnels was enormous, but if it rained on that day it was awful.

When I outgrew Sunday school I went to Girls' Bible Class in the church rooms. The boys had their Bible Class in the little room by the clock in the church. When I was 14 I was confirmed and Mother made me a dress from butter muslin as everything was on ration at that time.

My eldest sister was married when I was ten years old and I was the bridesmaid. Father used to wear a bowler hat to weddings and as we were walking down the aisle in procession he caught his hat on the umbrella stand and it flew up into the air, landed and rolled down the aisle. I picked it up and did not even smile. One did not laugh in church.

Sunday tea was always home-made apple tart and sometimes, in the summer, we would walk to North Growen and pick watercress from the stream for sandwiches, but that was a real treat.

When I was ten years old I passed the scholarship to Tiverton Girls' School. One thing going to a girls' school teaches you is that 'boy' is spelt with a capital 'B'. At that age I had to go on the train to Tiverton. The train left at 8.00a.m. and I had to walk two miles to get to the station. Mother walked into town with me on dark mornings in the winter. I knew no-one at the school when I started but settled down and made friends after a time. At the same time as I began we had girls from Europe, refugees who spoke no English, join us. They must have learnt English with a Devonshire accent. They did however pass their School Certificate with better grades than we did. There was no pressure placed on me at school and I remember when I told my mother I had passed my School Certificate with nine passes, she said 'Good, but that is what you went for'. My parents must have had a real struggle to send me to that school even though I had passed the scholarship.

At the same time as I went to Tiverton the war started. Everything changed. My sister Bet went to work in a munition factory and I cried all night when my brother-in-law left to go overseas. Things at home stayed about the same however, we had never had extravagant living and we still had chickens, rabbits, eggs and home-grown vegetables to help out the rations. Mother used to make her own butter and every week on a Wednesday she would make a pair of men's pyjamas to be sent to the soldiers by the Red Cross.

As the war continued all sorts of things began to change but more so in the town than in the country. There were no street lights and most of the young men were called up. There were soldiers everywhere. From our house we could hear the pipes being played as the Scottish troops marched to church from Hillersdon. Father dug a hole in the hedge to make an air-raid shelter and from our garden we could see the light from Exeter being bombed and this was even more horrendous for us as my sister was in hospital having a baby.

All the awful things were happening but as a child I don't think I understood. One has to remember there was no television and the newspapers were censored. It was not until the men came back after the war that it sunk in. My brother-in-law had been in Burma for 4½ years and he was a mere skeleton when he returned.

My father died and I had to leave school. I had always wanted to be a nurse but this was not possible now. I went to work in the office of Culm Leather. We were never teenagers but I was growing up.

Living in the country most of our spare time in the summer was spent out in the fields and then one summer when I was 15 years old we were watching the corn cutting and I noticed this boy. He had black hair, greased down with Brylcream, eyes like a gypsy and there must have been something else because he became my best friend, my husband, the father of my beloved sons and the love of my life, but that is another story...

Child of the Forties

Mrs Annie Minchin (née Symonds)

I was born in the early 1940s and, as a child, lived in Middle Mill Lane. At the bottom of the lane, where the CCA Fields are now, was Mingo's Farm. There was a dairy at the farm where they used to bottle the milk. We would walk along the Mill Path to Station Road to get to the station to catch the train.

Mr Kemp had a small grocery shop at the top of Middle Mill Lane, and he later moved to what is now Jeeves Sandwich Bar and then to what is now Londis. My mum used to buy all her groceries there. The library was in High Street, next door to the King's Head. I would sometimes go into Exeter with my Mum on the No. 27 bus, the fare was 1s.11d. and as a treat we would have hot dogs in Marks and Spencer.

I went to St Andrews Primary School, which was fairly newly built, but my first classroom was in the Victoria Hall. The reception classes were housed at the Victoria Hall and then we moved up to the St Andrews School building. The Victoria Hall later became a lace factory and then went on to house a children's clothing factory and then a soft-toy factory. It is now Young Ones Day Nursery.

As a child I went to Sunday school at the Methodist Church. Every year we would go on a Sunday school outing to the seaside, either to Dawlish or Teignmouth, sometimes we went by train from Cullompton Station and sometimes on a coach. I went to Brownies, which at that time was held in a wooden hut in Station Road and I also joined St John Ambulance and went along once a week.

After leaving St Andrews I went to Tiverton Grammar School but never completed my studies as, due to family circumstances, I left school when I was 15 and went to work at Fox's Factory in Higher Street (where Twyford Engineering is now). My job was to invisibly mend the woven material as it was taken off the loom. I worked from 7.45a.m. until 5.45p.m. going through the material as it came off the loom to check for any flaws and invisibly mend them. The pay was 'piecework' and one week, while I was saving up to get married, I earned £11.10s.0d. The Foreman, Wilfie, told me not to tell anyone how much I had earned as this was a lot of money at that time.

As a teenager I would go to the coffee bar in High Street or to the youth club at the Methodist Church. On Sundays we would walk down to the Cherry Tree to buy ice-creams and sit in the garden at the side of the shop to eat them. The shop was owned by Ron Dyer and his brother Len Dyer ran the unemployment office on the corner of Church Street.

At least once a week we would go to the Regal Cinema, in High Street, behind what is now the Cullompton Carpet Centre. There was no television and the cinema was the only entertainment. Mr and Mrs Copp owned the cinema and they also ran Copp's Fruit and Veg Shop, which is where Seddons Estate Agents is now. Pantomimes were held at the Assembly Rooms (now the Masonic Hall). These were the highlight of the year and everyone used to go.

I left Fox's when I got married in 1960. I was married at the Methodist Chapel in New Cut and we lived with my parents for a while. We bought our first house in Exeter Road for £800, it had no electricity and the toilet was at the bottom of the garden. My dad was a carpenter and he made new windows for the front and we built a bathroom on the back and had electricity installed. There was no central heating and no washing machine. I did all my washing by hand but had a boiler for the sheets.

In about 1962 I started working part-time as a waitress at the Cullompton Hotel, serving at dinner dances in the ballroom. It was all silver service with dancing to live bands. The hotel, at that time, was owned by Neville Jones.

There were two doctors' practices in Cullompton, Dr Shove and Dr Tallack in Church Street and Dr Hammond at Heyford House in High Street. The baby clinic was held in the Parish Rooms and the District Nurse, Nurse Hulbert, lived up the alley close to what was then the Rugby Club in Fore Street.

There was no supermarket in the town, and I remember the Co-op being where the library is now as well as a pub called the Half Moon in the middle of the town where Tavy Textiles is today. As a child my mum got all her shopping from Kemps but, just after I

Above: *The Cullompton Hotel, c.1960. Annie Minchin worked there part-time as a silver-service waitress.*

Below: *Fore Street, c.1950. The Half Moon public house (now Tavy Textiles) can be seen in the centre of the picture.*

St Andrews Primary School production, 1949. Those pictured include: *Brian Hales, Gillian Moore, Janet Graves?, Joan Gove, Janet Clarke, Anne Symonds, Alan Jones*

St Andrews Primary School production, c.1951. Left to right, front row: *Ray Hales, ?, Alan Shere, Bill Richardson, Nina Green, Pam Ross, Gwen Francis, Anne Symonds, Carol North, Pat Morgan, Mary Chubb, Joan Gove, Pat Budd, Margaret Whitfield, ?, Marie Luxton.*

Members of the Local Association celebrating the 30th Anniversary of Guiding in Cullompton, September 1950. Left to right, back row: *Ann Yendell* (Guide with colours), *Audrey Phillips, ?, Mrs Vickery, Kit Dyer, ?, Mrs Ley, Mrs Chas Carew, Muriel Whitton, Mrs Stewart, Mrs Radford, Margery Smith, Florrie Radford, Kathleen Mitchell, Margery Heard, Beth Woolcott;* kneeling: *Flo Owen, Muriel Coxhead, Mavis Force, Dr Audrey Baker, Greta Fear, Margaret Russ, Joan King, Miss Lorna Baker, Margery Woolcott;* seated: *?, ?, Lorna Butt.*

Cullompton Carnival Queen Jennifer Radford (centre) *and Carnival Queen Attendant Anne Symonds kicking off Cullompton Football Match, November 1957.*

married, Normans opened in Tiverton and we would go there once a month to do our main shop. We would take it in turns with my brother-in-law, he would take his car one month and my husband would take ours the following month to save on petrol.

When we first got married my husband had a motor-bike but we bought a van when our first child was born in 1962. I remember it used to rattle and shake. We would take the children to Sandy Bay in a caravan for holidays or sometimes to Weymouth or Cornwall.

My two sons went to St Andrews Primary School and then to Cullompton Comprehensive School, the oldest went on to university and the younger one learnt his trade as a motor mechanic at Clark's Motors, which has now been pulled down to make way for the new McCarthy & Stone development.

We left Cullompton in 1986 and now live in Colyford but I have very fond memories of my life in Cullompton.

Child of the Fifties

Steve Goffey

I was born in 1955, the youngest of Eileen and Bill Goffey's four children. We lived at 101 St Andrews Estate, the house my parents moved into when it was brand new. My dad worked as a stoker at the Gas Works in Station Road and my earliest memory is of being allowed to stay up and wait for him to come home from work as it was my birthday. He came home with a present, a corgi tipper lorry.

I started at St Andrews Primary School when I was five but not long after Stanley Hill dropped a bookcase on my foot and broke it. I had to stay off school for a couple of months which didn't upset me too much. My first teacher was Mrs Ashford, and her husband was the headmaster. In the years that followed my teachers

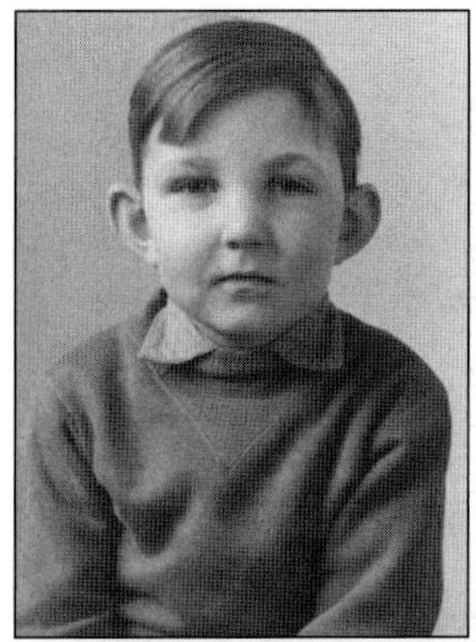

Steve Goffey, aged five, c.1960.

Below: *St Andrews Primary School teaching staff, 1952.* Left to right, back row: *M. Morgan, B. Roberts, Miss Hall, R. Chapman;* front row: *Miss I. Scorse, Miss B. Phillips, Mrs Ashford (headmaster), Mrs Ashford, Miss H. Cole.*

were: Mrs Crispin, Mrs Scorse, Mrs Bryant, Mrs Coles, who used to live in High Street where Bays Dental Surgery is now and was my favourite teacher, Mr Dobson, who used to collect butterflies and took us on lots of nature walks, Mr Pike and Mr Kerslake. I was always a bit scared of Mr Kerslake.

I wasn't too keen on school dinners and so I would go to my gran's house every lunchtime for beans on toast. I used to hate eating vegetables and I dreaded Sunday dinners as my dad would make me eat all my greens, now I only eat peas.

My mum would give me a wash sitting on the draining-board and we had a tin bath in front of the fire. We played in the recreation-field; there were lots of trees there then, we would climb the trees or play 'cowboys and indians'. The only play equipment was a big slide and a set of swings. There was an old water trough and a pump and in the late 1950s they built toilets behind the Victoria Hall – they are still there.

I got my first bike when I was about five or six, it was a Hercules, a hand-me-down from my brother. I think I got my first new bike when I was about 11. My family got a black-and-white television when I was about eight, we rented it from a shop in Station Road.

Every morning before I went to school I would go down to Browns in the High Street (next door to where Proberts Bakery is now) to buy 20 Senior Service for my mum. We would have to do chores for our pocket money. We would chop wood, clean out the fire and help with the gardening. I can also remember taking an old pram down to the Gas Works to collect coal. Mum and Dad reared chicks as we had an incubator unit and I would feed the chicks and would go to the West of England Hatcheries to collect new chicks.

At Christmas we would catch the bus into Exeter and go to Santa's Grotto at Waltons and then on to Fortes fish-and-chip shop for our lunch. The first holiday I can remember was to Starcross and we stayed in a caravan. We also went on coach trips and caught the train to the seaside; I still have vivid memories of the station. Opposite the station there was a football field and the cattle market pens.

Sunday school was at the Hebron Hall. We were picked up in a minibus and our teacher was Mrs Peters. Mr Callard would let all the Sunday school children use the tennis-courts at his house in Colebrooke Lane. There was a youth club on Monday evenings and I remember an outing to Paignton on the coach.

I went to Cubs, the hut was in New Street when I first started and the leader was Fred Read. I remember going to Plymouth on a camp – it was the first time I had been away from home and I was homesick for the entire week. I later went on to Scouts and then Venture Scouts and it was while I was a Venture Scout that the Scout headquarters moved to Tiverton Road. Later my brother Tony Goffey became a Cub leader.

I got my first pair of long trousers when I started at Cullompton Secondary Modern but I was the only person that started school without a blazer, or that's how it seemed at the time. All the new children congregated in the hall while they decided which classes to put us in. I was put into Mr Winter-Flood's class. Every Friday we had to run crosscountry up Old Hill, along Upton Lane and back down behind the mills, I can still remember the route.

We would go to the Regal Cinema on Saturday afternoon, it cost 3d. As I got older I would go to the Boys Club, which was at Community House on the corner of Church Street and we would play table tennis. We would often go to Bradninch as that was where all the decent girls lived. We went to the youth

West of England Hatcheries, Station Road (where the police station is now sited). Steve Goffey collected his day-old chicks from here.

The rear of Cullompton Hotel, c.1953, looking across to where Knightswood and Meadow Lane now sit.

club at the old Salvation Army Hall in Peter Street.

In order to leave school I needed a job and so I went along to the Labour Exchange with my mate and Len Dyer said 'I have just the job for you two lads'. That is how I became a 'Bobbin Boy' at Fox's Factory in Higher Street and soon progressed to a weaver. I was trained by Ken Squires. I didn't really enjoy the work and the pay was piecework. I spent a lot of time in the toilets smoking so didn't earn that much and left to work at Whitton's Transport in Station Road. I worked in the stores and my boss was Percy Cross.

About the same time I started courting my wife Dawn and we were married in 1975. I later went to work at Reid & Lee in Exeter and joined the army in 1973. I was sent to Ireland and spent five years in Germany before leaving the army and returning to live in my home town.

Child of the Sixties

Shirley Hector (née Harris)

I was born in 1959, the third daughter in a family of seven children. I had two older sisters, one younger sister and three younger brothers. Mr parents, Rosemary and Derek Harris, were living in a small terraced cottage in Colebrooke Lane when I was born. We later moved to Haymans Close and then to a brand new house in Orchard Way when I was about ten.

My earliest memories are of walking to the shops with my sister Sylv who is a year older than me. We would have been about four and five at the time; we would go to Mr Curtis the butcher or Mr Grant the baker to buy meat and bread for the family. Colebrooke Lane was just a small lane and it was considered quite safe for young children to be out on their own. Everyone you met knew you and you knew them.

I started at St Andrews Primary School when I was four, I should have gone into Mrs Yelland's class but I cried because I wanted to be in the same class as my sister and they let me go into Mrs Crispin's class with Sylv. I remember school dinners, which I quite liked; my favourite desert was shortcake with strawberry custard. We used to do sports on the recreation-field and I enjoyed netball, which we played in the school playground.

My sister and I would walk to school but were often late as we would stop to play in Tufty Park or have snowball fights when it had been snowing. When I was 11 I went to Cullompton Secondary Modern.

We had three bedrooms in our house and I shared one with my three sisters, we had two sets of bunk beds. We had a black-and-white television but it wasn't switched on until about 6p.m. for the news. I don't remember watching the TV much; we spent most of our spare time playing outside with the other children that lived roundabout, mainly in the fields or on the waste ground on the corner of Orchard Way, before they built the flats. Sometimes we would go to Tufty Park.

I went to Guides – the Guide leader was Mrs Owen and I remember camping at Powderham Castle and also at Hemyock. The Guide hut was in Station Road, next door to Labdon Building Supplies. I also went to Sunday school at the Methodist Church and we would buy sweets on the way to eat during the church service and then we would go into the Sunday school. I liked going to Sunday school, which was run by Mr Williams, as I could play with toys that we couldn't afford at home. I remember Sunday school outings to the seaside, Goodrington Sands and Exmouth by coach.

I would go shopping in the town with my mum. We would go to the International Stores where we would buy 1lb of broken biscuits from the barrel. We would also go to the Co-op and Knowles for fruit and vegetables. The highlight was going to Mrs Roger's sweetshop where we could pick what we wanted from all the jars of sweets lined up along the shelves and Mrs Rogers would weigh them out for us into a bag.

Shirley Hector (née Harris) age 14.

I remember going into Mr Mitchell's butcher's shop one day after I had been to the dentist and he gave me a sausage for my tea for being a brave girl. I don't remember ever buying any new clothes, I think I mainly had hand-me-downs from my two older sisters and my mum knitted our jumpers and cardigans. I can remember buying shoes though; we used to go to Mrs Yardley at the top of town.

We didn't have a lot but it didn't worry us, I remember one Christmas being particularly pleased with a present from my nan: a bag of liquorice sweets and a skipping rope. I also remember a secondhand scooter which my dad painted up for me. To earn pocket money I had to help wash the dishes in the morning before school and in the evenings and help with the housework on Saturdays. Every Saturday we would have chips for lunch and we would take it in turns to sit on the front step peeling the potatoes – we needed a lot of potatoes for a family of nine!

I would take my 6d. pocket money to Cherry Tree Stores and spend it on sweets. When I was older I had a paper round, I started by helping my sister with hers and then, when I was old enough, I think about 12 or 13, I got a paper round of my own. My mum used to

Fore Street, c.1960. Culm Meat Supply is in the foreground. Mr Mitchell gave Shirley a sausage for being a brave girl following a visit to the dentist.

do various part-time jobs, depending on the season; potato picking, turkey plucking, egg collecting, etc. I remember helping with the potato picking at Rull Farm and also with the turkey plucking.

My dad was a 'digger driver' and he worked away from home a lot, he worked on the construction of the M5. He later started his own plant hire business. We had a big estate car and Dad would take us out on Sundays when he was home. The three boys in the very back, the four girls on the back seat and Mum and Dad in the front. On the way home we could visit our nan and grandad in Broadclyst. Dad and Grandad would go into the pub and we children would sit in the pub car park with a coke, shared with two straws, and a packet of crisps.

Mum and Dad had a caravan at Ladrum Bay and Dad would take Mum and all us children down there during the summer holidays, he would drop us off and then come back for us two or three weeks later.

As I got older I would walk into Tiverton to go to the pictures or go to the youth club at either the Gospel Hall or in the Parish Rooms. On Friday nights there would be a disco in the Parish Rooms for teenagers, we would also go to dances at Willand Village Hall. I would also catch the bus to Bradninch and go to the 'Spiders Web' which was a room for youngsters at the Castle Inn, where there was music and a pool table. It was here that I met my husband Barry when I was about 13. We got married at St Andrews Church in 1980.

After leaving school I went to work in Mr Vicary's newsagents in Fore Street and then went to Bako Western until my daughter Emma was born in 1987. I have never left Cullompton and now live at Knightswood, in a house built on the fields where I used to play when I was a child.

Child of the Seventies
Sharon Snow

When I was born, in 1969, my family lived at 5 Pound Square in the house next door to where my nan, Win Moore, now lives. We moved to St Andrews Estate when I was about four but my earliest memory is of starting at St Andrews Primary School when I was five.

The headmaster at that time was Derrick Allen and teachers I remember are Mr Kerslake and Mr Murray who we nicknamed 'Murray mint'. I remember learning to swim in the outdoor pool in the grounds of the school and sports day on the recreation-field. At that time there were [school] houses: Drake, Grenville, Hawkins and Raleigh and I was in Hawkins. We had assembly every morning and a little bottle of milk at morning break. I also remember a school trip to the Devon County Show.

When we weren't at school we played in the street outside our house. I have an older sister Alison and a younger brother Kevin. I can remember Kevin once falling off the cemetery wall and dislocating his arm. We would play games such as skipping and hopscotch with the other children that lived close by. I particularly remember Mandy Newland and Stephen Pike. When I was about 11 or 12 Mandy's parents, George and Alison Newland, took me on holiday with them to Butlins at Minehead.

I went to Sunday school at the Baptist Church and Brownies, followed by Guides at the Guide hut in Station Road. My mum would take me and my brother and sister shopping in Exeter occasionally and we would sometimes go to the seaside, usually Exmouth, on the bus. My nan and grandad would often come as well.

Win Moore, who still lives in Duke Street, with granddaughters Alison (left) and Sharon Snow, c.1971.

Sharon Snow seated on the Cullompton Hotel entry in Cullompton Carnival c.1985.

My dad sometimes sent me down to Roberts Hardware shop to buy paraffin for his greenhouse heaters. I had to go round to the alley at the side of the shop and get it out of a sort of pump. The best place to buy sweets was Heards on the corner of Cockpit Hill, they also sold groceries and fruit and veg but they had a fantastic range of sweets. The other place we would go for our sweets was Jack Mills's shop on the corner of Station Road. He was a fishmonger but he also sold fruit and veg, groceries and sweets. Other shops I can remember at that time were a freezer shop selling frozen food where Bob Dalzell's shop is now, the Wine Shop, Battens Shoe Shop, Lawrence's Newsagents and the delicatessen in Fore Street where Fulfords Estate Agents is now.

On leaving St Andrews I went to Cullompton Comprehensive where Keith Turner was the headmaster. My favourite lesson was PE and crosscountry running, the teacher was Miss Cligg and I can still remember the route of the crosscountry runs. I represented the school at the East Devon trials. I also liked cookery classes, taught by Mrs Vallis and was not keen on French or German. Other teachers I can remember are Mr Davey who taught geography, Mr Button and Mr Kellaway. Several of the classrooms were prefabricated huts. The school uniform was a grey skirt with a white shirt and black jumper and we had to wear flat shoes; high heels weren't permitted.

In the evenings, as a teenager, I would hang around the town, although I had to be home by 9p.m. Where the Post Office is now there was a clothes shop with a pool room upstairs. It had a juke box and games and we would sometimes go there or otherwise to the youth club that was held at Community House in Church Street. There were also discos in the Parish Rooms where Tim Scrace was the DJ.

After leaving school I worked at the Old Vicarage Nursing Home for a short while before going to the Cullompton Hotel. My main jobs at the hotel were chambermaid and waitress but the work was varied and I enjoyed it. When I was 18 I was allowed to work behind the bar. I particularly remember the wedding receptions on Saturdays.

The hotel had a nightclub called 'Frankies', but was later refurbished and renamed 'Champs'. I sometimes worked in the nightclub, usually serving food and I remember the bouncers Dave Wannell and Mark Morgan. I also baby sat for the then hotel owners who had three sons: Neil, Alex and Colin Morris.

The hotel was sold in 1988 and renamed Toad Hall. For a short while after that I worked for Frank Clarke sorting vegetables but soon went to Car and Commercial Garage in Station Road. It was later renamed CCS Ford Ltd but it closed in 2001 as it couldn't compete with the motorway services area. I now work at Londis Stores in Fore Street so have never strayed far from Cullompton.

Child of the Eighties
Alex Morris

I was two years old when I went to live at the Cullompton Hotel, I don't remember moving there but I do remember how big it always seemed to me. It was 1983 and my family bought the hotel from Mr and Mrs Bazley and moved in en mass. There was my mum & dad (Steve and Judy Morris), my older brother Neil, my aunt and uncle (Dave and Sheila Mills) and their son, my cousin Lewis, plus my nan and grandad (Pauline and Stuart Mills). My cousin Amy was born in 1985 and my younger brother Colin came along in 1987.

My family lived in a flat at the front of the hotel, on the first floor, above the bars. As we came out of the flat there was a balcony from which we could look down into the large entrance hall. My brother and I liked to lie down on the floor and watch what was going on downstairs through the railings. There was also an outdoor balcony to stand and watch what was happening outside, but we weren't very often allowed to go onto the outside balcony.

One of my first memories was going out into the wilderness (my mum told me later it was Plymtree) to collect a new puppy. He ran about on the parcel shelf at the back of the car on the way home. We called him Sam and he watched over us, I loved that dog. He used to follow me to school and sit outside my classroom and my dad would be called to come and fetch him. I never worked out how he knew where to find me.

There were two big heavy wooden doors at the front of the hotel, these opened into the big entrance hall. In the hall was a reception desk with an office behind where my mum used to work. There was a big red rug in the middle of the floor and a big fireplace with armchairs either side. At Christmas we would have a great big Christmas tree in the hall that went right up to the roof. It was a struggle to get the tree in the front door.

Next to the reception desk there was a pair of double doors into the ballroom. We liked to play in there. It had a big stage where we would play our toy guitars and make believe we were a famous pop band. We also liked to slide on the dance floor after it had been polished. As I got older I would sometimes help to lay the tables for weddings, etc. My mum and auntie would give us the knives and forks and we would go along putting them on the tables.

At the back of the ballroom was a kitchen and the chef was called John Thomassen. Sometimes his children, Daniel and Sarah, would come and play with us. I remember Daniel had a remote control car and we would play with it in the ballroom. There was also a restaurant and my cousin Lewis and I would sneak in and pinch the After Eights, which were kept on top of the fish tank, when no-one was looking.

At the back of the hotel in a separate building was a nightclub. The youth club would hold under-18 discos there now and again, and when I was about five or six I would go in and get my hand stamped and all the older girls would 'mother' me. I remember we once sneaked in an open window and my mum caught us playing with the DJ equipment.

My favourite was playing in the garden. We had swings in the back garden and there was a big bush and we made a hiding space in the middle. Once we found a tramp sleeping under the trees. We used to use our old pram as a boat to sail along the leat at the front of the hotel. The gardener was called Arthur Clapp and he once made us wooden guns with a peg on the back with a rubber band attached to fire things. It worked really well.

One Christmas it snowed and we made a snowman in the front garden and slid down the drive on trays. My family had to work on Christmas Day as we would have lots of people for Christmas lunch and everyone was very busy. We would have our Christmas in the evening when we would all go to my nan's bungalow, which was in the grounds of the hotel, and open our presents. I remember getting a lego aeroplane one year.

I shared a bedroom with my brother and my dad decorated it with 'Super Ted' wallpaper. I also remember my Superman pyjamas. Birthdays at the hotel were great as we had parties with a magician in the ballroom and I could invite lots of friends.

When I was three I went to Brookgate Playschool in the grounds of the Community College, I didn't like it very much and would scream when my mum left me. I must have got used to it eventually though. I remember a wooden wendy house and a box full of dressing-up clothes. I remember painting pictures and making playdo, and falling asleep during story time.

I went to Willowbank Infants School. I can remember getting told off and having to stand outside the headmistress's office with some other boys and we swapped 'transformer' stickers. I also had to stand on the wall in the playground occasionally if I was naughty. After school we would sometimes stop to play in Tufty Park. Sharon Snow would occasionally take us to the CCA Fields to feed the ducks and one time I got too close and fell into the leat.

When I was eight I went to St Andrews Junior School and my best memories are of school trips, one to Paignton Zoo, where I bought a rubber snake, and the 'London trip'. I went to Cubs at the Scout hut in Tiverton Road.

We left the hotel in 1988 and the company which bought the hotel from my family changed the name to Toad Hall. I was upset to leave the hotel and I still have many fond memories of my life there. However, as we had come to like Cullompton my family decided to stay here and my parents bought a house close to Cullompton Community College and that suited me fine as I didn't have far to walk to school.

It also meant we were close to the John Tallack Centre where I went to youth club and I would sometimes act as DJ. We played tennis in the summer and swam at the outdoor swimming-pool, which was open to the public after school and in the holidays. I also joined a roller-hockey team and we played in the cages (tennis-courts) at the Community College.

One of the highlights of my time at the Community College was going on the French exchange. We had a French boy to stay with us and then I went to Ploudalmezeau, Cullompton's French twin town, to stay with Julian and his family.

I left school when I was 16 and trained as a hairdresser and I now run the Hair and Beauty Salon at Padbrook Park, not far from where the Cullompton Hotel once proudly stood.

Willowbank Primary School, c.1986. Left to right, back row: *Gary Butler, Emma Parker, Christopher Turner, Katy Foley, Damien Hornsey, Lucy ?, Beth Timbrell, Elizabeth Roberts, Carrie Matthews;* third row: *Heather Peek, Karen Mitchell, Stuart Pears, Richard Whitworth, Toby Brooks, Caroline Alford, Daniel Simm, Donna ?, Ian Harris;* second row: *Elaine ?, Sharon Bishop, Kevin Goffey, Mrs Roberts (teacher), Alex Morris, Natasha White, Natasha ?;* front row: *Ross Cottrell, Adam McNeil, Anthony Adams, David ?, Timothy Adams, Andrew ?, Timothy Simm.*

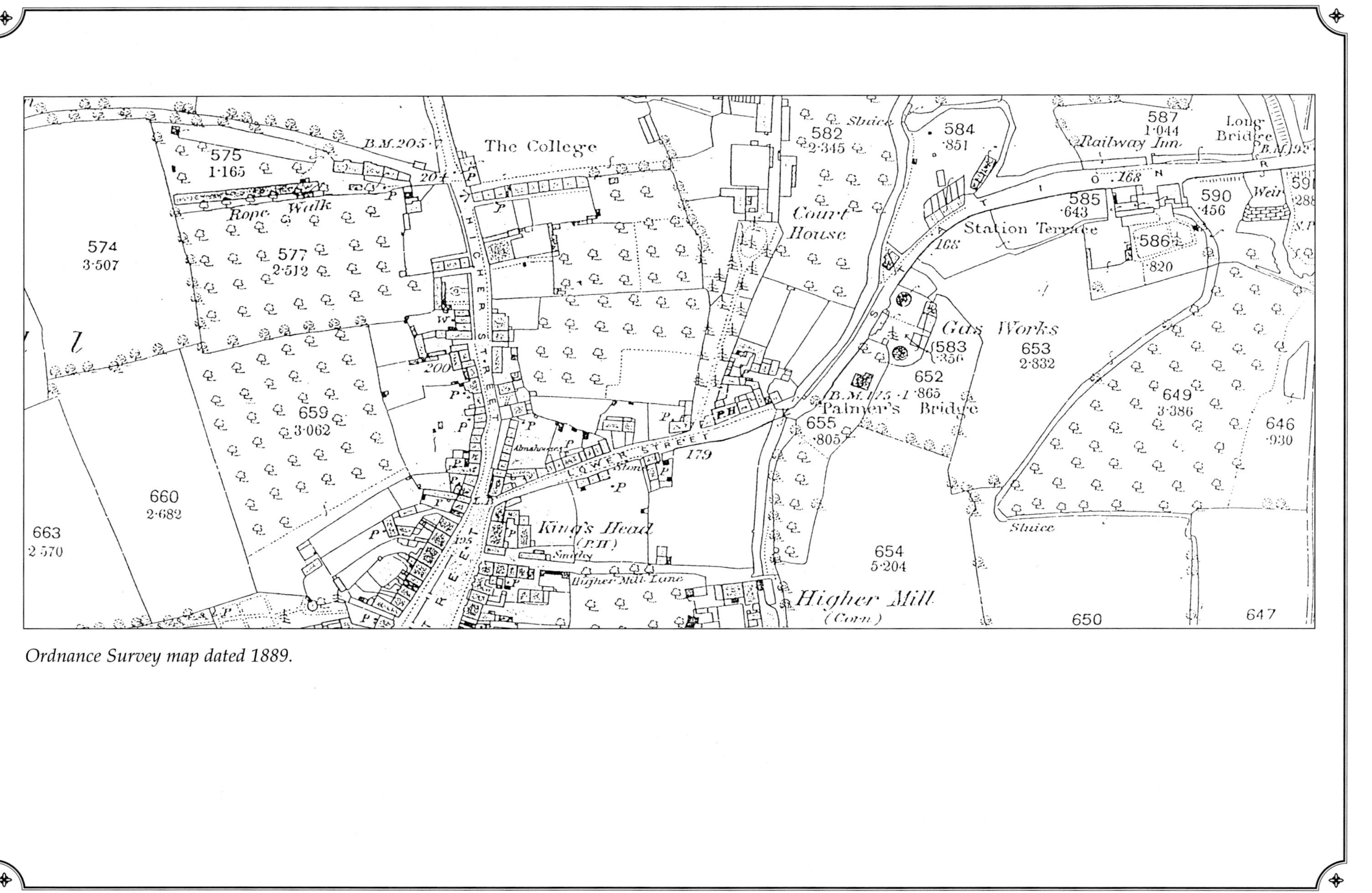

Ordnance Survey map dated 1889.

Chapter Six

Station Road

'Cocker's' was demolished in the 1960s to make the Station Road junction wider.

Station Road was originally called Lower or Low Street but residents didn't like living in 'lower' street. The name was changed in 1931 but the station that gave the street its new name no longer exists as it was closed in 1964. It has always been a busy entrance into the town, nowadays because of the motorway, but in years gone by quite a large proportion of the local industry was reached via Station Road as it still is today.

In the 'olden days' everyone, except the very rich, went to work on a bike or walked. The 'rush' hour was between 6a.m. and 7.30a.m. and, at home time, between 5.30p.m. and 6.30p.m. This is when Station Road would be full of people on bikes.

On the corner of Station Road and Higher Street, where the shelter is now, there was a shop called Cocker's. In the 1930s Mr Cocker could be seen sitting crosslegged on the floor doing his tailoring. His daughter ran a sweetshop in the same premises. This and a property on the opposite side of the road were demolished to make the road wider. Traffic lights were installed in 2004, mainly to make it easier for pedestrians to cross the road but also to ease the traffic congestion in Station Road at peak times.

At the turning from High Street into Station Road there was once a row of cottages with a cobbled pavement outside. Where the police station now stands was Gibbings and Earland Coach, Cart and Wagon Works. This later became the West of England Hatcheries. Here thousands of eggs would be taken in, hatched and then sent to customers all over the world via the station. Local people also bought the day-old chicks; those with plenty of money had an incubator but others used either a broody hen or put them in a box and kept them warm with a hot-water bottle. The Hatcheries moved to Dulford and the police station was built in 1974.

Labdon Builders Merchants has been on the same site since 1916 and was originally the base for their workforce of builders and carpenters.

Behind Labdons Yard was Whittons Transport, a haulage firm that started with a Foden's steam lorry. These lorries had a fire under the bonnet and underneath was the ash pan that all the red hot coals fell into. The company soon progressed to diesel- and petrol-fuelled vehicles, although the old 'steamers' were pressed back into service during the Second World War. The company carried mainly paper

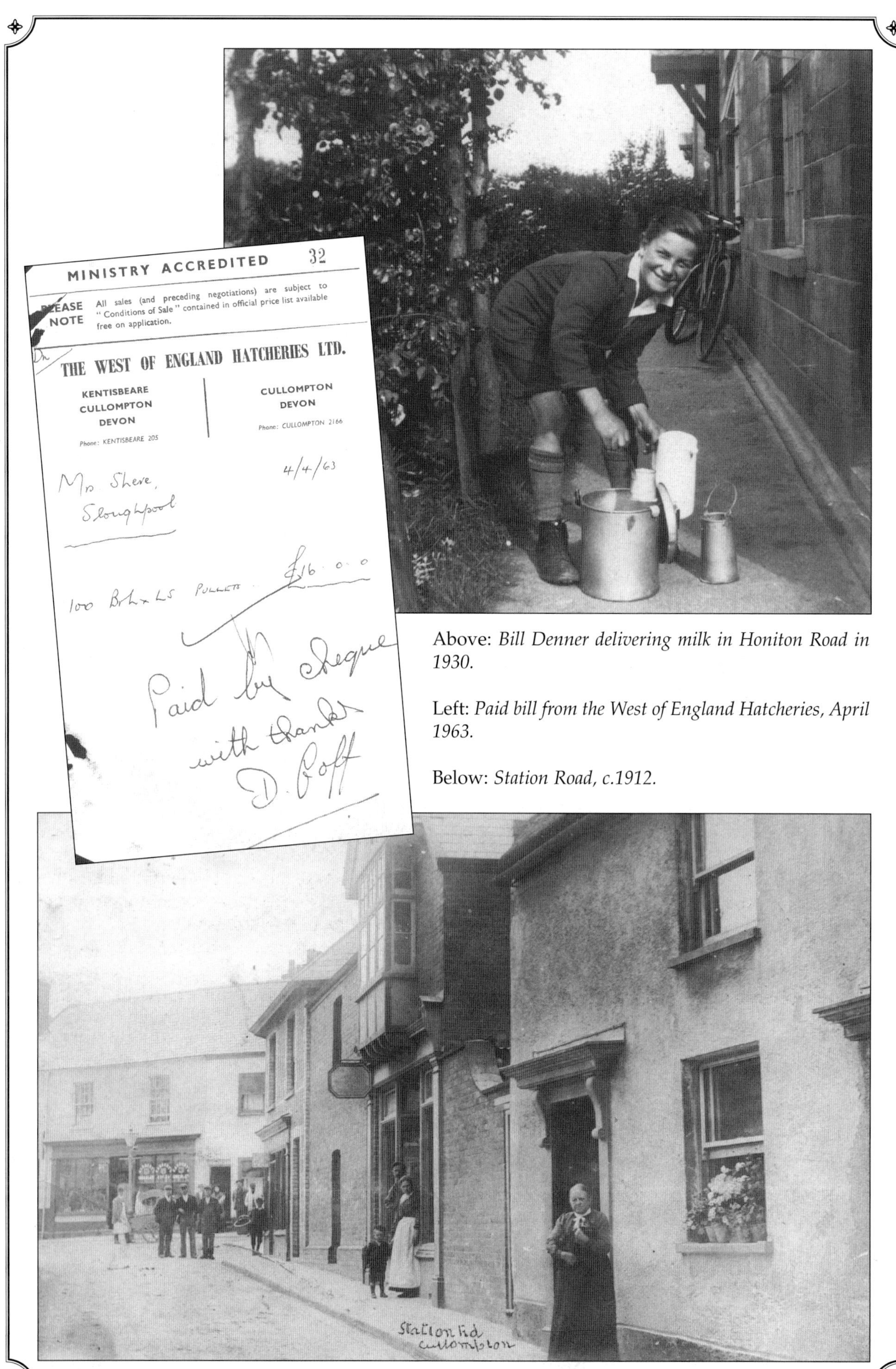
MINISTRY ACCREDITED 32

PLEASE NOTE All sales (and preceding negotiations) are subject to "Conditions of Sale" contained in official price list available free on application.

Dr.

THE WEST OF ENGLAND HATCHERIES LTD.

KENTISBEARE
CULLOMPTON
DEVON
Phone: KENTISBEARE 205

CULLOMPTON
DEVON
Phone: CULLOMPTON 2166

4/4/63

Mr Shere,
Sloughpool

100 BrL x LS Pullets £16. 0. 0

Paid by cheque
with thanks
D. Poff

Above: *Bill Denner delivering milk in Honiton Road in 1930.*

Left: *Paid bill from the West of England Hatcheries, April 1963.*

Below: *Station Road, c.1912.*

Gibbings Carriage Works, c.1904, situated in Station Road where the police station is now. It later became Gibbings and Earland and then West Country Hatcheries.

Whittons Transport lorries in the 1940s.

produced at the Cullompton, Hele and Silverton mills. They also collected paper from places such as Ivybridge Mill. This paper, all of various grades and quality, was taken to destinations throughout Britain. As the company expanded it was not only paper that was carried; a fleet of 'tippers' worked the local quarries. Loads of cattle hides were also transported, which were, by their nature, known to the drivers as the 'smellies'. In its heyday there was a fleet of approximately 100 vehicles.

For a brief while the site became a BRS depot during the years the haulage industry was nationalised, but reverted back to Whittons on denationalisation. Further companies were formed, including Whittons Garages specialising in both commercial and car retail repairs and sales together with a filling station. Whittons Heavy Haulage specialised in heavy duty 'low-loaders' and mobile cranes and the 'Green & Cream' Coach Company did school runs and daytrips.

By the end of the 1960s the prosperity of Whittons began to wane and in 1973 the receivers were called in. The Wild Group obtained the company in 1975 and many of the operations were closed down in order to concentrate on warehousing. It was then that the present London Brick warehouses were built and it became known as the Western Way Industrial Estate until the land was sold to Tesco in about 2004 and companies in the industrial units were relocated.

Next to the garage was the Gas Works. There was a gas holder which increased in size according to the pressure of the gas. In the 1930s children were sent there to get clinkers for the garden paths and would also take a tin or a pan to get a few pennies worth of tar. This was used to paint around the bottom of a house or paint out the chicken house.

The gas retorts were installed by Messrs Willey and Co. in 1865 for the Cullompton Gas Light and Coke Co. With its three beds of coke chambers and 20 horizontal retorts the works could supply 150,000 cubic feet of gas per day. At first it only supplied Cullompton but later Bradninch was also supplied from this site. In 1929 the Cullompton Gas Company passed into the hands of Devon Gas Association until it was nationalised in 1949.

When the works closed in 1956 the manager, Mr F.G. White, who had been at the works for 33 years, as well as eight other men were offered work in Exeter by the gas board. Only he and two other men accepted the offer as the others were able to obtain work locally. The last of the gas holders went in the early 1970s with the introduction of North Sea gas.

The Weary Traveller, as it is known today, was originally The Railway Hotel and later became the Showman, in recognition of the fairground people that live nearby during the winter. It changed its name to the Weary Traveller in 1990. Ern and Dolly Goff were the landlord and landlady of the of The Railway Hotel between 1959 and 1969.

The following is a copy of an advert found in a local newspaper dated 11 January 1855:

To be sold by Auction, by Mr THOMAS HART at LUXTON'S RAILWAY INN, CULLOMPTON on WEDNESDAY the 24th of JANUARY instant at Two o'clock p.m.: 758 Oak, 176 Ash, 120 Elm, 87 Beech, 5 Chesnut Trees, 233 pollards and 475 saplings with their Tops, Lops and Bark, as they now stand on Crankland, Paulsland, Rull and other Lands, in the Parish of Cullompton, near the Cullompton and Tiverton Junction Station and well situated for removal.

For viewing please apply to the Auctioneer, who will direct a person to show the same; and further particulars may be obtained of him, or at the offices of Messrs CROSSE and LEIGH, Solicitors, Cullompton.

A deposit of twenty per cent will be required at the close of the Sale.

The town's cattle market was moved from the town centre to Station Road in 1918 and the entrance was beside The Railway Hotel. The market was held on the first Wednesday in every month in a field behind the hotel and farmers from all around would bring their animals to sell. It was common for young lads to miss school on market days to help out.

Sometimes, if dealers from further afield came to the market to buy beef cattle it would be loaded onto cattle trucks at the station and taken out by train.

The Railway Hotel, c.1957.

G. Shore's sawmills, which were in Station Road, c.1913.

The Railway Hotel c. 1908.

Aerial view of The Railway Hotel, c.1950. The land to the rear is where the cattle market was held.

Flooding at The Railway Hotel before the water-course was altered. The man in the foreground is Johnny Jones, c.1958.

The Railway Hotel, Station Road, 1908.

There was always a lot of noise and confusion on market days: men shouting, dogs barking and animals not always going where they ought, and of course the latter did make quite a mess. The market closed in 1957 due to lack of support.

Opposite The Railway Hotel was the 'fair field' where a fair was held every Good Friday and for the young people of the area this was one of the highlights of the year.

The land on which Cullompton Hire Centre was established was bought by Mr Terry Snow in the early 1980s and after several years of wrangling he eventually obtained the necessary planning permission and opened in 1986. He later expanded the business to include Direct Building Supplies. The business was sold to Ian Briggs in 1996.

Behind the Hire Centre is Sumpters Farm. During the building of the Great Western Railway the 'New Found Out', a beer shop for 'navvies' could be found here.

Across the bridge is Stoneyford, and on the right-hand side, just over the bridge, was a marshy field where beautiful King Cups used to grow. During the Second World War the Royal Engineers were stationed in Cullompton. They used to build bridges and carry out exercises in that marsh. There was a bungalow a bit further down which was later demolished to make way for the motorway.

Mr and Mrs Clarke outside 1 Grants Cottage, c.1935.

Bungalow between Stoneyford and the railway bridge demolished to make way for the bypass.

Gertie Clarke dressed as a daffodil for Cullompton Carnival, c.1925.

Mr and Mrs Clarke, who lived at 1 Grants Cottages, Stoneyford. Mr Clarke worked for Mr Grant who farmed at Newlands. They had 14 children: Henry, William, Frederick, Alfred, Sidney, Maud, Minnie, Alice, Hilda, Edith, Elsie, Bessie, Gertie and Ivy.

From left to right: *Bessie, Gertie, Hilda, Elsie and their mother, c.1932.*

Devon Growers or 'the fruit farm' as it was once known, was founded by Mr S.R. Cummings in 1928 and their first directors' meeting was held at The Railway Hotel. The Great Western Railway Company provided a special siding from which they could dispatch their produce. Over the next few years a glasshouse nursery was erected and their main crops were tomatoes and cucumbers which were dispatched, by rail, to markets all over the UK. As well as dispatching produce they also received large quantities of Welsh steam coal for the 21 boilers. The nursery continued to be heated by coal until 1957 when it was changed to oil.

At the end of 1932 the nursery acquired land from the Western Counties Brick Company (the old brick yard had, until then, produced a considerable amount of bricks for local use). During the Second World War the nurseries held emergency supplies of steam coal as it was felt that this was an area unlikely to be bombed and therefore a reasonably safe place to store coal. It is also thought that the nurseries were used as a turning point for German aircraft during their night bombing raids as, by night, they resembled a large lake and could not be camouflaged.

In 1945 additional land was purchased and a separate department was set up which dealt entirely with farming. They had a herd of Jersey cattle, known as the Blackdown Herd as well as a considerable acreage of potatoes and cereals. They were among the first farms to install a complete bulk grain handling and drying system.

Aerial view of Devon Growers c.1950.

In the early 1960s it became evident that the company needed to invest to remain competitive. The farming operations were reduced and the glasshouses were rebuilt and in the late 1960s and early 1970s the production of flowers was gradually introduced. In 1978, when the company celebrated its 50th anniversary, it was the largest producer in the South West of year-round pot chrysanthemums and also still produced a large amount of tomatoes. Devon Growers has now closed but the glasshouses can still be seen.

Not far from Devon Growers are the first council-houses to be built in Cullompton, constructed in 1927.

Crossing the road and coming back towards Cullompton one comes to Higher Kingsmill Road which leads down towards the Kingsmill Industrial Estate and St Regis Paper Mill. The paper mill has always been a major employer in the town, and at the time of writing employs about 120 people. Initially it was run intermittently to fit in with farming – people worked on the farms during the summer and made paper in the winter. Now the mill works 24 hours per day, 357 days per year and the workforce works in shifts. At one time the hooter could be heard several times a day summoning people to work.

Paper mill workers, 1934–36. Left to right, back row: *Billie Willis, Enid Osborn, Bertie Clarke;* front row: *Chrissie Osmond, Molly Drew, Queenie Heale, Glynis Luxton.*

The layout of Station Road altered with the motorway; the original road to the paper mill roughly followed the line of the sliproad up onto the bridge and if you look carefully just before you come to Kingsmill House there is a little stone road bridge that carried the original road.

The railway station itself was where the M5 junction is now situated. It was reached by the road next to the Alexandria Industrial Estate and the stationmaster's house is still there. There were extensive buildings on the other side of the line because there was quite a big goods depot as well as a couple of coal yards which supplied the town with its fuel. It was a reasonably sized station with several little loop lines enabling trains to come in and pick up passengers. All the local factories used the station to transport their wares. The 'up' platform was on the town side of the station and one had to cross a bridge to get to the 'down' platform.

At one time the station was widely used by both industry and the general public. Children went to school in Tiverton, Exeter and Wellington on the train and the very few people who worked outside of Cullompton would use the train to get to work. Many people recalled that there was a lovely smell around the station as the steam trains and the furniture were always highly polished.

Top: *Cullompton Station, late 1950s.*

Above: *Cullompton Station goods yard, late 1950s.*

Left: *The bridge over the Culm on Kingsmill Road showing the station goods yard in the late 1950s.*

Right: *The entrance to station's good yards, with a stable on the left, c.late 1950s.*

Below: *The bridge over the River Culm at Stoneyford before the M5 was built.*

Cullompton Young Farmers Club: show and sale in the late 1950s at Bill Hill's Station Yard (once used as a coal yard for Reynolds Coal Merchants. Left to right, back row: *Jack Shere, John Berry, Robin Hussy, Alan Shere, Colin Reed, Robin Saunders, Edwin Derham, Peter Shere, ?, ? Churchill;* front row: *Josephine Richards, Marion Cligg, Kathleen Lock, Charles Vicary, Mrs Berdoe, Derek Cole, Rita Fisher, Kenneth Cole, Anthony Retter.*

One Man's Memories of Cullompton Station
By Ken Vigar

I was born in Station Road, Cullompton, in January 1933 and one of my first memories is of the circus coming to town. The animals were led through the town from the station to a field near the then Cullompton Hotel where the Big Top was set up. It was the first time I had seen elephants and they were led along the road, each one holding the tail of the one in front with his trunk.

Another early memory is of the 'Walls' ice-cream man coming by train from Exeter with his tricycle freezer box in the guard's van. He would then cycle around the town selling his ice-creams before returning to Exeter by train.

In 1939 my parents moved to Duke Street so I was further away from the station but the railway was still very much a part of my life. There were four coal merchants in the town who all had sidings at the station. The coal was unloaded from the open carriages to the bays, made of old railway sleepers, and was then weighed and bagged by hand and put onto lorries for delivery to the houses.

Cattle cake and feed was also stored at the goods yard in bags and delivered by lorry to the farms.

William Thomas Builder's Merchant was another part of the goods yard. Many heavy goods were brought in by train for onward delivery to other sites or to be collected.

In 1947 small goods destined for shops, etc., were sorted on arrival and delivered by horse and wagon to the shops. I well remember the first ice-cream delivery to the town after the war: it was packed in insulated boxes and again delivered to the shops by horse and wagon.

At the age of 11 (1944) I was lucky enough to gain entry to Tiverton Grammar School and this was to make the trains a part of my life again as the only way to get to Tiverton was by train. A good number of us had to catch the 7.45a.m. train to Tiverton Junction then transfer onto the branch line for Tiverton by the Tivvy Bumper. Most of us rode our bicycles to Cullompton Station where they were locked in the bike shed. On arrival at Tiverton we would walk to the school just in time for morning assembly.

I think it was a credit to the GWR that for the three years I did this trip I was never late for school; of course we had the same journey to do to get home, arriving back at Cullompton at approximately 4.50p.m.

Papers and milk were also brought to Cullompton on the 7.45a.m. train and collected by the tradesmen.

One Woman's Memories of Cullompton Station
By Jane Pidgeon

I was born and brought up in Cullompton although I now live in Truro and I have many happy memories of my grandparents Cecil and Florence Knight who used to live at East Culm. Grandad was discharged from the army after the First World War and joined the Great Western Railway in 1919. They moved to Cullompton around 1930 and Grandad worked as a signalman at Cullompton Station, and occasionally covered Sampford Peverell, Hele & Bradninch and Silverton Stations. He then served in the Second World War from 1939 to 1945 and on his discharge returned to Cullompton and rejoined the railway once again as a signalman.

I used to occasionally cycle down to the signal-box to meet him after his shift and he would allow me to pull the levers which changed the points on the track and I was amazed at how clean and sparkling everything was. Grandad was also a keen gardener and spent a lot of his spare time at his railway allotment which was situated close to Cullompton Station. He retired in 1960. His daughter, my Auntie Grace, worked in the station booking office for a number of years until she married Mr Percy Phillips from Exeter in 1950 and then transferred to Exeter St Davids Station booking office.

Cullompton Carnival, 1926: the Great Western Railway entry.

Above: *Staff from Drevon and Brown, a glove factory located close to the station on what is now the Alexandria Industrial Estate, c.1939.*

Below: *The London Inn, Station Road (then Lower Street) c.1895. Elias White, haulier, is in his pony and trap.*

Coming back up Station Road there was a tannery where the Alexandria Industrial Estate is now situated. Culm Leather Dressing Co. closed in 1982 with the loss of 98 jobs; at that time, it was the second biggest employer in Cullompton. Culm Leather's hooter made a squeaky sort of noise and would blow at 7.30a.m., 1p.m., 2p.m. and 5.30p.m. There was also Drevon and Brown's glove factory which employed quite a few girls making gloves.

The original Station Road Garage was situated where Colin & Martin Discount Tyres is now. In 1952 it was owned by Mr E.A. Watts and during the 1940s by Ron Kirkham.

The London Inn was situated opposite Belle Vue Terrace, but closed in 1903 as the magistrates refused to renew the licence, the reason being that it had changed hands three times since 1896 and there had been complaints of people loitering there on Sunday mornings. It is now a private house.

The layout of houses in Station Road hasn't altered a great deal over the years. College Road is new, and Bramblehaies Surgery opened in May 1994 and College Surgery in 1988. Where the ambulance station is now were once two cottages in country gardens and Court House was a private house belonging to Dr Cardell who held fêtes and garden parties there.

No. 3 Station Road is now Home Finders, but in 1962 it was Goffin Bros, builders and funeral directors. At one time it was a shoe shop but was closed for about eight years in the 1960s when Station Road was being widened. Mr and Mrs Collins bought the site from the Council in 1970 and opened a DIY shop. It later became a sports shop, owned firstly by Mr and Mrs Coaley and then by Mark Eakers. Mr Eakers sold the premises when he retired in 2001.

Palmers Bridge, Station Road, with Belle Vue Terrace in the background, c.1916.

Chapter Seven

High Street, Higher Street and Willand Road

What follows is a stroll up one side of High Street and back down the other side.

No. 1, Cullompton Town Hall: Originally known as the Parish Rooms the Council decided to rename it 1995 and it still looks very much as it did in the 1930s. It is built on land which may, at one time, have been the Green Dragon and later the Half Moon. The Half Moon was a coaching inn that took in all the land from the Town Hall to Middle Mill Lane down to the Mill Leat, including Labdon's Yard, Londis Stores, etc. The cottages in Middle Mill Lane were originally quarters for the ostlers (someone employed in a stable to take care of the horses) working at the inn. In 1870 some of the land was sold to the town and the Town Hall was built. The Labdon family bought the remaining land in about 1896.

Before the Second World War the fire-engine was kept at the front and during the war the hall became the first-aid post. At the time of writing the Town Hall houses the Town Council offices, which are on the first floor. The Council meetings are held in the main hall, which is also used for events such as jumble sales and coffee mornings, bingo, slimming classes and a regular market on Wednesday mornings.

On 1 January 1845 the following article appeared in the local press:

CULLOMPTON, DEVON

To be SOLD, by Auction, at the Half Moon Hotel, Cullompton on MONDAY the 26th day of January next, at five o'clock in the afternoon, the following: MEADOW, ORCHARD, INN and PREMISES

Lot 1 All that excellent watered Meadow called GREAT MILL MEADOW, situate in Cullompton aforesaid, containing by estimation, Six acres.

Lot 2 All this Orchard called FRY'S ORCHARD, containing by estimation an acre and three quarters situate in Mill Lane in Cullompton aforesaid, with the Curtilage and Buildings at the upper end thereof.

Lot 3 The HALF MOON HOTEL aforesaid with the Yard, Stables and Two Gardens, thereto adjoining.

Lot 1 is held for the remainder of a Term of One Thousand years, under the yearly rent of Fifteen Shillings and Two pence. Lots 2 and 3 are held in Fee Simple. The Premises are now in the occupation of Mr WILLIAM HODGES whose Term expires at Lady-Day next, when possession will be given.

High Street, c.1950.

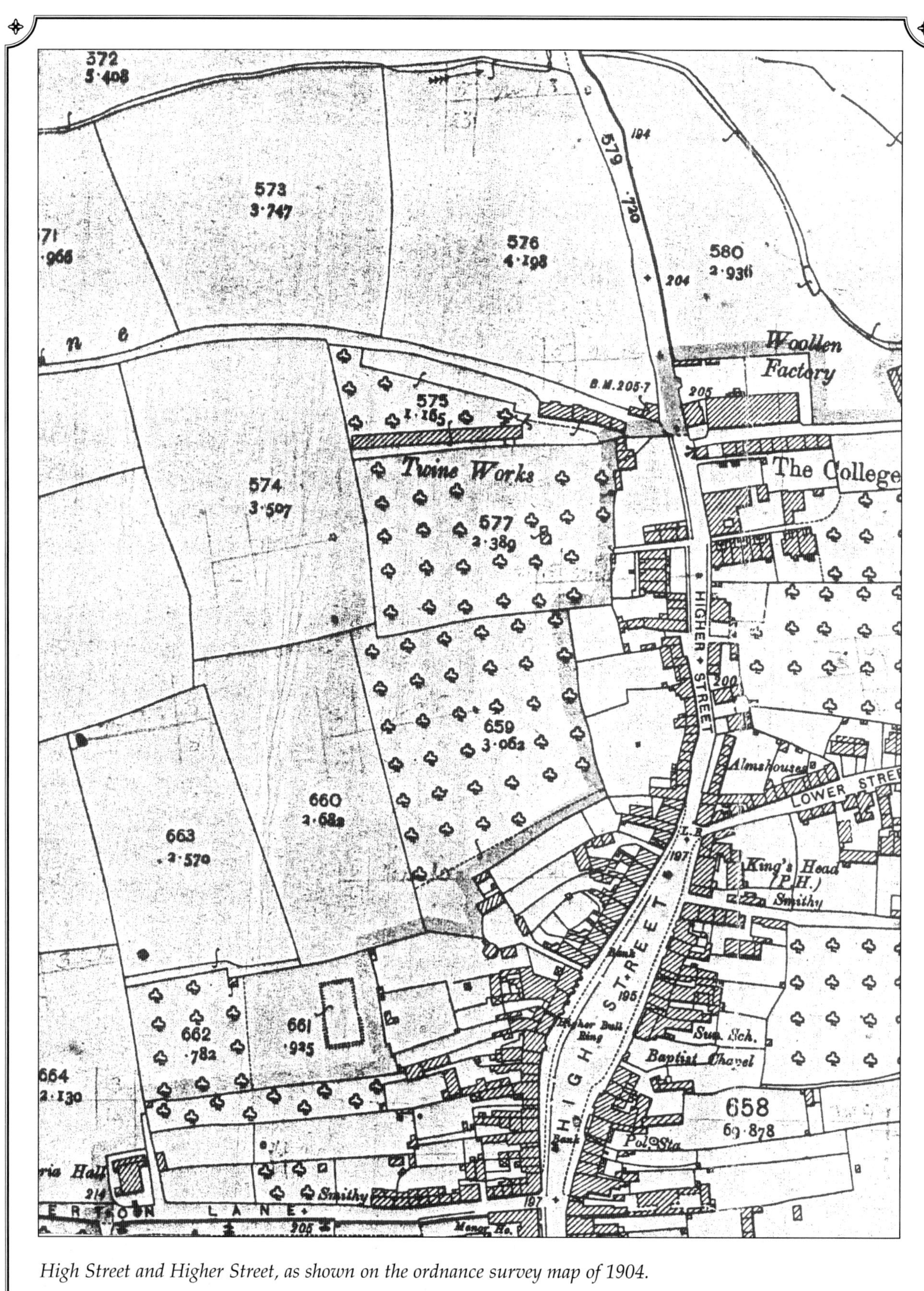

High Street and Higher Street, as shown on the ordnance survey map of 1904.

Horse and cart used for damping down the roads in High Street. Elias White is seated on the cart, c.1912.

Building the manse next door to the Baptist Church, c.1905.

The Premises and a Map thereof, can be seen on application to Mr HODGES, the Tenant, or to Mr ELIAS JARMAN of Cullompton, and further particulars may be obtained of Mr JOHN H. TERRELL, Solicitor, St Martins Lane, Exeter.

It is thought that the land referred to above is the land from Middle Mill Lane to the Town Hall, including Labdon's Yard.

No. 3, Proberts Bakery: In the 1930s this was Fare & Son Grocers, where the floorboards used to be covered in sawdust and the provisions counter was on the right. On the left was a counter with big square tins of biscuits all along the front and customers could pick out whatever they wanted. It later became Proberts High Class Grocers and Delicatessen.

No. 5, private dwelling: In the 1930s this was a sweetshop run by a family called Cook who also had an interest in the cinema opposite. It was also R. & M. Ward Sweets, Chocolates and Tobacco for a while. It was later taken over by the Brown family and run as a sweetshop with a wholesale business next door.

No. 7, Oakleys Accountants: At one time this site belonged to Mr and Mrs Hallet who sold gloves, but by 1977 it was called F. Brown Wholesale, dealing with confectionery and tobacco.

No. 9, Culm Florist: In the 1930s this was the Westminster Bank with Mr Ellis working as the manager. It was really just a big private house, with the bank making use of a couple of rooms on the ground floor. It was later transformed into a cake shop and tea rooms known as Pat's Pantry before it was used by Clark's Motors as its car showroom and then Bike Zone.

Nos 11&13, Thorne & Carter: This building was built by public subscription in about 1853 as a Town Hall and Sessions House, with the court being held upstairs. It was sold to the Police Authority in 1870 and land on the north side was purchased from Mr Alfred Thomas Batten for the erection of a garage to accommodate the police patrol vehicle for the resident sergeant's car. There was accommodation behind for the resident sergeant who always lived on-site. There were cells in the building, which meant that instead of troublemakers being taken into Exeter to be charged they could be charged and put into the cells in Cullompton.

The building was sold to 'Alfie' Dolbear in 1978 after a new police station was built in Station Road and and it became Thorne & Carter Estate Agents in 2000.

No. 15, Clark's Court: It is thought that this may, at one time, have been the site of the Red Lion Inn which was destroyed by fire in 1843. It later became a garage, originally known as Cullompton Garage and owned by Batten Bros. It was renamed Clark's Motors and, following the death of the then owner Mr Galliver, the site was put on the market. It lay derelict for several years before being sold to McCarthy & Stone.

No. 17, Foster Care Associates: Originally the Manse for the Baptist Church next door this property was let when a new Manse was built in Manitoba Gardens. It was sold to Jock Campbell in 1978/79 and he ran his solicitor's practice from here until he retired in 1994. The building is still owned by the Campbell family and is currently leased to Foster Care Associates.

No. 19, Harlequin Valet: Previously Smalls animal feed and seed merchants this site was converted into two shop units in about 2003.

No. 21&23, The Market House Inn: Named after the monthly cattle market that was held in Higher Bullring until 1917. It was then moved to a field behind what is now the Weary Traveller in Station Road. The hurdles which made up the pens for the animals were stored

The Cattle Market in Higher Bullring. It was moved to a field behind the Weary Traveller in 1917.

Above: *Celebrations in High Street on the occasion of the coronation of George V on 22 June 1911. The Market House Inn sign can be read in the background and Earlands is next to the Baptist Church.*

THE

CULLOMPTON GARAGE

— CO. —

Automobile Engineers and Agents

SALES AND SERVICE

FOR THE WELL-KNOWN

AUSTIN & MORRIS CARS

All Best Makes of Cars supplied

ADVICE AND TUITION.

Proprietors—BATTEN BROS, Tel. 27 Cullompton

A. MORTIMORE

Game :: :: Poulterer
Butter & Egg Merchant

Guaranteed Products of Devonshire.

3, High Street, Cullompton

DEVON.

Higher Bullring on market day, c.1910.

here. It is possible that it may have originally been called the Bishop Blaize.

No. 25, The Bays Dental Practice: In the 1930s this was a private house where Miss Hope Cole, a teacher from St Andrews School, lived.

No. 27, Honeycomb Animations: Originally a private house this building has been as used as offices for several companies. In the 1950s, for example, it was the office of Ford & Son decorators, painters and plumbers. Honeycomb Animations arrived in 2000 and is the home of *Binka* a well-known and well-loved cartoon cat who often attends local events. Founded by Simon and Sara Bor, Honeycomb Animation has been producing animation since 1982, including *Mop & Smiff* (1985 for BBC), the award winning *Tube Mice* (1988 for TSW/CiTV), 'Frootie Tooties' (1992 for TSW) and two series of the adult production *Beastly Behaviour* (1994–95 for WDR and Channel 4). Four series and two Christmas specials of *Wolves, Witches and Giants* (1995–98) were made for CiTV. Narrated by Spike Milligan, the series gained awards, notably the Royal Television Society's 'Best Children's Entertainment'. Sales have been made to over 50 countries including the Disney Channel in the US.

'Binka' the cartoon cat produced in Cullompton by Honeycomb Animation of 27 High Street.

Honeycomb Animation moved into its High Street, Cullompton, premises in 2000, increasing its output with several long-running series for ITV, BBC and Five. These include *Binka* for CBeebies, *Lost in the Snow* for CiTV, *Funky Valley* and a spin-off series *Funky Town* for Five, as well as the Bafta-nominated *Grizzly Tales for Gruesome Kids* (a Honeycomb/Elephant Production for CiTV) which has received many awards, including 'Best Children's Series' at Cartoon on the Bay and 'Best Childrens' and 'Childrens' Choice' at the British Animation Awards. Six series were broadcast between 2000 and 2006.

Since first appearing on TV in 2001, fat cat Binka has become a Cullompton favourite, attending the Farmer's Market and helping to switch on the Christmas lights. As well as CBeebies, Binka has also appeared on DVD, CD, in comics, on key rings, and a range of pet products including cat toys, cat litter and even a cat toilet!

No. 29, Originally a private house it became Thorne & Baker Auctioners, Valuers and Estate Agents and later Thorne & Carter Estate Agents before divided into several separate units. Currently houses Cullompton Chiropody, Mary Dunn Financial Advisor, and Top to Toe holistic services for dogs.

No. 31, Susan's Hair Boutique: Previously Miss Paul's Bakers and Chorley-Hallett Grocers. In the 1960s the shop belonged to Mr Holly who was renowned for selling the best bacon in town. It became a clothes shop in the 1980s before becoming a hairdresser's.

No. 35, King's Head: Named after Charles II, what is now the restaurant was a shop, which during the 1930s was run as Graves Poultry and Rabbits. Its use was changed to the public library in November 1938, with the librarian at that time being Miss Harding.

No. 37, Ian's Fish Bar: In the 1930s this was the International Stores and then S. Mills Fishmonger and Greengrocers. Another building on the corner of Station Road which was demolished for road widening was run for a time as Nex's Sweet Shop.

International Stores (now Ian's Fish Bar). From left to right: *Mr Stone, Mr Snow, Miss Quant, Mr Frist and Mr Gilly.*

Above: *Conservative Club Darts Team in the 1950s.* Left to right, back row: *Wilf Saunders, Reg Heaman, Bill Cording, Ern Goff;* front row: *Bob Weadon, ?, George Lewitt, ?, Ron Harris.*

Below: *Conservative Club, c.1960s.* Left to right: *?, Les Partridge, John Vicary, ?, Cecily Chambers, Mr Chambers, ?, Margaret Coates, Ann Hiscox, Mrs Holly, Mr Hiscox, Cecily Hiscox.*

High Street, c.1950, with cars double parked outside the police station.

On the Opposite Side of the Road...

No. 44, private dwelling: Formerly Holcon House Barber's Shop and before that Holcon House Restaurant. It was an antiques shop and café in the 1970s.

42. Ingleby House Dental Practice: Previously a private house owned by the Snow family, it was sold to Mr Bourne in around 2002 and he converted it to a dental surgery.

No. 40, Conservative Club: The idea of a Conservative Club was suggested in December 1885 by Colonel Lionel Walrond after his election as a Member of Parliament for the Tiverton Division. He envisaged 'a club in which working men might learn the true bearing of Conservatives upon the politics of the day'. A meeting was held in January 1886 and the following month the Cullompton and District Conservative Working Men's Club rented rooms at the Coffee Tavern owned by Mr Frank Sellwood. The club proved a success and within a year it had 200 members.

After a succession of one-room premises it was suggested by president Mr W.J. Grant that the club buy its present premises in High Street. Mr Grant bought the building and offered it to the 138 members for rental of £20 per year. Following the death of Colonel Walrond during the First World War the club members became the sole owners of the property.

No. 38, Dunn & Baker Solicitors: In the 1930s this was the manse for the Unitarian Chapel and Revd Pocock lived here. It later became a doctors' surgery until the doctors moved to Bramblehaies, a purpose-built surgery in College Road in May 1994.

No. 36, Watts & Son Estate Agents: Previously Hamiltons Estate Agents and originally a private house, in 1977 it became 'His Place', a craft centre selling local leather work and other hand-made items.

No. 34, The Vale Vets: In the 1930s Mr and Mrs Bill Hill lived here and it is believed that Mrs Hill started Glanherne School here and later moved it, first to the Victoria Hall and then to 12–14 High Street. Mr Hill was a very prominent farmer in the area.

No. 32, Batchelor & Co Accountants and Manchester Building Society: At one time this was Phyllis Potter's hairdressers.

Formerly No. 30: There was once a house between Barclays Bank and the Manchester Building Society, which was home to Mrs Evans and family. However, it was knocked down to widen the access to St Andrews Estate.

No. 28, Barclays Bank: Originally a private house it became an office and showroom for Culm Vale Electricity Company in the 1920s and the manager lived there. It was later taken over by SWEB but was closed in the mid-1970s.

No. 26, Vacant: In the 1930s Mr William Moorcroft had a home and a dental practice here, and was quite a prominent man in Cullompton. Other dentists that followed were Bill Woolcott, Mr Jefferies and Mr Leigh-Brown. The house originally had a large garden and Bill Woolcott used to open it up to the public for garden parties. There is still a dental practice on the first floor of the building.

Nos 22–24, private dwellings.

No. 20, China Orchids: Originally a doctors' surgery, where Drs Hammond, Murphy and Gidley

Denners Hardware Shop dressed up to celebrate Queen Elizabeth II's golden jubilee in 2002.

SPEAR Bros. & CLARK Ltd.
Wiltshire Bacon Curers
Ask for—
Spear's Finest Wiltshire Bacon
STOCKED BY ALL HIGH-CLASS GROCERS
CULLOMPTON
Also at
Bristol, Bath, London, Birmingham, Redruth, Cardiff, Swansea, Chippenham

RUTLEY & SON
ALL KINDS OF REPAIRS UNDERTAKEN.
Auto Engineers
Agents for SWIFT and SINGER CARS.
NORTON & LEWIS MOTOR CYCLES.
Garage .·. Cullompton

R. DYER
MOTOR & CYCLE ENGINEER

Any Make of Motor Cycle Supplied or Repaired
— B.S.A. SPECIALIST —
High Street .·. Cullompton

Girls from Fox Bros enjoying a Christmas dinner in 1958. Left to right: *Betty Thomas, Barbara Stocker, Olive Pipe, Eileen Burrows, Sheila Radford, Marlene Spear, Pauline Broom, Dianne Tolhurst.*

practiced. In the 1960s it was 'Smile and Charm' with a coffee shop on one side and a hair boutique on the other, but later became the Bullring Restaurant, Teapots, and Junction 28 Restaurant and craft shop.

No. 18, private dwelling.

No. 16, Chic Hairdressers: Originally a private house.

Nos 12–14, Harris Fowler: Heyford House was built for Dr Gidley in 1901–03 by Labdon & Sons. It was purchased from Dr Gidley in the mid-1930s by the Order of our Lady of Mercy who set up Our Lady of Dolours Convent School. The site later became home to Glanherne School. It was a doctors' surgery again in the 1960s for Drs Hammond and Finch.

No. 10, Bradleys Estate Agents: Originally part of the Convent School this building then became a fruit and vegetable shop before becoming Yardley's shoe shop. It was Proberts Estate Agents before becoming Bradleys.

No. 8, vacant: Originally part of the Convent School it later became Cullompton Weavers and in 1952 it was Culm Cycle Works. By 1962 it had been sold to Mr W.R. Denner who sold cycles, toys and ironmongery. It closed in 2005.

No. 6, Seddon Estate Agents: This site was Copp's Fruit, Veg and Flowers, Good Companions Fruit and Flowers and Colonels' Fruit and Veg before becoming an estate agents.

No. 4, Cullompton Carpet Centre: In the 1970s this was D.A. Moore, house furnishers, but prior to that it was a private house with the Regal Cinema behind.

No. 2, HSBC Bank: At one time Huxtables Sweets and Groceries.

Higher Street and Willand Road

Walking out of town towards Willand on the right-hand side are the John Trotte's Almshouses in Higher Street, built of the same sandstone as the Walronds. John Trotte, in his will dated 28 January 1523, declared that his executors should (with the remains of his goods, and with all the debts owing to him) build an almshouse for six poor men, and purchase land to provide them with sixpence a week, to pray for his soul and the souls of his wife and children.

Nothing is known about the Almshouses between 1670 and 1816. From 1816 until 1862 they appear to have been left in the control of the vicar, who repaired it in a temporary way and put in as occupants, old people in receipt of parish allowance. In the early-nineteenth century they were used as a bell foundry. In 1883 James Martin left £400 to restore them, and at this time a room was added. In 1906 Frank Sellwood gave £100 to provide an income for their upkeep. At the time of writing the Almshouses are currently administered by Cullompton United Charities.

Escotts was, at one time, occupied by Mr Bradbeer who was the manager of William Plumpton's Plumbers, whose stores and workshops adjoined the house. About 20 men were employed by Plumpton's and there are still manhole covers bearing the company name around the town. The company closed in 1964. The brick lock-up garage on the corner of Court Farm drive was later converted to a warehouse for Stone's Gloves, a glove wholesaler. Some of the gloves came from Drevon and Brown, glove makers located in Station Road adjoining Culm Leather. This site is now occupied by a confectionery wholesale depot.

To the rear of this building is an old brick cottage which formed part of The College, a religious foundation which extended down to the area now occupied by College Surgery and College Road. A branch of Fox Bros of Wellington once occupied the site now used by Twyford Engineering. The brick house in Higher Street, on the corner of Court Farm Drive was once the home of the Fox Bros factory manager. In the 1930s the company employed several hundred people. It closed in the 1970s and the tall brick wall surrounding the site was demolished. It became Crown Furniture Works and at the time of writing is Twyford Engineering.

The site now occupied by Astra Print was previously Culm Garage and before that Rutley & Son Garage, which was started in the 1920s by George Rutley. It was later taken over by his son Wilfred who was instrumental in setting up the St John Ambulance Brigade in Cullompton. The garage was the first home of the ambulance.

Turning around and coming back towards the town on the right-hand side, on the corner of Goblin Lane, there was a branch of the Western Memorial Co. owned by Mr Real and Bill Plumpton. All the headstones were displayed in the front of the place where they made them. The business closed in about 1956.

No. 10, Eastern Eye: In the 1950s this was Jack Heard Model dairy. It then became Frank Clarke's Dairy and later a fish-and-chip shop.

No. 8, Cullompton Clocks: In the 1930s this site was occupied by a pork butcher's called Spear Bros & Clark Ltd that only sold pork. It later became Mr Pring Butchers and Radford's Butchers. Mr Lesley Munn took over the business in about 1971, before his son Paul took it over from him. Paul later moved next door to help run the fish-and-chip shop and his younger brother Geoff took over the business. During the 1970s Sheila Greenslade's hairdresser's was above the shop.

No. 6, private dwelling.

Nos 2–4, Cullompton Dental Centre: In the 1930s this was Dyers Cycle Shop, but it was also a bakery at one time and people would take their sunday joint there to be cooked if they didn't have big enough ovens in which to cook it. The baker would take a slice off the joint in payment. The site, at various times, also served as office space for J. Bibby, Dulford Nurseries and Clem Lear Insurance Brokers.

Left: *High Street, c.1970.*

Below: *Karen and Stuart Spurway, High Street, Cullompton Carnival, c.1976.*

Fore Street looking towards High Street, c.1905.

E. & E. M. SOUL

Drapers and Milliners

FORE ST. CULLOMPTON

Below: *The Leisure Shop at 15 Fore Street with its window dressed in celebration of Queen Elizabeth II Golden Jubilee in June 2002.*

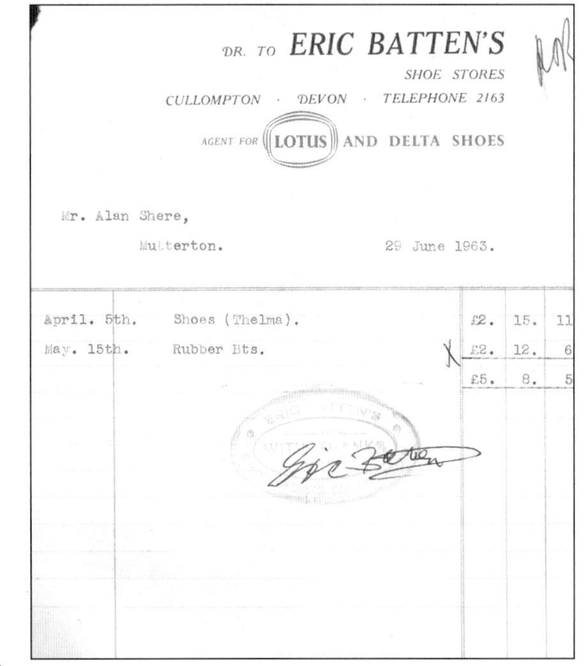

DR. TO ERIC BATTEN'S
SHOE STORES
CULLOMPTON · DEVON · TELEPHONE 2163
AGENT FOR LOTUS AND DELTA SHOES

Mr. Alan Shere,
Mutterton. 29 June 1963.

April. 5th.	Shoes (Thelma).	£2.	15.	11
May. 15th.	Rubber Bts.	£2.	12.	6
		£5.	8.	5

FRANK STEVENS (ELECTRICAL) LTD
RADIO AND ELECTRICAL SPECIALISTS.

Phone 2102
EVERTHING ELECTRICAL.
WIRING CONTRACTORS.

17, FORE STREET,
CULLOMPTON

10th. January 1964

Mr. A. Shere,
Mutterton Dairy
Cullompton

	Taking mains from back door through loft and on continary to dairy in heavy 7044 earth core cable to feed splitter in dairy, using 48 yds cable	£10.	3.	6
	Long Shippen and Meal House To wiring 4 light circuits controlled by one switch and altering position of switch for Yard Light	4.	5.	6
	Dairy To wiring one light circuit, one 15 amp plug circuit, supplying and fitting one Wylex fused box, wiringcircuit for milking machine motor, supplying ad fitting isolator switch fitting up press button starter, fitting slide rails for motor and pump	8.	12.	0
	Milking Parlour Wiring two light circuits and one outside light to work off dairy light, supplying and fitting one Waterproof Fitting	3.	18.	6
	One Brook 1 H.P. Motor	17.	18.	6
	One 5"x1.A. Pulley		9.	6
	One A.48 Vee Belt		8.	6
	One Pair Slide Rails	1.	7.	6
	One MEM Press Button Starter	3.	2.	6
	One Compressor Pump	25.	10.	0
	Eight Bulbs @ 1/10 each		14.	8
8/10/63	Three 100 Watt [illegible]		5.	6
		£ 76.	16.	2
		23	18	2
		100 -	14 ·	4

RECEIVED WITH THANKS 3/3/64
p.p. FRANK STEVENS (Electrical) LTD.

Chapter Eight

Fore Street

What follows is a stroll up one side of Fore Street and back down the other side.

No. 1, First Choice Travel Agents: At one time this was the site of a coaching-inn but the land has been owned by the Labdon family for over 100 years. Labdon & Sons Building Contractors are the oldest family business still in existence in Cullompton, having been established about five years longer than Veysey & Son. The shop was a builder's merchants and the offices and builders yard were at the rear. The shop has had numerous short-term tenants since the 1970s including Gas & Oil Burners, Hipkiss Lyne & Sargeant Estate Agents, Wessex Taverns, Roger Williams Solicitor, Malcolm Trump, Architect, and Mr Pheasant, Chiropodist.

No. 3, Londis: This site was formerly Steers Drapers and Ladies' and Gents' Outfitters from the early 1930s until the late 1950s. The shop front was changed from two windows with a recessed door to the present design when it became Kemps Grocers in 1977.

No. 5, Lloyds Bank:

No. 7, National Westminster Bank: The front is completely false; in the 1930s it was a cottage with a front room from where Mrs Endicott sold fruit and sweets. It was later taken over by National Provincial Bank.

No. 9, Dalzells: In the 1930s Nos 9 and 11 were combined and was Fry's Ladies' and Gents' Outfitters. By 1963 it was Smiths Drapers and by 1977 it was Spendfreeze and Spendsave, a freezer shop.

No. 11, Barber shop: Known as London House and previously Dalzells it became a barber's shop in 2006. Fry's Ladies' and Gents' Outfitters and before that the Misses Soul kept it – in 1908 it was Soul & Co., general drapers, milliners, clothiers and hatters. It was also Stanley Labdon Butchers at one time.

No. 13, Jeeves' Sandwich Shop: In the 1930s this was the London Central Meat Company and by 1938

Above: *Visit of General Sir Redvers Buller, Fore Street (note the street light in the foreground), 1906.*

Right: *Methodist Church, New Cut c.1908.*

it was the Central Dairy. It later became Kemps Grocers until Kemps moved into 3 Fore Street and the shop became Mr Vicary's card shop. It became Fresh 'n' Fruity for approximately two years before becoming a sandwich shop.

No. 15, The Leisure Shop: Battens Shoe Shop until the early 2000s. At one time there was a shoe repair shop behind, which could be accessed from Matthews Court. Mr Discombe worked here repairing shoes between the 1930s and 1970s. Keith Lambert took over the shop from Eric Batten in the 1980s but the name remained the same.

No. 17, Bubbles Launderette: In 1962 this was Frank Stevens' wireless shop, which later sold televisions. Mr Stevens' daughter, Susan, opened a hairdressing business in rooms on the first floor. This later became Vicky's Hair Stylist. Prior to Mr Stevens taking over the premises it was Baker's and before that Beeston's music shop. In 1977 it became a fishmongers and fruit shop run by Roger Stone and his wife.

My First Job and My First Long Trousers

Mr Derrick Kellaway

I left school in 1941, and went to work at Frank Stevens' Electrical and Radio Shop in Fore Street where Bubbles Launderette is now. I was paid 5s. a week! My duties included charging accumulators, which were used for radios where there was no mains electricity. Most farms and outlying dwellings had no mains. After I had charged these wet batteries I took them to the butcher's and baker's shops. They were taken on the country rounds and distributed where needed, and the discharged ones brought back for me to collect and repeat the process.

I had to wear a shop coat or overall. After a few weeks my coat had several holes burnt by the acid! My boss told me that I must buy a new coat and I replied 'If I don't get a rise I'm leaving', his reply was 'You had better leave'. I left and went to work at Labdons for the princely sum of 7s.6d.

No. 19, White Hart Inn: In its coaching days it had its own ostler and stables at the rear. There was also a field at the back where horses could graze. Mrs Coxhead can remember it on market days in the 1930s – at that time the market was held in fields behind what is now the Weary Traveller, and the farmers would come into town in their pony and trap which they would leave behind the inn. Then they would go into the White Hart for what was called a 'market day dinner' which cost a shilling.

Left: *Devon & Dorsets Reunion at the White Hart, March 1980.* Left to right, back row: *Eric Batten, Reg Hales, Ted Sampson, Mr Sanders, ?, Cliff Denner, ?, Peter Patterson, Tom Batting, ?, Ralph Mitchell, ?;* middle row: *J. Parsons, W. Bird, Lou Partridge, ?, Vic Tidborough, Bill Heale;* front row: *?, Jack Hake, Cyril Warren, Ern Goff, Col Young, ?, Ken Saunders, ?.*

Below: *White Hart Inn.*

Sole Local Agent for Cullompton Guide

W. E. LAWRENCE

NEWSAGENT, STATIONER,
PRINTER & BOOKSELLER

Greaseproofs, Wrappings and all Office Sundries

THE LIBRARY

Fore Street :: Cullompton

DEVON

No. 21, Vranch House: Lawrence's Newsagents, which was taken over by Bill and June Frost in the late 1950s. It was sold in the 1980s to a Mr Fish.

No. 23–25, Co-op: In the 1930s this was Reynolds' Ironmongers & Coal Merchants, who did a good trade in coal because everyone had a coal fire in those days. They had premises out by the station where all the coal was kept. They would bring it into town in lorries, bag it up and deliver it to people's houses. It was still John Reynolds & Sons in 1962 but later became Stan Doyle's Ironmongers and DIY, then Roberts & Cotterill Ironmongers and then Balfour Newsagents.

No. 27, Cancer Research (UK): Once Tiny Hellier's Toy Shop, which sold everything from safety pins and hair grips to toys and sweets... and if you wanted a car he also did a bit of dealing. It later became Stan Doyle's Wallpaper and Decorating Shop. Mr Derrick Kellaway remembers:

When I was a boy in the late 1930s and early 1940s there were two toy shops in the town. One was Phil Sweet's and the other 'Tiny' Hellier's, both in Fore Street. Phil Sweet's shop was at the bottom of the Cut and Tiny's shop was opposite. Tiny was well known for competing with Woolworths for custom: Woolworths, at that time, was famous for 'nothing in the store over sixpence' and many items were only threepence! Tiny would sell items at fivepence three-farthings and twopence threefarthings thus being one farthing cheaper than that famous store.

Also he would sell simple toys for as little as one penny! I remember buying a little toy yacht for that price, complete with mast and two little sails, all for a penny! At that time there were two main gutters in Fore Street, one on each side of the road, fed by the town leat. These streams had, at intervals, short wider parts called 'hutches' where people could dip out a bucket of water.

Also leading from the gutters down the courts were smaller streams for the houses there. I can remember when Cullompton was first supplied with mains water. I remember our teacher Mr Trevor Jones asking us to find out what the little signs put along the course of the pipeline meant – such as FH, SV, AV, etc. Going back to the town gutters, we children used to sail these boats, etc., in them, often losing them under a bridged section!

Fore Street, c.1950. Reynolds Ironmongers is in the foreground.

Cancer Research (UK): 'Cullompton Friends'

Mrs Thelma Shere

March 1990 saw the opening of Imperial Cancer Research Fund at 27 Fore Street, Cullompton. Over the 16 years it was in operation £53,000 was donated to the fund due to the hard work of all the volunteers who manned the shop. In 2000 the name was changed to Cancer Research (UK) and, even though money was still being raised for the charity, the management decided to close all shops in small towns, Cullompton being one of them. The doors closed after 16 years of trading on 3 March 2006.

The volunteers were very upset by this news, so a meeting was called with all 33 volunteers attending and it was decided that we would re-open ourselves as a fund-raising shop. The landlord was approached and terms were agreed, all the other services were contacted and all we had to do was dot the 'i's and cross the 't's. We would now be known as 'Cullompton Friends' and we would still raise money but each year it would be donated to a cancer charity.

A committee was formed under the leadership of the Manager (Mrs Thelma Shere) and with the help of all the volunteers. Mrs Wendy Pring was appointed as Assistant-Manager with Miss Joan Levett as Treasurer and Mrs Marjory Huxham as her assistant.

As soon as the public heard the shop was to re-open the goods poured in. The shop was repainted, the interior redesigned and shelving was put in place. The volunteers worked tirelessly to get everything ready and with bunting and balloons in place we were ready for the grand opening on the Wednesday morning.

On 3 May 2006 queues started to form outside the shop ready for Ross from Gemini Radio and the Town Mayor, Mrs Eileen Andrews, to cut the ribbon to open the shop once again. A large cake was cut and champagne was served to all the volunteers as a thank you for a job well done.

The takings from the first day were staggering and as I write the goods are still pouring in, as are the customers and again we shall be able to send a large donation to the fund, which in our first year will be the Bobby Moore Appeal.

No. 29, Fulfords Estate Agents: Originally Rawlings & Sons Grocers established in 1895. Along one side there were tins of biscuits which were weighed and put into a bag by hand (no gloves were used). On the other side was the provisions counter where customers would ask staff for a piece of cheese, for example half-a-pound of cheese (a big round one). Nothing was pre-packed and the assistants could judge within a whisker how much customers wanted. Sugar was kept in a sack on the floor and the quantity you wanted was scooped into a blue bag. Bacon was sliced in front of customers and the floor was bare with sawdust on it.

By 1977 this shop had become Standford Family Grocer and later was a delicatessen owned by Mr and Mrs Rosatti.

No. 31, Instep: Known as West End House it was a tailor and outfitters for many years in the 1930s owned by Harry Ball. It was also also Battens Gents' Outfitters before being taken over by Wakefields Men's Outfitters. It became Windsors Tailors and Outfitters in the 1980s.

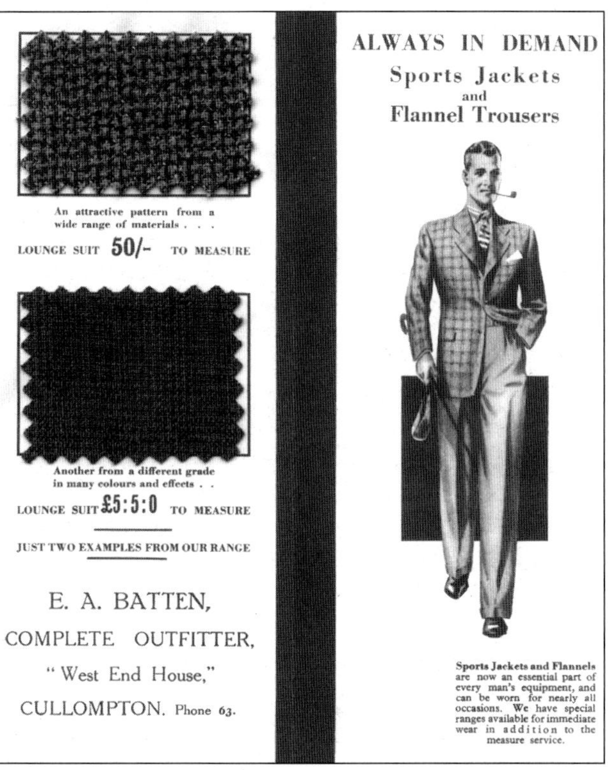

E.A. Batten Outfitter c. 1950.

No. 33. Streamers: In 1903 this was the Temperance House, a place for travellers to stay if they didn't want to stay in a public house. Since then it has had many owners/tenants including Tappers Vegetables, Sweets and Tobacco, and Halletts Models and Toys. By 1963 it was R.H. & R.E. Stone, Tobacconists, Confectioners, Fruiterers and Florists, but it has also been in its time Smugglers and Let's Go Travel.

No. 35, Stephen Ash: Formerly Denner's sweetshop, this site then became a barber's run by Mr O'Neil and then Bolham Dry Cleaners. It was Cullompton Wine Store in 1977 run by Mrs Dean before being bought by Mr Ash in the 1980s.

No. 37, vacant shop: One-time location of Fred Stephens Jewellers then Mr & Mrs Pope Jewellers.

No. 39, Moonlight Pizzas: Reg Paul Bakers had a bakery on the premises and baked lovely cakes and bread. It later became Hilton's Antiques and then Mills' Antiques until George and Veronica Mills moved to Tanyard Antiques opposite the present Somerfield store in Exeter Road.

No. 41, Cullompton Photographic: Formerly

Left: *The Post Office (now Pickwicks).*

E. J. HILL

Purveyor of *Best Ox & Heifer Beef*

MUTTON, LAMB
and
DAIRY FED PORK
DELICIOUS SAUSAGES
PRIME PICKLED BEEF
AND TONGUES

A TRIAL IS ALL THAT WE ASK.

FORE ST., CULLOMPTON

Cullompton Post Office Staff, 1890. Left to right, back row: *W. Field, ? Harris, Bob Rutley, H. Nex, A. Potter, ? Milford, ? Venner, ? Reynolds, J. Nex, ? Sanders, ? Kerslake;* middle row: *J. Harris, J. Reynolds, M. Knight, Mr and Mrs Heard, J. Bale, W. Spurway;* front row: *F. Rugg, F. Taylor, ? Webster, ? Ingersent.*

Frisby's Shoe Shop, which by 1977 had become Marie Footwear.

No. 43, Pickwicks: The original site of the Post Office it was moved to a new purpose-built complex on the opposite side of the road. There was a telephone exchange and telegraphic office here. In the 1930s all the phone numbers in Fore Street only had two numbers. In 1962 the site was occupied by the International Stores and it later became Lewin Peplow Chemist, Wines and Spirits. The chemist moved to Station Road and it then became Peggy's Pantry.

No. 45, First Studio: In 1895 this was Brooks' Ironmongers, owned by George Brooks who was also the fire chief. In the 1930s it was the gas showroom with a workshop down the alley behind. It was later taken over by Barclays Bank and then became Virginia's Hairdressers. It has been a hairdressers ever since, although it has had several different names.

No. 51, vacant shop: Originally part of the Angel Inn this site later became Culm Meat Supplies run by several different people including Bill Hill, Mr Radford and finally Brian Mitchell, who sold the business for development in 2005 when he could find no-one interested in taking it on as a butcher's shop.

No. 53, the Golden Eagle: Was once part of the Angel Inn, which had its licence revoked in 1903. It became a photographic shop, run firstly by Mr Haley, then by George Cross and finally Margery Heard took it over in 1962. It was where everyone went to have their wedding photos and such like taken. When Mrs Heard died the shop was sold to Mr Hong and became a Chinese take-away.

Views of the Neighbourhood

IN GREAT VARIETY.

A. HALEY

Artistic Photography

:: OF EVERY DESCRIPTION ::

The Studio, Cullompton

No. 55, Charcoal Grill : At one time Dick Carter barber's, and later Joe Simmonds barber's and by 1977 had become Mark Hellier & Son Electrical Shop.

No. 57, Community House: This was originally the Rising Sun public house. There is a view that Mr Sellwood was offended by the number of public houses in the town and purchased the Rising Sun for conversion into a YMCA. Later the Labour Exchange, run by Len Dyer, took over the front of the ground floor and the rear was used as a Boys' Club. During the war the ladies of Cullompton ran a teetotal canteen on the ground floor and the old skittle alley from the days when it was a public house was still there.

No. 59, Bill & Taylor Opticians: This site was occupied by Sid Salter, butcher, from the 1930s but by 1977 it was Guys & Dolls Boutique.

No. 61, Cameron's Books and Maps: From the 1930s to the 1950s this was Bill Moore Optician, later to become Dunn's Shoe Shop, Henry's Hair Salon and finally Franks Fencing.

No. 61a, Post Office: Originally the Brethren Chapel, in the 1980s it was a shop selling jeans, t-shirts, etc., with a pool table and gaming machines above.

No. 63, Lavington House: This spot has housed a variety of different office-based companies including Peter Bartlett solicitors. At one time it was owned by a Mr Reynolds who rebuilt Tower View on the opposite side of the road (currently Alfies) it is believed with the intention of setting the building alight as part of an insurance claim. He was sent to prison for setting fire to other property he owned in Cullompton and Exeter.

Mr Haley's photography shop at No. 53 Fore Street (now the Golden Eagle).

The Rising Sun (now Community House) on the corner of Church Street and Fore Street c.1910.

Cullompton Carnival: Cullompton Boys Club. In the photograph are Brian Gillard, Bill Bird and Edmund Pratt, c.1950.

No. 65, Claremont House: In the late 1980s this was Cullompton Antique and Collectors' Centre and later became Mid-Devon District Council's Office but this closed in March 2007. Claremont House has traditionally been occupied by the police; not only did the Sergeant live at the police station but the Superintendent of the Division also lived here.

On the Opposite Side of the Road...

No. 66, Hatch a Hobby, formerlyTenboly, was originally a private house, the home of Mr and Mrs Mingo who farmed at the bottom of Middle Mill Lane, it later became Mrs Sanders' Newsagents until about 1996. It was Patch Pocket in the early 2000s

No. 66, Craft Centre: In the 1930s this was Battens Butcher's and all the carcasses were hung outside. It later became Mr Vicary's Newsagents and then Mrs Sanders took it over in about 1976, though she later moved next door. In recent years it has also been a taxi office and secondhand book shop.

No. 64, Dynamix Hair Salon: In the 1930s this was Rossiter's Chemist and by 1962 it was E.E. Langdon's Chemist with Mr Nolan Trezise running the pharmacy. It later opened as Nikki's Hair Salon and recently became Dynamix.

No. 62, Nanna's Toy Chest: In 1851 this was a butcher's shop owned by John Read, in 1891 it appears to have become Alfred Battens butcher's shop and in 1901 Sarah Ann Budd, grocer and shopkeeper was registered as living here. From about 1920 it became Battens Cycle Shop until about the late 1950s when it became Maynards Cycle Shop. Culm Florist moved here from the shop a couple of doors up, it was then Crossley & Son Undertakers for a short time and was empty for a while before re-opening as Nanna's Toy Chest in 2006.

No. 60, vacant shop: In 1891 this was a furniture shop and in 1901 the census records show Lester Archer, tobacconist, was living here. The property was rebuilt by Mr Reynolds and in 1911 it was taken over by Mr and Mrs Easterbrook who sold sweets and tobacco. Len Rogers, Edith Easterbrook's son from her first marriage, spoke of cycling out to the station to collect buckets of ice from the train, which was then carried to the outhouse in Shepherd's Court at the rear of the shop to make ice-cream. This had to be done before going to school or work. Tobacco or snuff were kept in jars behind the counter and weighed out in small packets. It was usual for snuff to be bought in quarter ounces (5 gms) in small triangular bags and tobacco in ounces (25 gms).

E. Easterbrook's sweetshop and tobacconist, 60 Fore Street, in the 1950s.

Fore Street with Battens Cycle Shop in the foreground (left) *in the 1940s.*

Above: *Fore Street 1953.*

Left: *Fore Street c.1960.*

In 1918 Leonard went to work for Alfred Burrow, solicitor, but went back to run the shop when his mother retired in 1948. Leonard and Beatrice Rogers retired in the 1980s and the premises was converted for use as a hairdresser's called 'Haircraft' for many years, run by Janet Slater. The shop was closed in 2006 when she retired.

No. 56/58, vacant shop: Originally two shops this became one when Mr Cowley moved his electrical business here in about 1970. In the 1930s one shop sold wallpaper, etc., and was run by Mr Gardner and the other was Culm Weavers, which was run by Mrs Batten who sold knitted clothes and had a workshop at the back.

In the 1930s No. 56 was a fruit and vegetable shop run by Arthur Hellier, who was also a prominent Cullompton cricketer. In the 1970s the shop was taken over by Mr Knowles who had been a farmer at Paulsland Farm, on the outskirts of Cullompton. He ran it as a Farm Shop before it was taken over by Liz and Brian Wakeley who later moved to No. 62.

No. 54/52: Originally the Globe Inn this site became the Rugby Club in the 1960s. The building was later a shop occupied by Applegates off-licence and then it was converted to two shops which have both had a number of tenants. No. 54 has been a pet shop, Options, and a bike shop while No. 52 has been Weigh-it, a Sue Ryder shop and is now a Hospiscare charity shop.

No. 50, Crossley's Funeral Directors: In 1841 this site was a bakers and continued to be a bakers until 2005 when it was purchased by the Crossley family, who are funeral directors. Other owners have included Culm Bakery, Grants Bakery (1952) Bailey's Bakery, Thos Hart (1851) and Agnes Paisley (1881–1901).

No. 48/46, Alfies: In 1851 it belonged to John Benham, clock- and watchmaker but by 1881 it had become Devon Stores owned by Thomas Purchase. It later became Kelly Luxton's Furniture Store, then Welsh's Furniture Store. It was divided into two shops and became David Broom Drapers from the mid-1970s until Mr and Mrs Broom retired in 1999.

No. 46, Alfies: In the 1950s this site was occupied by Murray's Barber's with a ladies' hairdresser's upstairs. It later became Mr Vile's Barber's and then had a variety of tenants before being merged once again with No. 48.

No. 40, Hairmania: In the 1930s this was the private residence of the Ellicott family that ran the bakery next door. Taylor's China and Glass of

WM. BROOM

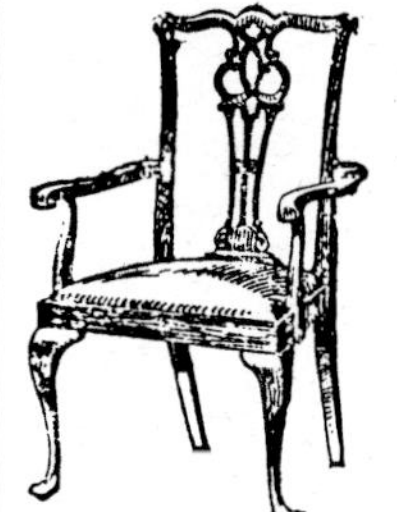

Manufacturer of Furniture

Restorer of Antiques

AND

General House Furnisher

ESTIMATES FREE.

Fore Street——CULLOMPTON

Fore Street with Devon Stores in the foreground, c.1925.

Taunton opened in the 1970s and it later became Dave Edwards Bookmakers until they moved further up the street.

No. 38, Peggy's Pantry: In 1891 this was George Brooks' Ironmongers and by 1901 it was Ellicott's Bakers, where bread and cakes were baked on site. It was a thriving business from the 1930s until the 1970s. In recent years it has been run as Jumping Frogs card shop and Lawes Electrical.

No. 36/34 Post Office Sorting Office: This was originally a double-fronted shop. In 1841 it was a drapery and remained as such for many years. By 1901 it was owned by Bowermans Drapers and House Furnisher. They sold all sorts of things including china which would be stacked up on the pavement outside. It became the Post Office in 1937.

No. 32, Murray's Fruit & Veg: John Knight is recorded as living here in the 1881, 1891 and 1901 census. In the 1930s it was Sharland's Dairy. A lovely bowl of clotted cream was often displayed in the window and they must have sold quite a lot of it because it never seemed to go off – but then nobody worried too much about health and safety back then. Indeed, Mrs Muriel Coxhead can remember seeing a few flies buzzing around it. This site has had a number of tenants including Tipples, Kingdoms Drapers and Dry Cleaners , Gone Bananas and J & L Cosmetics.

No. 30, Veysey Butchers: The oldest retail business in the town centre. In 1851 William Weald, butcher, was here, but Alfred Veysey purchased the shop from Ian Hornsey in c.1890 and the premises have been owned and run as a butcher's shop by the Veysey family ever since. The shop was closed for a while during the First World War and when Harold Veysey decided to reopen the shop he needed to find seven people willing to use their ration books in his shop. He had difficulty finding those seven customers as people felt he had let them down by closing the shop.

There was a slaughterhouse at the back of the shop but it eventually became uneconomic to slaughter their own cattle so this was closed in 1999. Until that

S. J. SHARLAND

Caters Especially for Tourists Picnic Baskets

DEVONSHIRE CLOTTED CREAM a Speciality.

DAIRY PRODUCE and TRUSSED POULTRY sent to all Parts.

The Dairy House, CULLOMPTON

JOHN VEYSEY

Family Butcher

HOME-MADE SAUSAGES A SPECIALITY.

Fore Street .·. Cullompton

Four American servicemen who were stationed in Cullompton. The Assembly Rooms (now the Masonic Hall) was their 'mess' and they became regulars at the Half Moon Inn, which was then owned by Mrs Percy and Mr and Mrs Cross.

time Veysey's had slaughtered all the meat for themselves and Culm Meat Supply on the opposite side of the road.

No. 28, vacant shop: Originally the Dolphin Inn, it is listed in the 1841 census and in 1903 it had a yard with stabling for 15 or 16 horses and plenty of bedroom accommodation. It had its licence taken way in the 1920s as there were too many pubs in the town. It was subsequently empty for several years until it became the Dolphin Fish & Chip Shop in around 1936, selling very good fish and chips. By the the 1950s it was Tancock's Ironmongers, and later became Bolhams Dry Cleaners, then the Co-op, Cullompton General Stores and finally Gone Bananas, which closed in 2006.

No. 26, Westward Counties Insurance Brokers: This was a grocer's store at least between 1861 and 1901. In the 1920s it was Cullompton Weavers run by Mrs Gidley who revived the hand-weaving trade with a handloom at the back of the shop. Mr Terry ran the shop for Mrs Gidley and it became Terry Weavers. In 1932 Mr Terry bought the shop and it became Terry's Electrics and later Acland's Radio and TV in 1960. Mr Cowley was the manager and he later took over the shop and moved the business to larger premises.

No. 24, Tavy Textiles: Originally an inn known as the Three Mariners it changed its name to the Half Moon Inn. It was owned by the Percy family who also owned the Assembly Rooms behind. A succession of troops were stationed in Cullompton during the Second World War and the soldiers were billeted in various halls throughout the town. The Assembly Rooms became their mess, while the mess kitchen was situated in The Green (where the British Legion bowling alley is now).

Mr and Mrs Cross became particularly friendly with some of the American soldiers billeted in Cullompton towards the end of the war. The inn was sold to Whitbread in 1945. It later became a textile shop called Forty Winks selling household textiles.

The Assembly Rooms, now the Masonic Hall, was used for dances, etc., in the 1930s and '40s with Ron Harris and his band, including Harry Chubb, Ken Dyer on the piano and singer Jim Kerslake.

Percy Cross, whose parents ran the Half Moon, can remember being given a knife and a candle to prepare the floor for dances; he would flick thin slices of candle wax onto the floor so that it was suitable for the 'soft shoe shuffle'. For many years Cullompton Amateur Dramatic Society put on two plays a year here and the Pantomime Club performed their annual pantomime here until 2004.

No. 22, Saunders Pet Shop: In 1871, 1881 and 1891 the census shows the premises as belonging to John and Ann Budd, grocers. In the 1930s Mr Frost, a tailor, had the shop. He used to sit crosslegged on the floor making trousers, etc. It then became Phil

Tavy Textiles; Winners of the Best Dressed Christmas Window Competition, 2004. Back, left to right: *Judith Trevellyan, Beverley Palfrey, Irene Kerslake (Tavy Textiles);* Front: *(holding certificate) Rebecca ? and Alison Palmer.*

Hand Woven Tweeds
AND
High grade Knit Wear
TO TONE.

ENTIRELY OUR
OWN PRODUCTIONS.

Look for the Name.

——TERRY,——

Warwick House, Cullompton.

'Phone 2249 CENTRAL CORN STORES 76
FORE STREET, CULLOMPTON

Received of ....

By **H. F. HEARD**

EGG AND POULTRY MERCHANT. LICENSED DEALER — IN GAME —

	CHICKEN
	HENS
	DUCKS
	RABBITS (Trapped)
	„ (Shot)
	GEESE
	PHEASANTS
	PARTRIDGES
	TURKEYS

TELEPHONE: CULLOMPTON 2278

PRIVATE ADDRESS: "WOODHEY," 4 LOWER HILL BARTON ROAD, EXETER
TELEPHONE: EXETER 67970

A. G. HEYWOOD

MILLER, CORN & CAKE MERCHANT
LOWER MILLS, CULLOMPTON

19

CWTS

5366 LOWER MILL, CULLOMPTON 'Phone: CULLOMPTON 2278 Date 19
RECEIVED from
the sum of Pounds
Shillings Pence
Cash
Cheque
Returns
Discount
Total £
A. G. HEYWOOD
Per

YOU MAY DEDUCT .... DISCOUNT IF PAID BY ....

Fore Street, c.1960, with Acland Electrical in the foreground.

F. WELLINGTON
High Class Confectionery
TOBACCO, CIGARETTES
CIGARS, ETC., ETC.
PURE SWEETS
Speciality:—ICES—in Season
FORE ST., CULLOMPTON

MURRAY T. FOSTER
M.P.S.
Pharmacist
Wine and Spirit Merchant
"Tonax" The Tonic Wine
Seed Merchant
COLLUMPTON, DEVON

STATEMENT EST. 1798 TELEPHONE: 2279 DAY AND NIGHT
WINE · SPIRIT AND ALE MERCHANTS · SEEDSMEN
M. T. FOSTER LTD.
MANAGING DIRECTOR: N. T. TREZISE, M.P.S. DIRECTOR & SECRETARY E. M. TREZISE
SUPPLIERS OF VETERINARY MEDICINES · CHEMISTS · AGRICULTURAL HORTICULTURAL & DAIRY REQUISITES
14, FORE STREET, CULLOMPTON.
DEVON
M A.W.Shere,Esq., Mutterton Dairy, Cullompton. 31 DEC 1963 19
31 DEC 1963

DATE	REF. NO.	DETAILS	DEBITS	CREDITS	BALANCE
1963 Oct/Nov.		A/C			10 3 4
Dec 10	298			19 5	2 3 11
3	164	1			2 14 5
18	342	1x6			
					5 4 2
1964 Jan 7	23			3 11	3 - 3

3-3-1964
RECEIVED from Mr A Shere
the Sum of Three Pounds
— Shillings on behalf of M. T. FOSTER LIMITED
and Three Pence
WITH THANKS
£ 3-0-3

Sweet's Toys and China and then Mrs Saunders' Toys and China. The business closed in the 1980s since when it has been a mobile phone shop and Streamers cards and sweets, who moved across the road.

No. 20, Ye Olde Tea Shoppe: Once the premises of William Broom, cabinetmaker, who also had a workshop in The Green, in what is now the British Legion. He sold furniture and other bits and pieces here.

No. 18/16, Prescotts: In the 1930s this was a sweetshop run by Mr Wellington and then it became an exclusive hat and gown shop run by Mrs Cole; her name was Lavinia and so was the shop. Many older town residents still refer to the shop as Lavinia's. The shop was then purchased by Mr Nolan Trezise and managed by his wife prior to the property being purchased by Mr and Mrs Wickham.

No. 14, Alliance Pharmacy: Established in 1798 and originally the Fountain Inn it had a licence to sell alcohol until very recently. In 1841 it belonged to the Foster family and later became known as Foster's Chemist. Although it has had several owners the name stayed the same until 2005 when it was changed to Moss Chemist and then Alliance. Murray Foster was a very prominent figure in Cullompton: as well as being a chemist he wrote a history of the town.

Mr Nolan Trezise took over the pharmacy in the 1940s and was joined by Mr and Mrs Wickham in 1968. In the 1930s Muriel Coxhead remembers it being a proper Victorian chemist with big bottles of coloured fluid in the window, which all chemist shops had in those days. There was a long counter along the left-hand side and behind it there were drawers with all sorts of drugs, herbs, etc., painted on the front. The chemists took pinches out of the drawers and made up pills, powders, etc., with these ingredients.

No. 12, Early Days: Nos 10 and 12 were originally one shop and for a long time was a drapery. In 1861 John Bowerman is recorded as owning the premises employing two girls and two boys in his draper's shop (he had another shop further along Fore Street). It later became Welch's Ladies' and Gents' Wear, David Martin Outfitters and Eulay Ltd. It was eventually divided in two and No. 12 became Toogoods selling items such as costume jewellery, handbags, general nick-nacks and gifts.

No. 10, Dave Edwards Bookmakers: Previously a dry cleaners, it was also a sports shop.

No. 8, The Merchant's House: In 1841 Richard Western is recorded as living here, and he was still here in 1881 but in 1891 the house was empty and in 1901 it was 'used for business only'. Mr Frederic Burrow had his solicitor's offices here and the practice was taken over by his son Alfred Burrow. Following his death in the 1940s it was, in turn, taken over by the Nichols family solicitors and then Ashford Sparkes and Harward until the office closed in 1994.

An extension was added to the rear of the property soon after the Second World War and a solicitor and his family lived there for some years. Later the modern extension was used as a print works and then as a courtyard café. The property was also used for a secondhand book shop before being auctioned in 1996.

No. 6, The Walronds: In 1551 it was owned by Henry Paris and then his son and granddaughter Emlyn who married John Peters or Petres of Compton Pool. Emlyn and John enlarged and enhanced the property between 1578 and 1605, since when it has remained largely unchanged. In 1785 it was owned by the Portman family and purchased by Revd John Sydenham in 1825. In 1888 it was acquired by Frederic Burrow who carried out extensive repairs to the property. His son Alfred also owned the property for many years and let it to numerous tenants including the Plumpton family who lived there in the 1920s.

The first Catholic church in the town was established at the rear of the property by Mrs Plumpton and Mrs De Las Casas. When St Boniface Church was built the chapel was unused until it was leased to the nuns from the Order of the Sister of Mercy who ran a convent school at Heyford House. It was then leased to a number of different people until it was purchased by Miss Severn and her aunt Miss Yeoman.

No. 4, Veryards: Home of Mr Edwin Lawrence in the 1930s. Mr Lawrence was a missionary but retired to live in the house in the 1970s. During his absence it was leased to a number of families and after his death it was sold and incorporated into the Manor House Hotel.

No. 2, Manor House Hotel: Built as a private house, it is thought that the original house consisted of the present front part only – i.e. three rooms with a passage on the ground floor with three rooms above which opened into each other, plus attics

The Merchant's House, Fore Street, c.1930.

The Walronds (foreground), *c.1930s.*

Guigette Langran (née Plumpton) and her brother Peter Plumpton at the Walronds, their family home, 1920s.

Veryards: home of Mr Edwin Lawrence in the 1930s and later incorporated into the Manor House Hotel.

above. The title deeds show it to have been in the occupation of: Thomas Trock (on the top corners of the front are panels that are inscribed '1603 T.T'. and 'T.T. – A'); Henry Skinner; John Kerslake; William Sellocke (Sellick); Bernard Wright, surgeon; John Garrett, Clerk 1785; William Tanner 1791; Robert Baker 1791; William Upcott 1828; John Samuel Upcott 1842.

Thomas Trock was probably the T.T. of the inscription and may have been the builder but it is thought that the original house was probably built in the sixteenth century and refurbished by T.T. in 1603.

The Ainsworth family lived in the house in the 1930s but during the Second World War it was requisitioned by the army and the officers were billeted here. The iron railings outside were removed as part of the war effort. After the war the owners of the house opened part of the property as a tearoom. Mr Neville Jones and his wife ran it as a hotel in the 1950s and carried out a great deal of work to the property before moving to take over the Cullompton Hotel (now Heyridge Meadow).

Manor House, the iron railings were removed during the Second World War to make munitions as part of the war effort, c.1928.

Fore Street, c.1949.

Cullompton Pantomime, c.1974. The picture includes: *Linda Wilbourne, Sandra Chambers, SallyAnn Herring, Susan Check, Beverley Brookes, Susan Attewell.*

Chapter Nine

Exeter Hill, Exeter Road and New Street

Hebron Hall (on the corner of Cockpit Hill), Christmas party in the late 1950s.

Cockpit Hill

On the corner of Cockpit Hill and Exeter Hill, where Aspen Properties is located, was for many years Heards corn merchants and poulturers. The Heard family also ran a transport business from the yard further down Cockpit Hill opposite the entrance to Brooke Road. Their transport depot on the corner of Queen Square was originally the workshops of Luxton's who made furniture to order.

At the back of the shop there was a little fridge which would be full of boiling hens, rabbits or pheasant according to season. Heards acted as a collection point for turkeys; people brought their turkeys in and during December the company would transport thousands of turkeys to Bristol and sell them on the market. During the big freeze of 1962/63 one farmer was unable to get his turkeys into town and instead stored them in a shed. By the time they went to collect them ten weeks later they were frozen solid but perfectly fresh.

Pound Square, early 1900s.

Further down Cockpit Hill is Hongs Fish and Chip Shop, this was once the Crown and Thistle public house.

On the corner of Cockpit Hill and Pound Square is the Unitarian Chapel. In about 1695 the congregation built a meeting house which remained until 1814 when another was built on the same site as it was considered dangerous. Jerome Murch in a *History of the Presbyterian and General Baptist Churches in the West of England* published in 1835 wrote:

> *... adjoining the chapel are two schoolrooms, of still more modern date, used for the religious instruction of about sixty boys and girls. The congregation also support a library, a fellowship fund and a brotherly society. These institutions have lessened the evils of ignorance and poverty and strengthened the union that subsists among the worshipers. In promoting the happiness and improvement of this interesting society their pastor, Mr Yeates, has been lately assisted by Mr N.S. Heineken.*

Sunday School prize-giving at the Unitarian Chapel, February 1957. Left to right, back row: *Tony Moore, Margaret Clarke, Martin Rutley, Jean Din?;* middle row: *? Veale, Janet Moore, ? Joan Rutley, ?;* front row: *Roger Hill, Caroline White, Lynette Rutley, Decima Veale.*

Harvest Supper at the Unitarian Chapel, 1958.

Right: *Cullompton Secondary Modern: Prefects' Room Rules, 1962.*

DEVON COUNTY EDUCATION COMMITTEE

Headmaster:
F. A. CHAPMAN

Telephone:
CULLOMPTON 3164

THE COUNTY SECONDARY SCHOOL
CULLOMPTON
DEVON

17/9/62.

PREFECTS ROOM - RULES OF.

1. Room to be kept CLEAN and TIDY.
2. No marking on walls.
3. Prefects only allowed in room.
4. Windows to be closed every night.
5. Prefects not to enter attic.

PREFECTS:

Head Girl - Susan Young Deputy Head - Queenie Cole.
Head Boy - David Abrahams Deputy Head - Alan Sleigh.

Denise Carnell
Elizabeth Medcroft
Mary Jarvis
Patricia Hodge.

Allen Broom.
Peter Goffin.
Stuart Kemp.
Michael Palmer.

Cullompton Secondary Modern School outing to Bristol Zoo, 23 June 1949.

This chapel collapsed in 1911 and the present chapel was erected in 1913.

Exeter Hill

There were several shops on Exeter Hill but these have all gradually closed. In 1977 No. 7 was Fresh Farm Supplies and No. 9 was Heritage Crafts. Other shops on this side of Exeter Hill in years past have included: Nex Bicycle Repairs, Kingdoms Drapers and Tailors, Eales fruit and veg and Forse Butchers.

On the opposite side of the road where the Magistrates' Court and Health Centre is now was the site of the original school.

The public elementary school on Exeter Hill was an edifice of brick with stone dressing in the Elizabethan style built in 1872 from designs by architect W.H. Stafford Esq., at a cost of £2,000. In 1893–94 the school was enlarged at a cost of about £500 for 240 boys, 200 girls and 250 infants. In 1914 the average attendance was 165 boys, 144 girls and 127 infants. Mrs Muriel Coxhead recalls:

There was only one school in Cullompton and the children went to the same school until they were 14. The bakers used to bring a tray of buns for the children, a halfpenny for plain and a penny for fruit buns. The mothers used to give their children money to buy buns to have with their midday milk, it was a third of a pint of milk for all schoolchildren.

In 1921 when Audrey Abbott was six years old she won a knitting competition at the school. She won a shilling which was an awful lot of money to a six year old. In 1937 St Andrews Primary School was built for the younger children and it eventually became 'Cullompton Senior Secondary School Mixed'. It closed in 1964 following the construction of a new school in Exeter Road.

Next door to the Health Centre is the public library. In the 1930s this was the Co-op which contained a provisions counter and bakery on the left and, on the right, a drapery and shoe shop, with furnishings upstairs. The Co-op later moved to Fore Street and the library moved from premises on the opposite side of the road.

Above: *Staff and friends at Cullompton Secondary Modern School's centenary, 1970.*

Right: *Cullompton Secondary Modern School centenary, 1970. Left to right: ?, Mr F. Chapman (former headmaster), Mr K. Edwards (headmaster).*

The private dwelling that is now No. 4 Exeter Hill was Mrs Farrant's wool shop during the 1980 and '90s. It then had a number of tenants before being converted into flats.

No. 12, the Pony & Trap: Formerly the Commercial Inn and renamed in 1976. Mrs Pring, wife of the then landlord Mr Alan Pring, suggested changing the name in memory of Mr Oburn (Obi) Luxton and his horse Snowball who was stabled under the skittle alley for many years. The pub sign hence shows Mr Luxton and Snowball. It is thought that the pub may have originally been called the Admiral Hawke.

The private dwelling that is now No. 16 Exeter Hill was L. & S. Insurance Brokers until the early 2000s.

Exeter Road

The house on the corner of Crow Green and Fore Street was at one time H. Battens, a butcher's shop before they moved to Fore Street. They displayed some big bullock horns over the door *(see below)*.

The shop on the corner at the entrance to the Old Tannery was at one time Vicary's card shop and later a newsagents and tobacconist.

Commercial Inn Darts Champions, c.1959 (now the Pony & Trap). Left to right, back row: *Anstey Lane, Frank Ewings, Dennis Pollard;* front row: *Norman Gooding, Jack Luxton, Cecil Barrs, Charlie Radford, Sid Stiling and Lou Webb.*

H. Batten, butcher's shop on the corner of Crow Green and Exeter Road.

Presentation to Major Sellwood on his retirement from the tannery. Included in the photograph are: *Major Sellwood and Mrs Sellwood, Mr Percy, Mr Brook, Mr Rainey, Mr Greenslade, Mr Denner, Mr Hales, Mr Lane, Mr Gillard, Mr Jones, Mr C. Hodge, Mr Radford, Mr Hooper.*

Above: *Fire at the Sellwood Bros tannery (currently the site of Somerfield supermarket), October 1958.*

Left: *Jaffa House, Brooke Road. This was originally the home of the Sellwood family who owned the tanyard adjacent.*

The Bell Inn, Exeter Road, c.1910.

Exeter Road with, what is now Cherry Tree Stores, in the foreground.

The Old Tannery Industrial Estate was, at one time, all part of Sellwood Bros (Tanneries) Ltd, and the main building is where Somerfield supermarket is now situated. It later became Tremletts Tannery.

Jaffa House, thought to have got its name from a biblical quote about Simon the tanner who came from Joppa or Jaffa, was the home of the tannery owners, the Sellwood family. The foreman's cottage was in Way's Lane.

The Bell Inn has been on the same site since at least 1856 when it was listed as the 'New Bell Inn', as at that time there was also a Bell Inn near the church. The Himalayan was previously the Silver Bridge Fish and Chip Shop and The Golden Lion was previously called the Inglenook Restaurant, but was renamed the Golden Lion when it was purchased by Mr Cheung in 2004.

Cherry Tree Stores (Nos 106–110) was started by Joe Dyer in his front room between 1913 and 1914, but at that time it was called Joe Dyers Café and Ice Cream Parlour; he later renamed it Cherry Tree Stores after the tree in the garden. In 1957 Harold Denning took over the shop and in 1963 the top two cottages were pulled down and a new shop, Dennings, was built. It was later taken over by Ivor and Greta Brock and renamed Brocks, until Mrs Jean Baker purchased the store in around 2002 and changed the name back to Cherry Tree.

Padbrook Park, originally farmland and mentioned as far back as the Domesday Book, was purchased by the Chard family in 1963 who farmed there until selling off some of the land for housing development in the late 1980s. The money was used to develop the golf complex which was started in 1991 and officially opened in March 1992. The complex included the golf course and pavilion suite, an indoor bowls rink and a fitness studio. The complex was sold to Mr and Mrs Gary Scargill in October 2003 and the hotel bedroom block was opened in 2005. At the time of writing planning permission is being sought to expand the golf course from nine holes to eighteen.

Toad Hall was demolished in 2006 to make way for housing development. Originally known as the Cullompton Hotel it was built in 1930 as a

Above and below: *Stages in the building work at Padbrook Park.*

Left: *John Chard assisting with demolition work at Padbrook Park, c.1990.*

Above: *The building in the foreground was originally a golf shop but is now the Hair and Beauty salon.*

Padbrook Park, 1992. The golf course can be seen behind the main buildings.

The Cullompton Hotel

EXETER ROAD
CULLOMPTON

Telephone:
Reception 2272
Residents 2445

EAST DEVON and THE CULLOMPTON HOTEL

The beauty of Devon attracts people from all over the world. The County is fortunate in offering numerous places of beauty and interest. In the centre of these places is situated the attractive building and gardens of the CULLOMPTON HOTEL. The Hotel is set in five acres of garden. It is a purpose built hotel built in 1932 by local Master Builders to an exceedingly high standard of construction. The stone mullions and stone windows are unique and the design is of early eighteenth century. Truly a magnificent building.

CULLOMPTON HOTEL specialises in Weddings, Private Parties, Conferences, Meetings etc. large or small, the service especially congenial, friendly and personal.

This hotel is popular as a base for holidaymakers who like to visit more than one resort, there are many holiday resorts within one hours journey from the hotel.

FOYER – This Foyer is impressive and unusual. Instantly welcoming by its homely atmosphere.

POLYGON LOUNGE BAR – A small intimate Bar. Popular for the very wide selection of drinks and cocktails available. Adjacent is a Lounge Bar for those who like space and comfort while out for an evening.

FUNCTION ROOM BAR – tasteful and efficient Bar to cope with 200 persons.

HOW TO FIND US:

Travelling south on the M5 motorway will bring you into the lovely county of Devon.

Coming off the motorway at junction 28, drive through the country town of Cullompton and on the right hand side is the impressively built Cullompton Hotel.

In this Hotel awaits good service and hospitality of experienced proprietors and staff who are concerned with making your visit a pleasant one.

EXPLORING:

The Hotel is within easy reach of Exmoor and Dartmoor and many fossil areas in Devon. There are Trout Fishing facilities within minutes of the Hotel. Several Golf Courses in the vicinity. Two National Trust Houses are within ten minutes car ride from the Hotel. Knightshaye with its beautiful formal gardens and Killerton Park with its fine old house and miles of parkland.

Cullompton Hotel promotional leaflet, c.1980.

purpose-built hotel and gentlemen's club and included what is now the Culm Valley Bowling Club. Its name was changed to Toad Hall in 1988 when it was purchased by Mr Peter Radford and partners. It changed hands a couple of years later and the new owners went into the liquidation and the premises were empty for some time before being purchased by the Mana and converted into a residential home. It was sold for development in 2005.

New Street

In years gone by New Street was decorated with oak branches on Whit Monday and the street had its own 'revel' and 'mayor choosing'. Climbing a greasy pole for a leg of mutton was a feature of the festival. There were sports in the street and a carnival atmosphere.

When John Wesley came to Cullompton he preached in a little orchard at one end of New Street where Vickery Close now stands.

Years ago many of the properties were rented at 1s.9d. a week and before mains water was available people paid 1d. to dip water from a well at the dairy which was opposite No. 30 New Street. At one time five houses here could have been bought for £200.

In June 1972 a report from the *Devon & Somerset News* visited New Street and met some of the residents. Mr Bill Hodge, for example, had lived in New Street all of his 81 years. He explained that instead of being rented the majority of homes were now privately owned and various businesses such as a dairy, a coal merchant, a sweetshop and bake houses had disappeared. Mr Hodge remembered the August carthorse parade at Cullompton.

Mr Hodge left school at the age of 12 and started work for 3s. a week in the Chick's Foundry in Middle Mill Lane. At that time sixpence would buy a pint of beer, a 'screw of baccy', a clay pipe and a box of matches – leaving a halfpenny change. He then became an ostler at the White Hart before army service in Mesopotamia.

After leaving the army he worked for 26 years at Kingsmill and was then at the local tannery until the disastrous fire of 1958. He then went to work part-time for the Post Office and retired in 1971.

Left: *Duke Street before Rivermead was built, August 1952.*

Below: *Cullompton Carnival, Duke Street (now Cullompton Community College playing-fields), 1950.* Left to right, back row: *?, June Rutley, Margaret Whitfield;* front row: *Martin Rutley, Jean Whitfield, Lynnette Rutley, Celia Force, Bert Whitfield.*

TO THE PEACEABLE

ELECTORS

OF THE

BOOT QUARTER,

OF THE TOWN OF

COLLUMPTON.

GENTLEMEN,

In presenting myself before you as a Candidate for the office of Mayor I desire to draw your attention to my fitness for that important post by reminding you of the many and varied occupations I am now so successfully engaged in, though ill-tempered people say I have too many irons in the fire.

My upright character will I believe, cause me to fill the office of Mayor with credit to myself & satisfaction to the residents in the Quarter, for if elected I am determined to keep order amongst you by supplying all necessary information to the Police, so as to suppress all wrong doing, especially drunkenness & gambling in Public Houses, and by closing and doing away with all Skittle Allies in the Quarter.

I can with confidence promise to attend to all the affairs of this district in a proper manner for having lately given up an un-important situation under Government in consequence of the slowness of promotion and from a sense of my general unfitness, I have some leisure time on my hands.

If you do me the honour of electing me, I should be glad to discharge the duty of Mayor on condition I receive a suitable recompense for my services, as the heavy expenses recently incurred by me in the Law Courts, do not incline me to do anything gratuitously.

Believe me, Gentlemen,

To remain, yours respectfully,

PASTE-POT.

Dated, Sneak's Terrace, May 14th, 1875.

As part of New Street's Whit Monday celebrations it traditionally had its own 'revel' and 'mayor choosing' ceremony. The above gives an insight into this election process for one of the candidates in May 1875.

Above: *Coronation Day celebrations, 1953, in the grounds of what is now Cullompton Community College.* Included in the photograph are: *Betty Stocker (née Wellington), Dianne Tolhurst (née Sanders), Jill Tolhurst (née Gunn), Janet Clarke, Arthur Tolhurst, Gertie Tolhurst, Mrs O'Neil, Joyce Cross, Betty Cross (née Patchett), Ted Sampson with daughter Margaret on his shoulders, Mrs Bellamy, Miss Bake (schoolteacher), Ernest Hill's four daughters, Mrs Hake with daughter Sarah, ? Voisey, Mary Grabham, Mrs Hooper, Mr and Mrs Shopland, Barbara Shopland (née Budd), Mr Jones, Terry Jones, Rita Jones (née Wheller) John Cross, Diane Bellamy, Mrs Budd.*

Left: *New Street on Coronation Day 1953.* Left to Right: *Olive Gold, Stephen Gooding (in pram) and Mavis Gooding.*

The Golgotha.

The pulpit.

The font.

Chapter Ten

The Parish Church of St Andrew

By Percy Cross

Church parade at St Andrews Church.

The Church lays away from Fore Street down its own 'Church Lane', which for some unexplained reason in these latter years has become known as Church Street.

Cullompton's Parish Church of St Andrew stands as a proud monument to the English Perpendicular Gothic Style. The tower, roof, screen and the Lane's and Moore's aisles or chapels, are all well preserved. The tower was built somewhat later than the main structure. It is built of sandstone and is dressed with Ham stone. It is adorned with small pinnacles and gargoyles astride the tops of the buttresses.

The west-facing front of the tower bears a fine clock; the present chimes were installed in the middle of the 19th century. It also bears a sculptured Ham-stone plaque, depicting the crucifixion. This is one of the few things that shows severe signs of deterioration; it is true that Ham stone is notoriously susceptible to erosion, but here, however, it appears to have been uncommonly selective. The heads of the Christ and of the two persons standing below on either side are completely missing, whilst the rest of the sculpture remains almost intact. I recall that during my infancy, sitting in the church attending Sunday school, we children were given the explanation of the 'missing heads' by the then incumbent: Revd Watkins-Grubb. He explained to us that during the English Civil War, a contingent of Parliamentary troops passed through Cullompton and on seeing the sculpture and being fervently Puritan, they condemned it as being idolatrous and an offence to their religion. They set up their firearms and executed the beheadings with powder and ball. Giving due respect to a Clerk in Holy Orders, this explanation may be apocryphal, but it does have a certain fanciful air and could be true. It is certainly a plausible explanation to the strangely selective pattern of erosion.

Before moving to the interior it is interesting to examine the north and south sides of the building; they are in distinct contrast, the north being modest whilst the south is ostentatious. This difference is even more apparent when one enters the church.

The first impression on stepping inside from under the west face of the tower is magnificence. The Ionic columns gently lead one's eye forward to the screen and upwards to Cullompton's highly renowned roof; although a 'wagon roof', it differs from others by having cross braces that one would expect to see with a flat roof. All are richly worked, each post having a carved angel. The church is said by some to be the church of a hundred angels. Above the screen, dividing chancel from nave there is a highly decorated rood beam bearing a coat of arms.

The screen was restored in the middle of the twentieth century, just after the end of the Second World War; those of us who remember it prior to its restoration, recall it had a beautifully carved plain-wood appearance of medium oak hue. One recalls that at the time there was a great divergence of opinion between those that supported the restoration and enhancement and those who felt it should remain as it was. Those in favour of restoration won the day.

After the work had been completed the pro-restoration faction itself became divided, some declaring that it was a beautiful enrichment to the church, whilst others proclaimed they had not expected it 'to go so far', being a most unnecessary 'gilding of the lily'. The controversy simmered on for some time but finally faded. The decorated screen still remains, to be admired by many, for its bright colours that are set off by the whiteness of the walls and pale stone dressings.

The contrast between the north and south exterior continues once inside the church. There are two aisles abutting the nave: on the north lays Moore's aisle and on the south, Lane's aisle. These aisles are testament to the rivalry between two families. The Moore's of Moorhayes House were typical wealthy landed gentry, whilst John Lane was in today's parlance an 'incomer', a cloth merchant of extreme wealth: a 'wool man'. They were the church's two main benefactors of their age, c.1520.

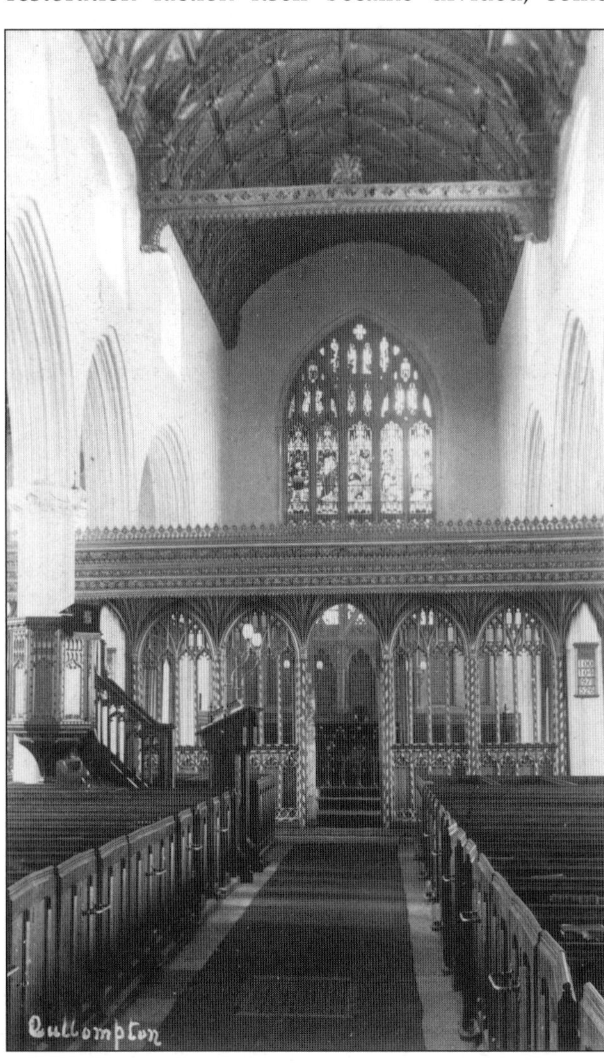

Moore's aisle.

Lane's aisle.

They were, however, very serious rivals. A full architectural description of these aisles would fill many pages; suffice it to say that if there has to be a winner, it has to be Lane. The Moore aisle is most admirable, but dims when compared with that of Lane; it is advantaged by its western aspect, thus being well lit on sunny days. Its pale stone fan-vaulted roof, a very rare sight in a parish church of this size, reflects the sunlight, creating a mood of soaring splendour. A very fine and exceptional Burne-Jones stained-glass window adds to this grandeur. At its southern end is piled the base of a medieval rood carved Golgotha: a most historic piece. It is perhaps that its skulls and bones are too harrowing for modern tastes that it does not occupy a more prominent place, as it did during my childhood.

There is a small chapel at the northeast corner of the church in which is laid the Stars and Stripes: the flag of the United States of America. There is a plaque on the wall bearing the names of the American servicemen who were billeted in Cullompton and later fell in the Second World War.

There have been many benefactors to this parish church, both past and present and one that stands out is William Froude Esq., who lived in Cullompton during the 1840s. He had chosen Cullompton to make his home because it lay approximately halfway between both Exeter and Taunton, and Plymouth and Bristol; for he was Brunel's chief engineer on this stretch of the Great Western Railway. Froude was a pious and wealthy man and he worshipped in St Andrews Church. He stated that the interior roof was in need of refurbishment. He offered, out of his personal purse, to fund the cost of the refurbishment of the chancel roof if the cost of doing the same for the nave roof would be borne by the local parishioners. Froude put up his money and the work on the chancel was completed, though no funds were received from the local parishioners. One today has only to look upward to compare the chancel roof with that of the nave, to be grateful for Froude's generosity and regret the parsimony of the locals.

From about 1910 until 1920 (work stopped during the First World War) a local firm of builders undertook to carry out repairs to the tower. Their scaffolding would have been more akin to their medieval predecessors. They erected a small hut at the base of the tower to store their tools and partake of their refreshments. One day after lunch they left the hut and prepared to mount the scaffolding, when one of the gargoyles dislodged itself and came hurtling down. The hut broke its fall and it survived in a reparable condition; the hut did not, being reduced to kindling wood. The next day, a customer congratulated the builder, who also happened to be the landlord of a local public house, on his lucky escape. He retorted, perhaps with tongue in cheek, that luck did not come into it and that things that fell from churches would never strike one of the righteous. This may sound fanciful, but my grandmother assured me it was true; the builder was my grandfather, Fred Percy.

Percy & Sons and Plumpton & Son: the workers who carried out repairs to St Andrews Church tower, c.1912. Fred Percy is standing in the back row sixth from the left; fourth from the left (back) is his father Bill Percy.

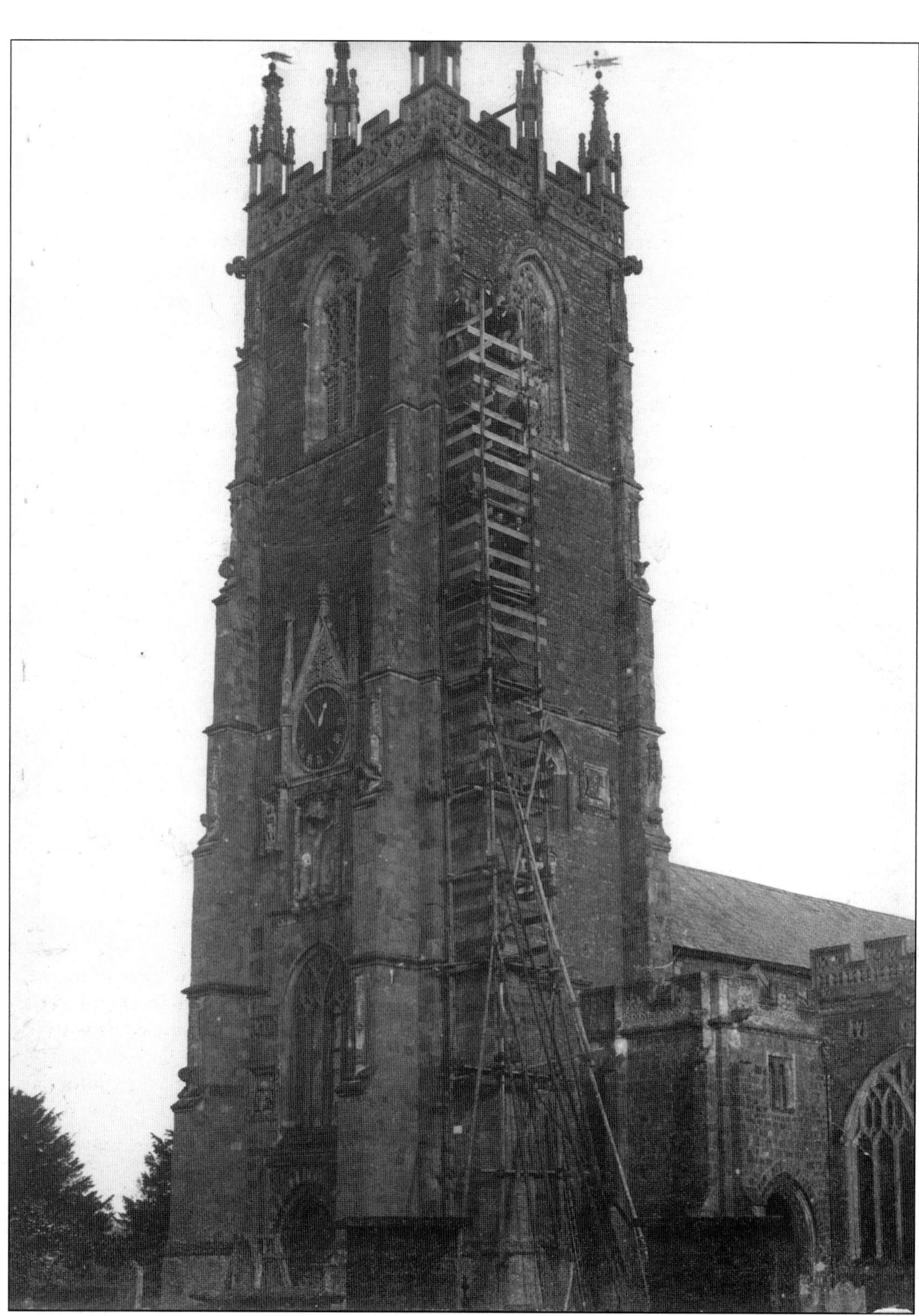

Repairs to St Andrews Church tower, c.1912. Messrs Percy are on top of the tower.

Chapter Eleven

The Walronds

By Mrs Jane Campbell

The first *Book of Cullompton* contained an article by Miss June Severn in which she told the history of the house and previous owners. June owned the freehold of the whole property but had sold leaseholds to the twin sisters Beatrice and Daphne Reeves. In the last paragraph she said that she, and the Misses Reeves, were thinking about the future ownership and guardianship of the property. June approached the National Trust to assume ownership but the Trust's properties have to support themselves by taking paying visitors. However, the delicate, old fabric of the Walronds would not be able to stand up to the number of visitors required for its upkeep and the Trust declined the offer; so June had to look for other solutions. She considered the Town Council, which duly investigated possible uses for the house but it was clear that a local authority would have difficulty in raising sufficient funds to carry out the repairs needed for the house or to ensure long-term maintenance.

June then decided to set up a Trust and invited a group of people to join together for that purpose. The Cullompton Walronds Preservation Trust was formed in 1996 and was incorporated as a Company Limited by Guarantee and as a Registered Charity in 1997. The Trust raised funds for a feasibility study, which included a detailed survey of the property and a business plan, which was submitted to the Heritage Lottery Fund in 1997. Unfortunately, the priorities of the Lottery Fund changed soon after the application was submitted and it was rejected. Although the Trust was asked to submit a reduced application, the three ladies, June Severn, with Beatrice and Daphne Reeves, decided that they would offer the property for sale on the open market and this they did in 1999.

The property went to auction but, although many prospective purchasers visited, none would buy it. The ladies therefore decided to stay where they were and to manage as best they could.

The Trust stayed in contact with the ladies and supported them with various projects such as protecting the glass in the front windows by the installation of polycarbonate shields, and investigating the possibility of gates for the front courtyard.

June loved the house and always made visitors welcome. She opened her home to many local groups to raise funds or to study the structure and internal features, such as the plasterwork. There were flower festivals, exhibitions of toys and clocks, coffee mornings and the National Trust Christmas shop, which was regularly held in the house. As the ladies grew older and funds more scarce these activities eventually ceased.

In June 2004 Miss Daphne Reeves, who had been in failing health, died in Taunton leaving her flat in the south wing and part of the garden to her twin sister Beatrice. June and Beatrice worked hard to sort out Daphne's estate but June had a stroke shortly thereafter. As a result she went to hospital and then to a nursing home in Tiverton where she died in September 2004. June left her property, consisting of the main house and Craft Cottage and a major part of the garden, to the Cullompton Walronds Preservation Trust. The Trustees were delighted but immediately realised the enormous responsibility placed upon them. June had always expressed her intention of leaving the property to the Trust, in order to ensure that the house would be restored and maintained and made available to as many people as possible, whilst realising that there would be a long-term need to cover the costs of such a wish. During her lifetime she had been in contact with the Landmark Trust, a registered charity which restores and maintains historic buildings and manages the properties as holiday accommodation, and the Trust reopened this negotiation.

Following June's death the Trustees made contact with the Heritage Lottery Fund to enquire about the possibility of raising funds for the restoration of the property. The Heritage Lottery Fund's response was that they would not consider an application for a property which was in more than one ownership and that the Trustees would have to look elsewhere for funds. It was clear that urgent repairs were required to make the roof and walls waterproof and applications were made to Devon County Council, Mid-Devon District Council and Cullompton Town Council for grants towards the cost of emergency repairs and a structural survey. Funds were provided by the Local Authorities and from the Regional Development Agency through the Gateway Trust. Jonathan Rhind Architects were appointed to carry out the survey and a steeplejack secured the roof tiles and one pinnacle, and repaired some of the guttering, which greatly helped to protect the property from further deterioration. A restorer was employed to prop up the lintels in the main hall and sitting room, secure the vulnerable plasterwork and ancient glass, the ceiling over the newel staircase, and to buttress loose stone from a failing lintel in the main staircase.

Funds for this work were raised by the sale of much of the furniture through the auctioneers, Bearne's of

Walronds. The garden at the rear where work has started on transforming the garden into a public park for everyone to enjoy.

Walronds. Fireplace in the main hall, the crest above is the family crest of Sir John Petre and his wife Emline Paris. It is dated 1605 and marks the completion of the interior of the house.

Exeter. The Awards for All scheme made a grant of £5,000 to enable a feasibility study and disability access audit for the garden.

June's death resulted in Miss Beatrice Reeves being the sole occupant of the Walronds. She was in poor health and decided to move from her flat upstairs to her late sister's flat on the ground floor. Work was done to enable her to move but unfortunately she went to hospital just before Christmas 2004 and never returned.

As the Trustees were unable to raise funds while the property was in two ownerships, a valuation of Miss Beatrice Reeves's property was obtained by her solicitor and the Trust borrowed sufficient funds from the Architectural Heritage Fund to purchase her two flats and her part of the garden. The transaction was completed in December 2005, which enabled the Trust to proceed with a feasibility study for the development of the garden as a public facility and plans for the future of the house. Beatrice Reeves died in January 2006 and very generously left her estate to the Trust. This enabled Trustees to pay off the loan from the Architectural Heritage Fund and to allot the residue towards the next stage of the restoration of the house and work on the garden.

Since the death of these three ladies the Trustees have been working to achieve their wish to secure the long-term future of the house, while opening it to the community as much as possible and of making the gardens accessible to everyone. The Trust has had volunteers from the students at East Devon College of Further Education over the last two years; their work in the garden has been a tremendous help. Other garden helpers include the local Army Cadet Force and the Rangers. Frequent events have been held in the house to show visitors around and to raise awareness of the project. The first major event in the house was the launch of the Culm Valley Community Plan in May 2005, since when there have been coffee mornings, antiques days, sales of books, plants and bric-a-brac, charity days, parties, working parties in the garden, tours by visiting history groups, and meetings of a range of organisations both local and national, such as Cullompton Chamber of Commerce and the Association of Preservation Trusts.

Planning permission has been obtained for the removal of the existing garages to enable the creation of an access from Fore Street to the garden for everyone and planning permission has also been granted for the change of use from a private to a public garden. The intention is to start work on demolition of the garages in the near future, together with changes in the garden which will take some time to mature.

A large and dangerous ash tree has been removed

Students from East Devon College working in the gardens at the Walronds, High Street, July 2006.

A student from East Devon College working in the gardens at the Walronds, July 2006.

as well as two cypress trees which limited access to the garden. Permission for further clearance has been obtained while tree preservation orders for the two fine limes and several ancient yews and a sweet chestnut have been prepared.

In the meantime the Trust is liaising with the Landmark Trust to agree the terms and conditions for the future management of the house and courtyard garden. It is intended that three rooms in the south wing will be used to provide a kitchen, lavatory and meeting room for use by the community, while the main house and courtyard garden will be made available for holiday lets and functions. The house will be made available to the community for at least three weeks during the year and local schools will be encouraged to visit the house to learn about its local significance.

Uffculme Community College is working on a website for the project and numerous volunteers have worked in the house and gardens: cleaning, clearing, removing partitions, making coffee and generally assisting with the project. The Trustees have been greatly encouraged by the involvement of Philip MacMillan Browse, a noted plantsman who was a founder member of the Eden Project and a former Director of RHS Wisley, among other prestigious appointments, who has volunteered his advice on the future planting of the garden.

Between May 2005 and September 2006 over 1,500 people visited the property and the Trust sends out regular newsletters to more than 300 people who have expressed a wish to support the project. None of the events would have been possible without the willing help of numerous volunteers and the Trustees recognise that the support shown by the community is vital to the achievement of their aims – to carry out the wishes of the three generous ladies who left their property to the Trust for the benefit of the community.

The Trustees are: Mrs Jane Campbell Chairman, Col M.J. Woodcock Retd, Company Secretary, Mrs Linda Holloway Secretary, Mrs Elizabeth Labdon, Treasurer, Mrs Muriel Coxhead, Mr John Cummings, Mr Charles Heeley, Mr Clive Madge, Mrs Elizabeth Whitely, Mr G.R.W. Wickham.

Chapter Twelve

In Conclusion

Cullompton has character, history and a strong sense of community. It is a place that people continue to want to live and bring up their families but it is no longer the self-sufficient market town that it once was. Its population is continuing to increase and there are plans for still more housing and industrial development. Where once most people lived and worked in the local area, nowadays many of the people that live in Cullompton travel out of the town to work and shop.

The railway station has been replaced by a motorway services area. The tanneries and factories that used the railway station, and employed large numbers of people, have closed and been replaced by distribution/warehousing companies. However, there are plans to expand the Kingsmill Industrial Estate and provide more local jobs. Plans have finally been approved for the long-awaited last section of the Northern Distributor Road to link Station Road with Willand Road. This will ease traffic congestion at the Station Road/Willand Road junction but will also mean another 200 homes and thus more cars.

Many of the traditional shops have closed as Cullompton's main street is unable to offer the variety that the larger towns and big shopping centres can provide. Changes in people's lifestyle has meant that where, at one time, there were four or five butchers' shops and one take-away, there are now four or five take-aways and one butcher's shop. But Cullompton still has a butcher, a baker and several individual shops that can provide something a little different. Planning permission has been granted for the development of a Tesco supermarket in Station Road, although at the present time there is no definite timescale for its construction. No-one is sure how this will affect the existing shops.

The garage in the centre of the town has been replaced by a sheltered housing development. Another garage in Willand Road has become a printing company and a third garage in Station Road closed soon after the opening of the motorway services area. If and when a new supermarket is built in Station Road it is planned that a petrol station will be reopened on this site.

The Cullompton Hotel, once the venue for many local wedding receptions and dinner dances, has been demolished and replaced with houses. But in its place there is Padbrook Park which caters for weddings, etc., but also has additional facilities such as a fitness studio and beauty salon. The owners, Sue and Gary Scargill, have recently completed the construction of a 40-bedroom hotel and conference suite and now intend to extend the golf course from nine holes to eighteen holes.

The Cullompton Community Association has been organising an annual firework display on the fields for as long as anyone can remember and intends to improve the play facilities on the community fields. There is also an intention to improve the present street sports facilities in Meadow Lane. The Town Picnic, which is arranged by the Town Council, has now become an annual event and is held on the community fields in the grounds of Cullompton Rangers Football Club, every year in June, as part of the town's Festival Week.

The town's Christmas lighting display continues to improve year on year. Local businesses provide the power for the lights and all the shops decorate their shop windows with a Christmas theme. There is a street procession which always includes the two local majorette troops: Ace Majorettes and Culmside Majorettes, when Father Christmas comes to visit. He rides into the town centre on an open-top bus provided courtesy of Stagecoach Bus Company, and the local children are able to visit him in his grotto. He says that the children in Cullompton are always the best behaved of all the children he visits.

The Farmers' Market, which was set up in 1998, is still thriving and has about 20 stalls every month. It is managed by a committee of volunteers and run by a paid manager. Local events are often timed to coincide with the market date as so many more people are in town on the second Saturday of the month. Local charities and organisations often have a free stall at the market to promote themselves and the Christmas Farmers' Market always has a very special atmosphere.

The location of the market, in Station Road car park, is still the same as it was eight years ago when it was first set up, but the producers come and go. The only remaining stallholder from the very first market is Alison Dibble. She has not missed a single market and her range of products has increased and always reflects the taste of the customers. Cullompton Farmers' Market is still the longest running farmers market in the South West.

The Regeneration Group, which was instrumental with Tracy Frankpitt in the setting up of the Farmers' Market, has now evolved to become the Devon Gateway Development Trust. It joined the South West Regional Development Agency's Market and

Tracy Frankpitt Left), founder of the Farmers' Market, and Alison Dibble who has been a stallholder since the market was set up in 1998.

Coastal Towns Initiative in 2002 and, following a great deal of consultation with local residents and businesses, produced a Culm Valley Community Plan in 2005. The aim of the Plan is to 'create a thriving community in control of its future'.

The Trust was set up to progress the community projects identified in the Community Plan. These are projects which are intended to reinforce a sense of identity and community spirit and improve the quality of life for people living in the local area. Successful projects to date include: the updating and improvement of the Cullompton website, the production of the Culm Valley Guide and the broadcasting of a community radio station, Culm Valley FM, for four weeks during June 2006. A business plan had been drafted for a permanent community radio station and the working group are currently looking for premises and funding.

Work has recently started on a new health centre in Willand Road and it is anticipated this will be completed by autumn 2007. Both St Andrews Primary School and Cullompton Community College have recently been improved and enlarged. A working group, set up by the Town Council, is currently investigating the setting up of a Youth Café in the town centre.

Cullompton's Town Crier at the time of writing, Gordon Pring, is very active and attends as many community events as he can. He is also a very good ambassador for Cullompton as he competes in many competitions in the Devon area and promotes Cullompton wherever he goes. Cullompton St John Ambulance Brigade attend all the local events in case of any medical emergencies and enthusiastically take part in the Christmas parade and other events. There is a strong contingent of Rainbows, Brownies and Guides and an Army Cadet unit was started at the beginning of 2006.

My Cullompton

Mrs Sexton

I never can tell what made my husband and I come to Cullompton, but as I have lived here for over 20 years, now I realise that I still enjoy being here and have very deep roots. Living in Salcombe in the South Hams for 25 years I had grown to love the sea and the beauty of my surroundings, and Cullompton was a town that I had to grow to love.

It has altered considerably since those early days. Two or three vast estates have grown up and more and more people have settled. I can remember Oak Park when I first went there to deliver envelopes for Christian Aid – just a row of houses – and as each year has past the great estate has sprung up.

Padbrook came up like a mushroom in the night. I was amazed when I first saw its size. The folk who move in always add something to the local organisations, such as the Women's Institute, the churches or the different clubs, where you make friends and learn about other cultures.

Being a churchgoer I found this easy as we are well endowed with churches in Cullompton. I joined the Baptist Church and have had a very full and happy life in consequence.

But with so many retired folk around, we didn't seem to have much for the elderly (the over sixties), but as I made friends I discovered that a Luncheon Club had recently been formed, and this has stood the test of time. Indeed, it is very successful giving joy to the many who attend.

A Disability Club cheers my lovely people each month, meals on wheels provides an outlet and the blind folk, who are many, have an interesting club which meets once a month. Most of these meetings are run only because of the interest and dedication of volunteers, and are well attended.

Cullompton is evolving to meet the needs of its population. These changes are coming about gradually and it is hoped that the town's warmth and sense of community will never change. Cullompton has a very interesting past and looks to have a very interesting future.

Judy Morris

Official Guides to Cullompton, one from c.1930 and one from c.1970.

Envoi
The Play's the Thing...

Pupils of the Convent High School, Cullompton, at their performance of Snow White and the Seven Dwarfs, 1938.

CAST LIST

Snow-white:	Carmel Fielding
Prince:	Kathleen Criddle
Wicked Queen:	Joy Melhuish
Huntsman:	Christl Kris
Herald:	M Raylings
Fawn:	J Hellier

Captain of the Guard: Monda Stone

Dwarfs: A. Skinner, M. Oxenham, J. Luxton, J. Keane, S. Thorne, S. Cook and L. Martin

Greek Girls: M. Terry, P. Barons, M. Harding, M. Taylor, C. Stevens, E. Hanney, M. Hibberd and B. Glass

Princes: S McCarthy, C Howe, D Hohla, E Gerstenberger and M Hughes

Fairies: L. Rees, E. Gollop, A. Reynolds, D. Hartnell, J. Stoddart, J. Squire, M. Mulcahy, E. Farmer, G. Hellier and M. Baker

Princesses: M. Kris, D. Haas, J. Clifford, P. Ransome and G. Baker

Rabbits: M. Wonnacott, P. Jarrett, M. Jarrett and T. Roberts

Programme

SNOW-WHITE AND THE SEVEN DWARFS

As performed by the pupils of the
CONVENT HIGH SCHOOL,
CULLOMPTON,
DEVON,
December 8th and 9th, 1938

PRICE - 2D.

Proceeds in aid of the District Nursing Associati[on]

The front and back of the original programme for the 1938 performances of Snow White.

Items introducing :—

1. Toe Dance .... J. Keane and S. Cook
2. Ballet Dance .... Muriel Terry
3. Ballet Dance..... Muriel Terry, M. Oxenham, Anne Reynolds
4. Tap Dance by the Seven Dwarfs.
5. Tap Dance .... C. Fielding, K. Criddle
6. Tap Dance .... A. Skinner, L. Martin
7. Song, "Little Old Lady" by Lorna Rees.

——o——

Music by the Tiverton Orchestra (Mrs. Newman), conducted by Mr. Stoddart (Cullompton).

Costumes designed by Messrs. Fred Ford & Sons (Exeter).

Lighting Effects by Mr. Terry (Cullompton).

Stage Management by Mr. Broom (Cullompton).

Subscribers

David. B. Addison, Cullompton, Devon
Hilary Anstis (née Hodge), Cullompton
Bobby Arbery, Rull Cottage, Cullompton, Devon
Pauline Atyeo (née Tidborough), Cullompton, Devon
Lewis S. Bale, Cullompton, Devon
Mrs H. Barker, Pound Close, Holbrook, Ipswich
Mr Russell Biss, Roadwater, Somerset
Patrick A.J. Blackmore, Cullompton, Devon
Albert F. Boundy, Willand
Dick Bradbeer, Cullompton, Devon
James C. Brooks, Cullompton, Devon
David J. Broom, Cullompton, Devon
Margaret Broucke (née Dyer), Cullompton, Devon
Mollie D.G. Brown, Cullompton, Devon
Darren J.W. Burns, Cullompton, Devon
K. J. Burrow, Bucks Cross, Devon
F.H. Butler
John, Christina, Jack and Harry Chambers, Cullompton, Devon
Gary P. Chambers, Cullompton, Devon
Christine Chapman, Willand, Devon
Muma and Alan Cheshire
John and Karen Cleaver (née Spurway)
Anthony and Iris Cole
Gordon F. Coombes, Cullompton, Devon
Vernon R. Copeland, Cullompton, Devon
Miss Sheila Cox, Canada
Robert Crispin, Bradninch, Devon
Charlie Crispin, Bradninch, Devon
Colin Crispin, Bradninch, Devon
Paul Crispin, Bradninch, Devon
Barbara. J. Crispin, Hele, Bradninch, Devon
Jasmine Crispin-Vile, Bradninch, Devon
Joyce G. Cross, Cullompton, Devon
Paul and Linda Curtis, Cullompton
Marie Davey (née Broucke), Granddaughter of Ron and Phyllis Dyer
Mr and Mrs H. Davis, Cullompton
William P. Discombe, Cullompton, Devon
John L. Drew, Cullompton, Devon
Eric and Marian Dummett MBE
Elaine Dunn (née White), Kentisbeare, Devon
Ann and Barry Edmonds, Cullompton, Devon
Mr and Mrs R. Edworthy
Mr and Mrs B. Edworthy
Mr and Mrs L. Edworthy
Mr and Mrs A. Edworthy
Anneli Farrant, Cullompton, Devon
Sally and Colin Farrelly, Plymouth, Devon
Roger and Jean Firbanks, Cullompton
Steve and Julie Firbanks, Cullompton
Lynnette J. Frayne, Cullompton, Devon
Suzanne. D. Frost, Cullompton, Devon
Mr G. And Mrs P. Frost, Mutterton, Cullompton
Angie Gascoigne (née Knight), Widnes, Cheshire (formerly of Cullompton)
B.L. and T.F. Goff, Cullompton, Devon
Geoff Goodhind, Leigh on Sea
Kay and Brian Gordon,
Kevin R. Grant, Willand, Devon
Ian B. Gunn, Cullompton, Devon
Barry L. Gunn, Cullompton, Devon
Janet C. Hancock (née Phillips)
Adrian J. Harris, Stoneyford, Cullompton, Devon
Mr C.V. Havill, Stoneleigh, Wellington
Leisa S. Hawkins, Cullompton, Devon
Steve Hellier, Cullompton, Devon
Barbara Hellier, Cullompton, Devon
Mike and Sarah Hill, Cullompton, Devon
Jack and Audrey Hill, Cullompton
Faye and Tony Hoare, Cullompton, Devon
Eileen Hollings, Cullompton, Devon
Mr Peter Hurfod, Cullompton, Devon
Brian Johns, Cullompton
Peter and Emma Jones, Cullompton, Devon
Tricia Jones, Montford Bridge, Shrewsbury
Douglas. A. Keen, Cullompton

Joyce and Derrick Kellaway, Cullompton
Sandra P. Kemp, Cullompton
B.M. King, Felixstowe
Mike Knight, East Grinstead, West Sussex (formerly of Cullompton)
Ronald Law, Cullompton, Devon
Mr and Mrs M. C. Lotz
Robin C. Luke, Cullompton, Devon
G and J Manfield, Cullompton
Alan Manning, Cullompton, Devon
Rodney Manning, Cullompton, Devon
Rosa Manson, Cullompton, Devon
Sheila Maughan (née Radford), Feltwell, Norfolk
Frances Maunder, Cullompton, Devon
Reith and Sarah May, Cullompton
Mrs S. Medlin, Upperheyford, Oxon
Sheila Medlin
Neil and Nicola Meffe, Cullompton, Devon
Colin and Julie Metcalf, Cullompton
Mrs Audrey Miller, Cullompton, Devon
Kelly and Lauren Morgan, Cullompton, Devon
Rose Neeves, Shrewsbury
Janet Newton (née Goff)
Nick, Barbara and Rex Nicholson, Cullompton
S.A. and E.M. Norman, Cullompton
Joyce Owens, Cullompton, Devon
Yvonne and Alan Parsons, Cullompton
Betty Patchett (née Cross), Cullompton
Sue and Roger Perry, Cullompton, Devon
Bernard Pragg, Kew, Surrey
Mr and Mrs A. Prettiejohn
Margot Pullen (née Denning), West Byfleet, Surrey
Heather Rabbage, Cullompton
Gladys M. Radford
Mr F.C. Richardson, Cullompton, Devon
Louise and John Roberts, Vernon, British Columbia, Canada
Claire and Steve Roberts, Beckenham, Kent
Colin and Judy Rorie, Clyst Hydon
Elaine L. Rowe, Cullompton, Devon
Martin J. Rutley, Exeter, Devon
Kathleen G. Sampson, Cullompton, Devon
Lance and Betty Schroeder, Cullompton, Devon
Mrs Debbie Sellick, The Cherry Tree, Cullompton
Gail and Chris Shepheard, Clyst Hydon, Devon
Richard Shere
Jane M. Short, Cullompton
Mrs Veronica Sparrow-Norton, Exeter, Devon
Mr and Mrs J. Spurway, Cullompton, Devon
Ronald W. Staddon
Mr and Mrs Anthony Stevens
Mr Don Stevens
Kaz, Sophie and Leah Stocker, Cullompton
Jo, Julian and Amelia Stocker, Gloucester
Tom and Margaret Stocker, Cullompton
Tim Stone, Dawlish (Formerly of Cullompton)
Marion Stone, Cullompton, Devon
Lucy D.M. Stoneman, Cullompton, Devon
Mrs Lena M. Stoneman (née Goff), Cullompton
Richard and Susan Strevens, Cullompton
Paul Taylor, Cullompton, Devon
Sarah L.G. Thomassen, Cullompton, Devon
(Cllr) Michael Thompson, Cullompton, Devon
Martyn Thornett, Blackborough, Devon
James and Dorothy Toomer, Cullompton
Peter Trayte, Cullompton, Devon
Luke Trayte, Cullompton, Devon
Jan, Jerry and Ben Tucker, Cullompton, Devon
Peter and Helen Vile
Anne Vile, Cullompton, Devon
Hazel C.H. Vinnicombe
John F.W. Walling, Newton Abbot, Devon
Joy Walters, Hemyock, Devon
Martyn N. Warren, Toronto, Canada
Mr and Mrs M. Webber
Malcom. F. Wellington, Cullompton, Devon
Mike and Sharon Wetherell, Cullompton
Roger A.J. White, Langford Green, Cullompton, Devon
Michael Whitfield and Mora Cotterell, Cullompton, Devon
S.B. Wickenden, Cullompton, Devon
L.E. Worley, Cullompton, Devon
Richard and Janet Young, Cullompton

Further Titles

For information regarding up-to-date availability, please check our website at www.halsgrove.com

The Book of Addiscombe • Canning and Clyde Road Residents Association and Friends
The Book of Addiscombe, Vol. II • Canning and Clyde Road Residents Association and Friends
The Book of Ashburton • Stuart Hands and Pete Webb
The Book of Axminster with Kilmington • Les Berry and Gerald Gosling
The Book of Axmouth & the Undercliff • Ted Gosling and Mike Clement
The Book of Bakewell • Trevor Brighton
The Book of Bampton • Caroline Seward
The Book of Barnstaple • Avril Stone
The Book of Barnstaple, Vol. II • Avril Stone
The Book of Beaminster • Beaminster Museum
The Book of The Bedwyns • Bedwyn History Society
The Book of Bere Regis • Rodney Legg and John Pitfield
The Book of Bergh Apton • Geoffrey I. Kelly
The Book of Bickington • Stuart Hands
The Book of Bideford • Peter Christie and Alison Grant
Blandford Forum: A Millennium Portrait • Blandford Forum Town Council
The Book of Bitterne • Bitterne Local Historical Society
The Book of Blofield • Barbara Pilch
The Book of Boscastle • Rod and Anne Knight
The Book of Bourton-on-the-Hill, Batsford and Sezincote • Allen Firth
The Book of Bramford • Bramford Local History Group
The Book of Breage & Germoe • Stephen Polglase
The Book of Bridestowe • D. Richard Cann
The Book of Bridgwater • Roger Evans
The Book of Bridport • Rodney Legg
The Book of Brixham • Frank Pearce
The Book of Brundall • Barbara Ayers and Group
The Book of Buckfastleigh • Sandra Coleman
The Book of Buckland Monachorum & Yelverton • Pauline Hamilton-Leggett
The Book of Budleigh Salterton • D. Richard Cann
The Book of Carharrack • Carharrack Old Cornwall Society
The Book of Carshalton • Stella Wilks and Gordon Rookledge
The Book of Carhampton • Hilary Binding
The Parish Book of Cerne Abbas • Vivian and Patricia Vale
The Book of Chagford • Iain Rice
The Book of Chapel-en-le-Frith • Mike Smith
The Book of Chittlehamholt with Warkleigh & Satterleigh • Richard Lethbridge
The Book of Chittlehampton • Various
The Book of Codford • Romy Wyeth
The Book of Colney Heath • Bryan Lilley
The Book of Constantine • Moore and Trethowan
The Book of Cornwood and Lutton • Compiled by the People of the Parish
The Book of Crediton • John Heal
The Book of Creech St Michael • June Small
The Book of Crowcombe, Bicknoller and Sampford Brett • Maurice and Joyce Chidgey
The Book of Crudwell • Tony Pain
The Book of Cullompton • Compiled by the People of the Parish
The Second Book of Cullompton • Compiled by the People of the Parish
The Book of Dawlish • Frank Pearce
The Book of Dulverton, Brushford, Bury & Exebridge • Dulverton and District Civic Society
The Book of Dunster • Hilary Binding
The Book of Easton • Easton Village History Project
The Book of Edale • Gordon Miller
The Ellacombe Book • Sydney R. Langmead
The Book of Elmsett • Elmsett Local History Group
The Book of Exmouth • W.H. Pascoe
The Book of Fareham • Lesley Burton and Brian Musselwhite
The Book of Grampound with Creed • Bane and Oliver
The Book of Gosport • Lesley Burton and

Brian Musselwhite
The Book of Haughley • Howard Stephens
The Book of Hayle • Harry Pascoe
The Book of Hayling Island & Langstone • Peter Rogers
The Book of Helston • Jenkin with Carter
The Book of Hemyock • Clist and Dracott
The Book of Herne Hill • Patricia Jenkyns
The Book of Hethersett • Hethersett Society Research Group
The Book of High Bickington • Avril Stone
The Book of Homersfield • Ken Palmer
The Book of Honiton • Gerald Gosling
The Book of Ilsington • Dick Wills
The Book of Kessingland • Maureen and Eric Long
The Book of Kingskerswell • Carsewella Local History Group
The Book of Lamerton • Ann Cole and Friends
Lanner, A Cornish Mining Parish • Sharron Schwartz and Roger Parker
The Book of Leigh & Bransford • Malcolm Scott
The Second Book of Leigh & Bransford • Malcolm Scott
The Book of Litcham with Lexham & Mileham • Litcham Historical and Amenity Society
The Book of Llangain • Haydn Williams
The Book of Loddiswell • Loddiswell Parish History Group
The Book of Looe • Mark Camp
The New Book of Lostwithiel • Barbara Fraser
The Book of Lulworth • Rodney Legg
The Book of Lustleigh • Joe Crowdy
The Book of Lydford • Compiled by Barbara Weeks
The Book of Lyme Regis • Rodney Legg
The Book of Manaton • Compiled by the People of the Parish
The Book of Markyate • Markyate Local History Society
The Book of Mawnan • Mawnan Local History Group
The Book of Meavy • Pauline Hemery
The Book of Mere • Dr David Longbourne
The Book of Minehead with Alcombe • Binding and Stevens
The Book of Monks Orchard and Eden Park • Ian Muir and Pat Manning
The Book of Morchard Bishop • Jeff Kingaby
Mount Batten – The Flying Boats of Plymouth • Gerald Wasley
The Book of Mulbarton • Jill and David Wright
The Book of Mylor • Mylor Local History Group
The Book of Narborough • Narborough Local History Society
The Book of Newdigate • John Callcut
The Book of Newtown • Keir Foss
The Book of Nidderdale • Nidderdale Museum Society
The Book of Northlew with Ashbury • Northlew History Group
The Book of North Newton • J.C. and K.C. Robins
The Book of North Tawton • Baker, Hoare and Shields
The Book of Notting Hill • Melvin Wilkinson
The Book of Nynehead • Nynehead & District History Society
The Book of Okehampton • Roy and Ursula Radford
The Book of Ottery St Mary • Gerald Gosling and Peter Harris
The Book of Paignton • Frank Pearce
The Book of Penge, Anerley & Crystal Palace • Peter Abbott
The Book of Peter Tavy with Cudlipptown • Peter Tavy Heritage Group
The Book of Pimperne • Jean Coull
The Book of Plymtree • Tony Eames
The Book of Poole • Rodney Legg
The Book of Porchfield & Locks Green • Keir Foss
The Book of Porlock • Dennis Corner
The Book of Portland • Rodney Legg
Postbridge – The Heart of Dartmoor • Reg Bellamy
The Book of Priddy • Albert Thompson
The Book of Princetown • Dr Gardner-Thorpe
The Book of Probus • Alan Kent and Danny Merrifield
The Book of Rattery • By the People of the Parish
The Book of Roadwater, Leighland and Treborough • Clare and Glyn Court
The Book of St Audries • Duncan Stafford
The Book of St Austell • Peter Hancock
The Book of St Day • Joseph Mills and Paul Annear
The Book of St Dennis and Goss Moor • Kenneth Rickard
The Book of St Ervan • Moira Tangye
The Book of St Levan • St Levan Local History Group
The Book of St Mawes • Chris Pollard
The Book of Sampford Courtenay with Honeychurch • Stephanie Pouya

The Book of Sculthorpe • Gary Windeler
The Book of Seaton • Ted Gosling
The Book of Sennen • Alison Weeks and Valerie Humphrys
The Book of Sidmouth • Ted Gosling and Sheila Luxton
The Book of Silverton • Silverton Local History Society
The Book of South Molton • Jonathan Edmunds
The Book of South Stoke with Midford • Edited by Robert Parfitt
South Tawton & South Zeal with Sticklepath • Roy and Ursula Radford
The Book of Sparkwell with Hemerdon & Lee Mill • Pam James
The Book of Spetisbury • Ann Taylor
The Book of Staverton • Pete Lavis
The Book of Stithians • Stithians Parish History Group
The Book of Stogumber, Monksilver, Nettlecombe & Elworthy • Maurice and Joyce Chidgey
The Book of South Brent • Greg Wall
The Book of Studland • Rodney Legg
The Book of Swanage • Rodney Legg
The Book of Tavistock • Gerry Woodcock
The Book of Thatcham • Peter Allen
The Book of Thorley • Sylvia McDonald and Bill Hardy
The Book of Torbay • Frank Pearce
The Book of Truro • Christine Parnell
The Book of Uplyme • Gerald Gosling and Jack Thomas
The Book of Veryan & Portloe • Diana Smith and Christine Parnell
The Book of Watchet • Compiled by David Banks
The Book of Watchet and Williton Revisited • Maurice and Joyce Chidgey and Ben Norman
The Book of Wendling, Longham and Beeston with Bittering • Stephen Olley
The Book of West Huntspill • By the People of the Parish
The Book of Weston-super-Mare • Sharon Poole
The Book of Whippingham • Sarah Burdett
The Book of Whitchurch • Gerry Woodcock
Widecombe-in-the-Moor • Stephen Woods
Widecombe – Uncle Tom Cobley & All • Stephen Woods
The Book of Willand • James Morrison and Willand History Group
The Book of Williton • Michael Williams
The Book of Wilton • Chris Rousell
The Book of Wincanton • Rodney Legg
The Book of Winscombe • Margaret Tucker
The Book of Witheridge • Peter and Freda Tout and John Usmar
The Book of Withycombe • Chris Boyles
Woodbury: The Twentieth Century Revisited • Roger Stokes
The Book of Woolmer Green • Compiled by the People of the Parish
The Book of Yetminster • Shelagh Hill

Ernest Denner who worked for the Co-op Bakery delivering bread in the 1930s